The Altars Where We Worship

THE ALTARS WHERE WE WORSHIP

The Religious Significance of Popular Culture

Juan M. Floyd-Thomas
Stacey M. Floyd-Thomas
Mark G. Toulouse

WESTMINSTER
JOHN KNOX PRESS
LOUISVILLE · KENTUCKY

First edition
Published by Westminster John Knox Press
Louisville, Kentucky

17 18 19 20 21 22 23 24 25—10 9 8 7 6 5 4 3 2

Book design by Sharon Adams
Cover design by Mary Ann Smith
Cover art: Mary Ann Smith

Library of Congress Cataloging-in-Publication Data

Names: Floyd-Thomas, Juan Marcial, author.
Title: The altars where we worship : the religious significance of popular
   culture / Juan Floyd-Thomas, Stacey Floyd-Thomas, Mark G. Toulouse.
Description: First edition. | Louisville, KY : Westminster John Knox Press,
   2016. | Includes index.
Identifiers: LCCN 2016032957 (print) | LCCN 2016040273 (ebook) | ISBN
   9780664235154 (pbk. : alk. paper) | ISBN 9781611647808 (ebook)
Subjects: LCSH: Christianity and culture--United States. | Popular
   culture--Religious aspects--Christianity. | Popular culture--United States.
Classification: LCC BR115.C8 F563 2016 (print) | LCC BR115.C8 (ebook) | DDC
   261.0973--dc23
LC record available at https://lccn.loc.gov/2016032957

♾ The paper used in this publication meets the minimum requirements of the
American National Standard for Information Sciences—Permanence of Paper for
Printed Library Materials, ANSI Z39.48-1992.

Most Westminster John Knox Press books are available at special quantity discounts
when purchased in bulk by corporations, organizations, and special-interest groups.
For more information, please e-mail SpecialSales@wjkbooks.com.

Dedicated to our little ones with big futures:

Lillian Makeda Floyd-Thomas,
Kylee Alexa Hunt,
Gavin Tyler Hunt,
William Anthony Wallace, and
Christopher Aaron Wallace

Contents

Foreword

"Altar-ization": this coinage does not make its appearance until the very last page of this text, but from page 1 on, readers will have no difficulty knowing what the book is about. The authors are focused, relentless, and admirably clear. Readers are invited to share in "rigorous reflection concerning altar-ization of [six] aspects of American culture." In case "reflection" sounds lulling, the coauthors wake readers up with the next sentence: "We cannot overlook the truth that religion is in crisis." Religion may be declining, they report and may prove, but at the same time, worship at popular culture altars is prospering.

Right off, some readers may want to protest the word "we" in the title. Do "we" worship at one or more or all of these alternative altars here described? Advertisers and other writers like to include many who do not belong when they say "we." Thus "this season we all are wearing orange," or "we are preferring violent horror films," or "we all are communicating with Apple Apps." "We"? Who asked my permission to be included?

Some protest: "But I wear red, not orange." Or "I like sentimental tearjerkers." Or "I don't even own a cell phone."

Yet some form of worship at some or all of these altars is almost inescapable. The authors state that they are less interested in inquiring about *whether* "we" worship at these altars, than about *how* we do so. The six chosen altars appear in sequence, and readers may pick and choose among them: "Body and Sex," "Big Business," "Entertainment," "Politics," "Sports," "Science and Technology" are the options here. Readers who think about the ubiquity and force of each of these will likely be ready for "rigorous reflection," and they will get it here.

ix

These authors reconceptualize cultural reflection by helping readers realize an alternative to the familiar "religious *versus* secular" polarity, rich as that is, but limited also as it is. They deserve credit for enriching the language of searchers. For instance, religion, they suggest, is more likely than not best conceived as the "meaning-making" element in personal, cultural, and social life. And the choice of focus on "worship" relieves the authors of the necessity to treat all dimensions of "meaning making" or "religion" or "what have you."

Still, the Floyd-Thomases and Mark Toulouse cannot avoid implicit and explicit references to religion. They very helpfully draw on seven dimensions of religion familiarly posed by scholar Ninian Smart, and in tour-de-force fashion stick to them patiently and consistently as they search and discover the altars that beckon and that serve the citizenry as contemporaries engage in "altar-ization."

Worship is the focus. In religion and meaning making, an altar is not a study or arena, though "worship" often encapsulates what scholarship and conflict provide as corollaries or supports. As for "altars," they are defined as elevated and attracting locales for worship, offerings, and sacrifices. Observers of "popular culture" notice innumerable evidences of the sacrifices "we" make to enhance devotion to sex, entertainment, politics, and the like. The authors are right: whether one is "religious" or not, it is clear that religion is in crisis in popular culture, a fact that demands rigorous reflection.

The Altars Where We Worship provides significant aid for those who would reflect on the crisis and join the authors in their search-and-discovery missions. One does not need to restrict the search to a particular academic discipline or cultural scope. Reporters, sociologists, prophets, advertisers, critics, theologians, literary critics, cartoonists, and more, whatever they reflexively bring to the reflection, will here find illustrations about and equipment for addressing popular culture.

The range of scholars on whom they draw or to whose work they point is broad. One finds pop-music celebrities jowl-by-cheek next to big thinkers such as Merleau-Ponty. I recall reading a book by Huston Smith some years ago in which he quoted that French philosopher. As I remember it, we pondered this line: "because we are present to a world, we are condemned to meaning." All sentient beings are present to a world, or worlds, and they are observably "condemned to meaning."

So here are "meaning makers" addressing readers who are also "meaning makers." They are not aspiring to be formal philosophers, and they do not parade their learning or hide their meanings behind obscure words. If I had to summarize all their gifts and achievements here, I would describe them as gifted and ambitious noticers. "Noticers"? The word is not in the dictionaries, but it is not hard to deduce what it means. I recall a poem, "Afterwards," in which Thomas Hardy was writing his virtual eulogy. He spoke of what he had seen but which many overlooked in the natural world around them: he was one who "used to notice such things."

The noticers who wrote this book do not advertise themselves as expert in nature watching, though they may be such. They instead notice many things in culture, in popular culture, objects and events that one can easily overlook because they seem obvious. Yet these authors subject such overlookable entities and lift them up for observation, reflection, and perhaps responding action.

Mercifully, while they are by no means uncritical about popular culture, they are not cultural snobs and they do not whine (much) because many entities that they cherish are scorned by this or that set of worshipers at the altars here described. They do not finish their task by demanding specific responses to all the crises of our time. But they may well inspire and equip others to join them in the company of "noticers" who may become responding and critical activists, and they are to be celebrated for their alluring achievement.

These scholars of religion offer a work that is at once prescient about the times in which we live and rigorously mindful of methodologies useful for the study of religion. As a result, the book is noteworthy both for the depth of its critical insights and for a style accessible to a wide variety of audiences. *The Altars Where We Worship* is an interdisciplinary book well worth the investment of one's time.

Martin E. Marty
Fairfax M. Cone Distinguished Professor Emeritus,
The University of Chicago

Preface

As authors, we come with our own popular proclivities. Mark figures the odds and the angles. Juan is a trivia and media buff. And Stacey is fascinated with mind-benders, solving puzzles or figuring out what the next popular trend will be. Admittedly, we are all *homo ludens*, creatures of play who are equally competitive in our own right. You could say we like to win. Perhaps for this reason, the game show provided a perfect context for immersing ourselves in pop culture. Although we are scholars, we knew that, like most Americans, we had our favorite game shows.

Families gather around the television to see if they can outplay other families as they watch *Family Feud*. We try to shout out as fast as we can random answers that come to mind as we watch *Password* or the *$100,000 Pyramid*. Others of us test our genius on *Jeopardy* or try to figure out the multiple-choice strategy of *Who Wants to Be a Millionaire*. What does this say about game shows? What does this say about us? Is the American Dream something we can achieve through random guesses or expertise in trivia? Do game shows confer upon us a certain social status or appearance of wisdom that we otherwise are denied in our everyday lives? Can all our dreams really come true (fame and riches) in the span of thirty minutes?

In order to play, you have to pass the initial "screening test." Such tests not only examine one's knowledge or skill suited to the game, but actually are interested at least as much in whether potential contestants will appeal to the audience. Will a contestant be a good "face for the show"? Game shows want somebody for whom the audience will root—this contestant "deserves" to win. Staff members attempt to assemble a group of players the audience can affirm, so that one among them can experience fifteen minutes of fame and be celebrated as a winner.

An opportunity presented itself for us to try our hand in a contestant lineup. So we dove into the pool of contestants on *Wheel of Fortune*, the longest-running syndicated game show in United States television history. Not only did we feel this game show best represented a combination of luck (spinning a roulette wheel) and basic knowledge (how to play hangman, ability to spell, know the parts of speech and American idioms and icons); it also conveyed something more poignant. Who deserves a chance at the wheel?

Wheel of Fortune was on tour in Texas featuring "Best Friends Week." We felt it was an ideal time to immerse ourselves in what social scientists call participant observation. We could test our hypothesis by putting together a participant-observation scheme wherein two of us would be participants and the other would observe. We knew our chances were slim. Mark sent an e-mail in response to the routine local appeal from the show. Each year the show receives over a million requests to be included in an audition. Only six hundred actual contestants are chosen. We knew we had to survive the lottery from the mass of e-mails in the Dallas-Fort Worth area before we would have any kind of chance.

Once we got through the lottery, Stacey was certain that if we presented ourselves the "right way," our team of friends would be chosen as one of fifteen couples from among hundreds of couples who showed up on a Friday to audition for their chance at spinning the wheel. We had to decide which two of us would be the "friends." Obviously, Mark would have to be a contestant. We felt that a man and woman pair would be the most "attractive." So, Mark and Stacey would be participants while Juan would be the observer who helped us process our experience. Stacey believed the right chemistry and narrative would get us the chance at spinning the wheel. We knew we had to exude in our audition a balanced mix of professionalism, excitement, lightheartedness, mystery, vitality, and open familiarity with one another. We came up with a strategy for the day, including a little routine to use with one another during our time in the lights.

On the day of our audition, we spent some six hours in a room with other "best friends" being carefully watched and profiled. Sure enough, the match of a fifty-something white man (Mark) and a thirty-something black woman (Stacey) worked—an unlikely couple of "best friends" who constituted together both a curiosity and an idealization of American racial harmony. Wheel representatives judged us on their general impression that we would represent the qualities of "a Wheel of Fortune player" and that the two of us represented a *good* cross section of the population in a supposedly postracist America. We passed!

With taping to take place on August 25, all fifteen chosen couples arrived at the Nokia Center at 7:30 that morning. Taping did not begin until 3:00 p.m. All of the contestants were coached about how important excitement was to the game's image, airbrushed by professionals (ours were makeup artists for the soaps), interviewed, protected, and herded by security, photographed, rehearsed, and placed under contract. We could not go to the bathroom without an escort. Mark met Vanna White in the hall and exchanged hellos while being escorted along with a few other male contestants to the bathroom. As time for taping came nearer, we actually talked seriously and quietly between ourselves about bolting. To make things worse, we were chosen to tape the first show.

We were nervous as jittery cats, less for being under the lights and more for the fact we knew our professional images were about to be tested in a number of ways. How would our scholarly colleagues in the American Academy of Religion respond? But as we walked on stage in front of the more than six thousand people packed into the hall, with Stacey sweating bullets and Mark's stomach turning flip-flops, we somehow composed ourselves and became a part of the culture itself. As for Juan, he was simultaneously scholar, friend, and very much a nervous husband desperate for his wife to win. Mark's family cheered from the audience as well.

After winning the first two puzzles, during the commercial break we were "toweled down," made-up again, and shouted at for not showing enough excitement. "You are on the *Wheel of Fortune*, and you are *winning*," the woman told Mark. "You've got to show more excitement! Clap your hands, jump up and down, shout for joy! *Do something*!" "Stacey, you need to show us more of the person we saw smiling, laughing, and being excited!" We were way ahead going into the last round. We had banked over $20,000 and had lost only one puzzle. But alas, Pat Sajak landed on the $5,000 space for the final puzzle. Our colleagues, two younger women, scored $18,000 on the last puzzle and barely passed us to go into the bonus round. In some ways, we were both winners and losers on the show.

We learned several things. At some point, each of us lost all our ability to be observers. We lost all scholarly detachment. We were fully immersed. Mark and Stacey actually became contestants, and Juan found himself transformed into the angst-ridden family member, sitting at the end of his seat, with all of the answers in tow. We wanted to win the "big money." The excited high five between us (which we swore we wouldn't do) after winning the trip to Buenos Aires, Argentina, is probably proof enough of the fact. We simply could not contain ourselves. At that point, Mark turned to Stacey and said quietly, "Let's win this thing!"

We became part of the game-show culture, and at least two of us had our fifteen minutes of fame (or infamy, depending on how you see it). We also learned how many church members in our own congregations and how many scholars of religion are actually fans of *Wheel of Fortune*. The day of taping, three members of Mark's congregation greeted him from the audience (and were they ever surprised to see who the contestants of the first show were). Moreover, Juan witnessed several people (audience members and contestants alike) participating in religious rituals, praying, calling on God, giving thanks, and so on. He confessed to having a prayerful posture right before Mark and Stacey lost their chance at the big money. Then, after that prayer failed, he prayed that Stacey wouldn't be too disappointed or hard on Mark for not attending to the "do not make Pat angry" rule she had previously articulated (and that made her certain Pat intentionally landed on the $5,000 so the younger blondes would have a shot at winning). After observing Pat's playful banter with the two women contestants during a commercial break, Mark rather upset Pat when he interrupted what both Mark and Stacey interpreted as flirting by cracking, "It is really good to meet you, Pat; I grew up watching you on television."

To our mutual surprise, our scholarly colleagues were not embarrassed to see us appear on the show; they actually celebrated the fact that they knew people who became contestants. Our university and divinity-school colleagues even held a "watch party." One of the sessions at the American Academy of Religion meeting, where over ten thousand scholars of religion gather, announced the appearance from the podium. We simply had not anticipated that result—that our game-show appearance could get applause, even win accolades, as easily as actual scholarly production. Our scholarly apprehension about laying our reputations on the line to become participant observers on an American game show gave way to being celebrated by religious scholars, who actually offered their own two cents about how we might have played the game better.

This preface represents our own way of making the point that we recognize ourselves as part of what is analyzed in this book. None of us, in fact, is ever exempt from the influences exercised by popular culture in America.

Acknowledgments

Interdisciplinary work . . . is not about confronting already constituted disciplines (none of which, in fact, is willing to let itself go). To do something interdisciplinary, it's not enough to choose a "subject" (a theme) and gather around it two or three sciences. Interdisciplinarity consists in creating a new object that belongs to no one.

—Roland Barthes, "Jeunes Chercheurs" in *Writing Culture*

One does not make or remake anything alone; one cannot ignore the relations one has. To know one's self and one's situation is to know one's company (or lack of it), is to know oneself with or against others.

—Toinette M. Eugene, "Appropriation/Reciprocity,"
in *Dictionary of Feminist Theologies*

Collaborative efforts to do interdisciplinary work demand trust. The knowledge and commitments each scholar brings to the table create a web of mutuality, rigor, and vulnerability so that each can better understand the complexity and limits of their own disciplines and social locations. In some ways, working on this book constituted a kind of religious praxis. The writing process involved call and response, labor and love, construction and deconstruction, vulnerability and vision, discipline and devotion, reason and revelation, text and spoken word. This text is a constellation of all that we commonly love and hold sacred: work, family, and friendship—a friendship born long before any writing began.

This process began one place and ended up another in a number of ways. We began conversations while Stacey and Mark were faculty members at Brite Divinity School and Juan was at Texas Christian University. In 2008, Stacey and Juan moved to Nashville and Mark to Toronto. The fast-paced change of our personal and professional lives, not to mention the world and its events, delayed our ability to finish this project expediently. Yet the project itself provided occasions for enjoyable and intentional get-togethers in the midst of our own professional changes.

The work required the support and assistance of many people, without whom this volume would have remained nothing more than a running dialogue among friends. While, due to space constraints, we cannot thank all who have played a role, we would like to mention a few. We thank our many editors at Westminster John Knox. We are grateful for the work of the late Stephanie Egnotovich, with whom we talked about the initial project; Jon Berquist, whose strong interest in it helped keep it alive; and Robert Ratcliff, our final editor, who saw the work through to completion.

We have long been bolstered by the steadfast support provided by our respective families: Jeffica Toulouse, Lillian Floyd, Janet Floyd, Desrine Thomas, Juan Thomas Sr., the memories of our parents, Charles Floyd, Joan Van Deventer Toulouse, Orville Jack Toulouse, Raymond Charles Smith, and Gwen O'Neal Smith, and our children, Lillian Makeda Floyd-Thomas, Joshua Toulouse, Marcie Toulouse Hunt, and Cara Toulouse Wallace. We are grateful for colleagues, the solid friendship and extended family provided by people like Anver Emon, Frederick Douglas Haynes, and Debra Peek Haynes, Anthony Pinn, and the members of Sisters of the Sabbath Book Club.

We offer this book with appreciation for our colleagues, faculty and staff, and students at our respective institutions, Vanderbilt University Divinity School and Emmanuel College of Victoria University in the University of Toronto, and the research support provided by them and by President Paul Gooch of Victoria University. Finally, we are grateful for the work provided by our student assistants, Kayla Brandt and Alexandra Chambers, both of Vanderbilt, and Johnathan Knight of Emmanuel College.

Introduction

Hidden in Plain Sight

The Religious Nature of American Popular Culture

We must therefore, from the experiential point of view, call these godless or quasi-godless creeds "religions"; and accordingly when in our definition we speak of the individual's relation to "what [s/he] considers the divine," we must interpret the term "divine" very broadly, as denoting any object that is god *like*, whether it be a concrete deity or not.
William James, *The Varieties of Religious Experience*

Religion *is* important to Americans. But the religion we practice is often *not* the religion we confess. From at least the time of Alexis de Toqueville, observers of the American scene have recognized the essence of religion in everything American. Let's be honest with ourselves. Even though some Americans claim the country's population is deeply divided, often described as engaged in a "culture war," most Americans tend to worship at similar altars. Americans form a nation of believers; but what do they believe? What is the object of their faithful devotion? In response to the query, "What does it mean to have a god?" the German theologian Martin Luther answered, "Trust and faith of the heart alone make both God and idol. . . . Whatever then thy heart clings to . . . and relies upon, that is properly thy God."[1] Several centuries later, H. Richard Niebuhr commented that "if this be true, that the word 'god' means the object of human faith in life's worthwhileness, it is evident that [people] have many gods, that our natural religion is polytheistic."[2]

One could argue that, according to this logic, genuine atheists do not exist, since everyone believes in some source of ultimate meaning or fulfillment. Americans believe, first, in a serviceable God. We want a God who meets our

1

needs, who provides altars where we can get good service. Second, we want a friendly God, who blesses us as we become comfortable, wealthy, and successful. Our altars provide places where we find blessing in a community of like-minded seekers. Americans are practical people, who want a pragmatic faith. The objects of our attention have become our God, and fulfilling our desires has become our religion.

This book attempts to describe religion as we find it in the United States. The central question for *The Altars Where We Worship* is not *whether* Americans are religious but *how* we are religious. Put another way, if we are going to go to the trouble to be faithful, the object of our devotion needs to be useful to us. This is something peculiarly North American, something that seems to affect or infect all of us, no matter what our social location—black or white, gay or straight, religious or atheist, liberal or conservative, Republican or Democrat. Though we claim to serve things that are sacred, in actuality we deem sacred those things that serve us. On the one hand, we recognize that if everything is religious, nothing is religious. But we also know that the way we respond to things (perhaps by acting with a devotion that attributes ultimacy) can make something religious that is not meant to be religious at all.

Statistics reveal a startling gap between confession and practice in American religion. Slightly more than 70 percent of Americans in 2014 considered themselves Christian (a drop of nearly 8 percent since 2007). Comparatively few actually show up at religious services in any given week.[3] When Gallup asks the question annually, the survey reports about 35 percent of Americans claimed to attend every week or almost every week, compared with 41 percent in 2007.[4] These claims by Americans are exaggerated. A serious study of church attendance by sociologists of religion, published in 1993 (the year before Gallup reported 45 percent attending weekly or almost every week), taking a congregation by congregation count, found that, though 35.8 percent of the Protestants in the area they studied *said* they attended church weekly, on any given Sunday only about 19.6 percent *actually* showed up.[5] Some are more honest than others about their habits; in 2015, 50 percent of Americans answered that they attended only "seldom," or "never." Though Americans claim a strong religious identity, the commitment to attend religious services is simply not very high among them.[6]

Where are Americans finding meaning within their lives, if not in the practices and contexts provided by traditional religions? Where are Americans making meaning for their lives, if not in those places? *The Altars Where We Worship* seeks to answer these provocative questions.

Within the last several decades, survey and poll data have revealed a fascinating tension within the American religious experience. Some 80 percent of Americans state that religion is either very important (58 percent) or somewhat important (22 percent) to them. In 2015, however, 22.8 percent of Americans, especially younger Americans, claimed to be "religiously unaffiliated."[7] As of 2012, for example, 15 percent of those born between 1946 and 1964 (baby boomers) are unaffiliated. But 34 percent of those born between 1990 and 1994 (younger millennials) are unaffiliated.[8]

For those who are affiliated, most treat religion in an eclectic fashion. They are comfortable mixing and matching beliefs and practices traditionally at odds with one another. As early as 1992, one study described how Americans had found "substitute faiths" through their memberships in Common Cause, Sierra Club, or the nearest yoga, ballet, or martial-arts classes. Others had found spirituality through various avenues enabling "self-awareness," whether through "Self-Realization Fellowships," self-help books, paranormal experiences, or the practice of witchcraft.[9] In addition, these consumers tend to blend Christian backgrounds with other ideologies, like astrology, reincarnation, popular psychology.[10] Christian Americans consult astrological charts and dabble in telekinesis, even though their religious communities condemn these practices and scientists argue that no scientific evidence supports them.[11] These trends are not found simply among the younger generation. During the 1980s, President Reagan and his spouse, Nancy, both traditional Christians, depended upon horoscopes to change their White House calendars and appearances.[12]

People are taking control of religion in their own lives, making it a home-based commodity where sacred altars can be privatized. In the American consciousness, religion and spirituality are increasingly divorced from one another. Tom Smith, who directed a major sociological study on the question, estimated that a quarter of Americans think of themselves as "spiritual but not religious." The same study showed decreasing support for organized religion and increasing support for the privatization of religious belief. A sizable number of Americans approach religion as if it were a large salad bar, where one can pick and choose goodies from a seemingly infinite variety of bowls and mix up their own favorite combinations.[13]

Commitment to religious freedom and a suspicion of traditional institutions and authorities have always been prominent features of American life, but contemporary Americans have turned them into an art form. American popular culture celebrates our ability to break with tradition and indulge ourselves by satisfying religious and spiritual needs in untraditional ways. In our culture these days, it's hip to be spiritual, but square to be a Methodist. It's no wonder that the mainline churches are turning to commercials to try to get their groove back. The problems for the traditional church obviously began several decades ago. In his 1998 study of religion's role in the lives of members of Generation X, whose oldest members are in their early fifties today, Tom

Beaudoin contended that young Americans have grown skeptical about traditional faith due to corruption and scandal among sacred and secular leaders of the nation.[14] In the past twenty years, nothing much has changed this picture for the generations following. As Beaudoin wrote, "I was awash in popular culture and alienated from official religion. Despite all this, I still considered myself unmistakably 'spiritual.' By this, I meant I thought about religion, I thought there was more to life than materialism, and I pieced together a set of beliefs from whatever traditions I was exposed to at the time."[15]

Who can blame these last few generations? The last forty years have seen their share of sex scandals, whether in the White House or the church house. Presidential leadership has given us Vietnam, Watergate, the Iran-Contra scandal, and the debacles in Iraq and Afghanistan. Acts of terror and acts of nature, from 9/11 to Hurricane Katrina, have shaken our faith in the ability of authorities to handle crises appropriately. We are a nation of skeptics desperately looking for hope. President Obama's quick rise to leader of the free world likely owes something to these sentiments. Whether entirely accurate or not, the perceived hypocrisy and myopia of organized religion has given Americans license to meet their spiritual needs in any way that works.

We are not arguing this is the first generation of Americans that has experienced such disappointment and disillusionment with traditional religion. But we do believe this is a watershed moment. Traditional religion is being fundamentally challenged in ways previous generations would never have dared to imagine. Americans secure order for their lives, find moral guidance, and uncover life's meaning in cultural locations their grandparents most likely tried to avoid. An older meaning associated with religion was "faith seeking understanding"; today's meaning is more likely "pleasure seeking opportunity."

Nor are we contending that traditional religions in the United States are dying. Nothing could be further from the truth. We do believe that mainline American religions have lost their standing as core entities entrusted by most Americans with constructing, maintaining, and perpetuating shared notions of morality, meaning, and community for modern society. In their places, Americans have constructed "altars" from the stuff of popular culture—namely, body and sex, entertainment, sports, politics, big business, and science and technology—to supplement or supplant the role once occupied by traditional faith. Whether consciously or not, many Americans have discovered they can meet their basic religious impulses and spiritual needs in overtly nonreligious endeavors that end up serving them, ironically, in markedly religious ways. This book seeks to demonstrate how this is the case.

There's a new "sacred" in town. As Paul Tillich, Peter Berger, Sigmund Freud, and Karl Marx remind us in differing contexts (theology, sociology, psychology, and economics), this notion of the sacred is not defined concretely by religious commitments, but rather by how those things associated with the sacred operate in concretely religious ways. In this instance, religion is no longer about the normative rhetoric and practices attached to communities of faith and related institutions, and how we derive meaning from them. Rather, it is about "meaning making" and our preferences for those places where we enjoy a greater sense of our own fulfillment. Consequently, Americans often derive more meaning from altars found in the supposedly secular arena than in traditionally sacred locations. But this schism between secular and sacred actually marks a key fallacy in contemporary parlance. We have created a dichotomy between the sacred and the secular to our own detriment. The distinction between the two is not as evident as it first appears.

Religion and popular culture are hot topics when considered separately, but when they are brought together, the result can be explosive. This kind of analysis is timely because it seeks to understand the way people actually live, not the way, perhaps in their better moments, they think they should live. Most books on popular culture that touch on religion attempt to understand popular culture as something distinct from the religion that surrounds it, or attempts to influence it, or is influenced by it. This book examines how popular culture itself is religious. In his analysis of fetishism in contemporary American culture and society, David Chidester has suggested that "the study of religion in popular culture is faced with the challenge of exploring and explicating the ways in which such 'artificial' religious constructions can generate genuine enthusiasms and produce real effects in the world."[16] Whereas Chidester's perspective is equally incisive and astute, his phraseology "'artificial' religious constructions" has a troubling connotation: if someone holds a particular object or belief as sacred, what makes it more or less artificial than any other? The designation of what is authentic as opposed to artificial becomes untenable if one realizes that all things religious are created and perpetuated by humans.

Today's media, since at least the presidency of Jimmy Carter and the "Year of the Evangelical," have understood religion as something completely distinct from popular culture. The media routinely address the religious nature of "values voters" who purportedly derive their social concerns from traditional religious expressions. They have tended to use the term "evangelical Christians," a traditional religious classification, for what more appropriately should be called "the religious right," itself a cultural phenomenon. These days, to make matters worse, some in the media, especially the more conservative news outlets, uncritically parrot the political right by using the phrase "radical Islam" as a synonym for global terrorism. In other words, media are generally confused, even when they are discussing the traditional religious communities. Mainstream media have virtually no understanding of the way religion operates outside these parameters. In our setting, the more significant power of religion is found outside the influences of traditional religion's ability to transform culture.

Today the power of religion rests in the way culture operates religiously in people's lives to sustain values and beliefs that have little to do with traditional faith expressions. Yet few are talking about it. People are passionate about the prevalence of religion and the power of culture, but few realize the two are becoming one. American constitutional law has even seen fit to protect culture from overbearing religion, and religion from overbearing state control. But there is little understanding that culture itself can take on religious characteristics unrecognized by most Americans, but operating in an extraordinarily powerful and effective manner. *The Altars Where We Worship* seeks to expose the wizard behind the curtain to reveal just how America is shaped by this largely unexplored phenomenon.

Americans nowadays are more clearly aware that religion participates within a larger marketplace of ideas and experiences. We are hesitant, however, to take the next steps to examine just how the marketplace of ideas and experiences is itself religious. The construction of these "altars" as alternative religious enterprises culled from various dimensions of popular culture appears at first glance to be a blasphemous, narcissistic, and manipulative sham fomented by the worldly and secular. Yet their very existence in American culture indicates a twofold paradox.

First, inherent within their structure, and due to the function and relevance they readily provide for the lives of millions of Americans, these altars combine aspects of religiosity that people experience as transformative, prescriptive, and inspiring. Through them true believers find meaning for their lives that they deem comparable to the meaning others claim to find through more overtly religious settings. Second, and even more interesting, however, is the fact that most Americans live with the both/and in this equation. They attest to being religious and/or spiritual in conventional ways while, at the same time, in actual practice, they find meaning in altars found in popular culture. These folk are able to find gratification and sustenance at these altars, and are able to offer adoration and reverence before them, all without experiencing even the slightest twinge of cognitive dissonance or pang of disloyalty where traditional religious associations are concerned.

For better or worse, we are faced with the reality that human experiences before these altars contain religious characteristics in common with experiences before more traditional altars. Such a discovery, at the very least, requires us to broaden our notions of the American religious experience. Without passing judgment over the worshipers at these altars, many of the core issues and themes found there—differentiating insider/outsider identity, constructing moral and ethical codes of living, providing a mythological as well as epistemological framework for understanding human existence, and asserting some rationale for transcendence and ultimate meaning—are common concerns within the history of religion writ large. Rather than trying to debunk these altars in any fashion, we believe it is important to recognize that these altars naturally connect with our human desire to locate the religious impulse in something we perceive to be greater than ourselves. Clearly, within these spheres of popular culture, Americans have been able to discover religious elements that had once been understood to be the sole province of the world's great faiths.

Our method for examining these altars will adapt the seven dimensions of religion outlined by Ninian Smart in his seminal volume *The Religious Experience of Mankind*. His sevenfold framework offers a useful device for deriving a more complete picture of the religiosity associated with each altar.[17] Like more formal religions, each of these altars provides followers with (1) a *mythic narrative* to aid in addressing matters of sacred meaning and holy significance, sometimes in epic fashion; (2) a system of *doctrines* that outlines appropriate relationships and offers guidance concerning how followers should orient themselves within the world; (3) a set of *ethical codes* defining key values, principles or precepts, and rules or laws; (4) an *organization or institution* to aid in perpetuating religious ideas and imbedding them in the societal fabric; (5) a *ritualistic dimension* within which the faithful engage in acts that define meaning for life and merge belief with exercises of experience and practice; (6) an *experiential dimension* that enables followers to express their feelings and experience extraordinary meaning; and (7) a *material dimension* with concrete and tangible expressions of the sacred that enliven the five senses of touch, smell, sight, hearing, and taste.

Using Smart's typology to analyze what to most observers is merely secular culture enlarges our understanding not only of American culture, but also of the fabric of religion now operating within it. It allows us a means of examining the internal logic found within these cultural contexts ("altars"), in order to demonstrate what precisely, in religious terms, is happening for those who find meaning there. The typology enables a comparison with more traditional expressions of religion.

Finally, we believe the application of Smart's typology effectively expands our understanding of religion and acknowledges more accurately the actual practices associated with the complexity of religious faith as it exists within contemporary American society. We hope that the chapters that follow will help draw each reader into this process of interpretation and allow personal and meaningful reflection about the complex interaction between religion and culture within American society.

In addition to this framework of interpretation, we believe it might be helpful to readers if we share the impetus behind this analysis. At present, the academic study of religion is about understanding religion, not about either proselytizing or naming the heretical. Put another way, it is about perceiving and not prescribing about what is religious in our daily lives. This is especially true in this era, marked by religious pluralism on one side and globalization on the other. The scholarly analysis of religion is also filled with jargon and academic rigmarole (i.e., what seems for many to be confused and meaningless talk). Even though much of it offers helpful analysis about the religious, one has to care passionately enough about it, and labor long to understand it, before receiving much benefit from it. This is too bad, since acquaintance with some conclusions of the scholarly study of religion could actually help people who are religious understand and appreciate religion in new and vital ways. Further, they might find that greater knowledge of religion in general could help them plumb the depths of their own beliefs and to become more tolerant of, and conversant with, religious difference.

Even given the enormous production of scholarship in religious studies and theological education, the average citizen has little access to, or interest in, the content found within it. Consequently, few Americans, in spite of the self-confessed importance of religion for their lives, reflect critically or analytically about how they might be caught off guard by the power of religious experiences and expressions that actually appear, on the face of things, to be something other than religious. No matter what the cultural context for a person's life might be, no matter what a person's line of work, and no matter how thoroughly socialized within congregation or temple or mosque, there is nearly always a considerable chasm between how Americans *profess* their respective faiths and how they *practice* them. We believe a consideration of how popular culture operates in religious ways might offer Americans who are intentionally religious in traditional ways an opportunity to reflect about this gap between profession and practice in their own expressions of religious piety, belief, and experience, perhaps even to work to close it if they so choose.

If existing formulations of religious studies accomplish little in furthering general understandings of religion, the same is true of scholarly tendencies to compartmentalize the distribution of knowledge into departments and academic fields. Simply put, the examination of these modern-day cultural altars offers a multilayered and multidisciplinary approach to knowledge about religion. Such a look requires a multidisciplinary gaze that is able to draw from anthropology, sociology, psychology, history, political science, economics, linguistics, and the natural sciences, among other fields, to provide insights into the innermost workings of religion as a part of daily life in contemporary America. This sort of intellectual hybridity (or mixture) is increasingly important, because our existences in contemporary society gravitate toward being gestalt affairs rather than piecemeal endeavors. To put it more colloquially, the thoughts and experiences of most Americans, when considered as a whole package, nearly always amount to more than the sum of their parts. To understand the whole, we need somehow to make sense of more than just the individual experiences that contribute to the whole.

Therefore, even though we are affected by the dynamics of the natural environment, we must remember that the principles associated with ecology and biology constitute only one facet of our human existence. We are all political citizens subject to mandates defined by governmental authority as a fact of our lives. As consumers and producers, we exist under the dictates of the market. Countless other forces affect our daily existence as Americans, among them religion. As religious beings, Americans yearn to orient themselves within the world and find meaning in and for life that is transcendent to mundane experiences.

Though some would claim otherwise, we believe human beings are essentially religious: all human beings seek meaning and purpose for life. Of course, there are some who deny seeking meaning and purpose, but who actually find their meaning and purpose for life in denying their need to seek it. When one recognizes that humans naturally seek meaning, and that this quest is essentially religious, then one is able also to see that the "religious" is capable of attaching itself to any number of seemingly "nonreligious" forms.

The altars we examine here operate religiously for people, especially in cases where the heart might experience what the mind has not yet fully understood. That is why they can operate religiously, without any sense of contradiction, and create community simultaneously between persons as different from one another as the fundamentalist Christian and the secular humanist. The religious dimensions of these cultural altars can gather to worship together an amazingly divergent group of persons who otherwise have very little in common, especially considering traditional religious commitments. And yet they contribute meaningfully—perhaps more so than traditional religious altars—to how Americans define their lives, how they interact with others on a regular basis, and ultimately how they make sense of the world around them.

Contrary to the assumptions found during the modern period of the Enlightenment, no community in today's world, whether secular or religious, possesses a monopoly on truth. Our contemporary postmodern context means we need to recognize that everybody has a point of view. There is no exclusive or extraordinary claim on objectivity. Instead, every person is shaped by some community of assumptions. You might grow up outside the church and believe that religion has no place in public discussions because religion is not rational. In that case, you might believe that only nonreligious people can be rational. You might even find your purpose and meaning in life making such a claim (and thus, by some definitions, be acting "religiously" in the faith you place in your commitment to nonreligion).

However, in a postmodern context, we can now recognize that this type of belief in secular assumptions is no more objective or inherently truthful than assumptions created and shared within any variety of religious communities. Every person, in a contemporary public discussion, needs to be aware that assumptions come from somewhere—that all persons are shaped by the assumptions of the community or communities that formed them. When you are aware that this is the case, you learn how to listen to others, and how to communicate with others without insisting that your way of seeing things is the only way to see things, or that your way is synonymous with the truth.

A postmodern context enables us to assess a central truth about an examination of the religious significance of these cultural altars, namely, the claim that they share modes of operation and practice that are common to major world religious traditions like Judaism, Christianity, Islam, and Buddhism. They operate as communities that form those who regularly inhabit their spheres of influence. In the complex features of contemporary society, rarely does one find individuals who are shaped solely by a traditional religious community (a remote Amish community might be able to make such a claim). Instead, contemporary Americans are shaped by multiple communities. Given the low attendance in most traditional religious communities even on one day per week, most Americans are more likely shaped at a fundamental level by the communities they inhabit with more frequency the other six days of the week.

In this study, we are engaged very much in an investigation of a particular time and place in human history: we are striving for the sense of what religious faith is like in the early twenty-first century in the United States. In our examination of these altars, the field known as history of religion informs an important aspect of our method. As pioneering historian of religion Mircea Eliade indicated in his classic work *The Sacred and the Profane* (1959), it is crucial that we operate with a definition of religion as dualistic concern that has a fluid dynamism at its core. In his far-ranging vision, Eliade depicted the boundary between sacred and secular as much more permeable than previous considerations had ever acknowledged. According to Eliade, "The threshold is the limit, the boundary, the frontier that distinguishes and opposes two worlds—and at the same time the paradoxical place where those worlds communicate, where passage from the profane to the sacred world becomes possible."[18] Ninian Smart suggests that "the washing away of a fundamental distinction between religion and secular worldviews enables us to ask more sensible questions about the functions of symptoms of belief."[19]

Without a discipline of historical inquiry with its attention to issues of chronology, causation, context, and consequence, our grappling with the religious worldview of another individual or group—even those who might ostensibly share a belief system or faith tradition similar to our own—eventually makes no sense and becomes mired in irrelevancy. The history of religion is useful because it helps us infer how present perspectives and structures of religion—ranging from traditional organized religion to seemingly secular forms acting religiously—have emerged from the deep, messy, and complex web of human interactions and historic events over the long passage of time. In this way, the history of religion challenges us to go beyond the immediately evident and readily available forms of proof that, in turn, can also allow greater insight into the sacred heart of traditions. This heart contains such things as the lure of myth and ritual, the forcefulness of religious doctrine and values, the dynamism of pious conduct and numinous experience, and the enduring strength of communities of faith and their respective institutions. These serve to indicate to what extent faith has shaped our society and, conversely, to what extent society has molded our notions of faith.

In a similar vein, historian of religion Charles Long's *Significations* offers many provocative means of understanding religion as something that stands at the heart of what it means to be human. Human life itself is a constant search for meaning and personal definition/distinction. Most especially, Long's assessment of "cargo cults" demonstrates how a human community can develop quasi-religious preoccupations with material culture and cultural artifacts in ways that lead them to make fetishes and begin to worship them.[20] In another useful insight, Long invites scholars to question whether the traditional distinction in Christian theology between the "visible church" and the "invisible church" of the saved might actually represent a perpetual human search to find new locations to enable communal salvation.[21] In other words, rather than being dismissive of nontraditional religious locations, it might be more important to explore how everything (and everyone) is linked to the grand quest for human meaning and transcendence.[22]

To get a broad picture of what is actually happening in religious life, people need to look at the nontraditional locations alongside the more traditional ones. When viewed through such a prism, the interplay between religion and popular culture in our society is a richly layered and reciprocal relationship. We might see how the virtual construction of these altars is neither fixed to one place on the map nor limited to a specific moment in human time. Instead, we can begin to see the building of these altars as a process. In worshiping at these altars, Americans share experiences with other human beings across countless generations who have attempted to fulfill the very human desire to create meaning for their lives.

Equally germane to this exploration are the numerous insights gleaned from the field most commonly referred to as "theology of culture." On face value, this phrase often seems to represent a paradox instead of a partnership of sorts. On the one hand, theology (understood literally as God-talk) in its pondering of the sacred, holy, and divine is not necessarily directly at odds with the realm of secular culture. On the other hand, secular culture for many people automatically assumes a sphere of existence free of God and devoid of notions of faith and spirit. When joined together in this fashion, the phrase "theology of culture" appears to be contradictory and internally divided. It is our contention, however, that nothing can be further from the truth. The notion of a radical separation between the sacred and the secular is an assumption more than an actuality. In many instances, a shared realm of human experience runs through them both. Human beings seek an escape from the mundane or a notion of transcendence in the sacred and a feeling of the presence (or immanence) of the divine in the everydayness of their lives.

Without question, theology of culture is deeply indebted to the theological reflections of Paul Tillich. In his rather ubiquitous statement that religion is the "ultimate concern" of a person, Tillich explores the religious dimensions of popular culture in terms of its ultimacy—the synergy of ultimate concern (or obsession, if taken to excess) and the pursuit of ultimate fulfillment (whether it is eternal or ephemeral).[23] Elsewhere, Tillich asserts, "Religion is the substance of culture [and] culture is the form of religion. Such a consideration definitely prevents the establishment of a dualism of religion and culture. Every religious act, not only in organized religion, but also in the most intimate movement of the soul, is culturally formed."[24]

In this and other meaningful ways, Tillich moves from basic considerations to concrete applications in his attempt to illustrate "the religious dimension in many special spheres of [human] cultural activity." He analyzes the symbiotic relationship of religion to art, science, education, philosophy, and psychology among other human endeavors, as an attempt to overcome the "fateful gap between religion and culture." Tillich makes considerable inroads in connecting theology to culture broadly conceived. He also draws heavily from various academic disciplines in order to bring theology into fuller and richer conversation with other fields of knowledge and research. For example, his seminal work on symbols helps scholars rethink the iconographic significance of theological language.

In an attempt to bring the conversation found in this introduction full circle, we would note that the rigorous exchange between Mircea Eliade and Paul Tillich (in his later years until his death) provides a critical bridge linking the history of religions with theological thinking that, since that time, has offered new vistas for imagining the world around us. An awareness of the importance of a notion like the theology of culture can provide a vision of what religious reflection is and aid an examination of how it exists in our present context. Perhaps a study like this one, a practical exercise examining the ways Americans worship, through attention to various cultural aspects of their lives, will prove fruitful in providing a better understanding of the essential nature of religion itself as it operates in the twenty-first century.

We want to make clear that our approach is not interested in trying to define which religious experiences are true and which are not. In the chapters that follow, we examine six aspects of American culture that function essentially as "altars" where Americans gather to worship and produce meaning for their lives. At these altars, Americans reconcile themselves to a "serviceable God" who promises to meet their every desire. By examining the major players, fads, trends, movements, and events associated with each of these altars, each chapter will examine the religious inner workings of the popular cultural phenomenon associated with them.

While each of these altars offers its own justifications about the truth, our claim here is rather that all these religious experiences are simply authentically religious, whether their justifications be true, false, or somewhere in between. This work approaches each cultural altar as a place where an inhabited and quite human worldview operates authentically and religiously in forming the people who frequently seek and often find some kind of meaning and sustenance for life from it. Our study of these altars as a uniquely American form of religious expression begins with the assumption that some kind of faith exists at its point of origin. Therefore, all these experiences are authentic religious experiences. Rather than narrowly defining religion by its description (formal or functional), its origination (ordinary or extraordinary), or its direction ("this-worldly" or "otherworldly"), our approach enables us as observers to assess what associated religious practice *means* to the social and historical actors within a particular setting, as these actors attempt to make sense of themselves, their world, and what they consider to be sacred. In sum, this examination of the altars where we worship is intended to suggest a new direction in the study of American religion that would make room for a broader understanding of how religion and religious experiences hidden within American popular culture actually shape the lives of nearly all Americans. We expect that many more capable scholars will take this study much further than we do here.

1

Body and Sex

"Vanity of vanities, all is vanity." What the biblical book of Ecclesiastes condemns, American society tends to celebrate. While beauty is the physical characteristic of a person that gives pleasure to our senses and stirs the observer to behold it, vanity is the excessive pride one has in how their image evokes that response in others. Taken from the Latin word *vanitas*, vanity corresponds to the temporary or fleeting nature of human existence, the transience of all earthly things, inasmuch as all beauty fades. Despite the term's indication of emptiness, futility, and the certainty of death, the picture of beauty as vanity has often evoked desire and invited fantasy.

We find an immediate correlation in Greek mythology's classical depiction of Narcissus. Legend has it that Narcissus was the product of the rape of his mother, the nymph Liriope, by a river god named Cephissus. Concerned about his ugly conception but caring for the attractive young child, Liriope talked with Tiresias, a prophet, about what might happen to her son in the future. The prophet told the nymph that Narcissus would live to a ripe old age—given one caveat: "if he didn't come to know himself." As a young man, his excessive pride in his beauty arrested his own social development. He obsessed over his beauty and refused to connect with anyone who loved him. Instead, he faced a punishment of the gods by falling in love with the mirror image of himself reflected in the water. Paralyzed by his beauty, he did nothing but stare into the water and lust after his own image. He never realized he loved merely a reflection of himself.[1]

Whether connected to sexual desire or an obsession with beauty, the focus on our flesh, to make ourselves beautiful, is our attempt to create a reality within which we can live not only as objects of desire but as the

15

actual embodiment of desire. We hope to become beauty incarnate. In an attempt to understand why people fixate on desire, Michel Foucault turns toward an analysis of the practices "by which individuals were led to focus their attention on themselves, to decipher, recognize, and acknowledge themselves as subjects of desire." He concludes that this kind of acknowledgment brings "into play between themselves and themselves a certain relationship that allows them to discover and desire the truth of their being, be it natural or fallen."[2]

The prophet told Liriope that Narcissus must not ever know himself. Foucault would say that Narcissus actually found himself. His desire took him to his end; in dying to it, he fulfilled his destiny and revealed the full truth of his being, which was wrapped up in his desire for himself. Foucault has said that the desirous preoccupation with the self is driven by the need to know oneself. Regardless of all the attempts to distract him and keep him from knowing himself, the desire of Narcissus led him to the truth. Conceived in lust, driven by lust, Narcissus ultimately came to know himself as lust; he was, in fact, the incarnation of lust.

As the half-human, half-divine offspring resulting from a divine rape, Narcissus serves as a metaphor for a grandiose conceit and egotism residing at the heart of a particular strain of theological anthropology. Whether one believes in the hopes of human perfectibility (as liberals are prone to do) or in the wretched irredeemability of humanity (often a conservative perspective), both posit the human as the center of God's energies and attention. At the core of the Narcissus story is the reductionism of divine thought and action to everything human. The gods are, in the end, no better than us. The narratives of Greco-Roman mythology often diminish the activity and will of the Divine, to mirror the worst qualities of human beings, in this case, the quality of human lust.

Originally, the qualities found in Western monotheistic traditions encouraged the elevation of human activity and will in the direction defined by the one God. In some respect, this is the contrast between *vanitas* and *veritas*, the former emphasizing what is false and fleeting, and the latter emphasizing what is true and lasting. Displacing the *imago dei* with the *imago homo*, we prioritize the ephemeral over the eternal, the carnal over the spiritual, and fulfillment over sacrifice. It is all part of being human, which is why those associated with traditional faiths tend to illustrate the same priorities.

Whether we call our preoccupation with beauty narcissism, self-love, or the pursuit of happiness, much of our meaning making in life is related to it. No matter how much we might claim that beauty is either frivolous or meaningless, according to Freud, civilization cannot do without it, because it drives human impulses for both love and sexuality.[3] Wherever beauty presents itself, we are compelled to enjoy it, to literally *feel* it. The more we encounter it, the more we want to embrace and embody it. In these ways, beauty yields to desire. Images of beauty invite us to narrate our own fantasies, which are not merely erotic fiction about some anonymous persona, but rather self-revelations that free us from our human torment and fulfill our most sacred longings. This peculiar sensation is intoxicating and relentless.

Nowhere is this more apparent than in popular culture, where vanity, beauty, and lust make up the stuff of fantasy. According to cultural critic bell hooks, more often than not, men have been the producers and women have been the products of fantasy, yet both have sought their desired ends in the roles they have played: men have created realities and women have found escape.[4] In American life, no popular figure represents this reality better than Marilyn Monroe.

Born Norma Jeane Mortensen on June 1, 1926, in Los Angeles, Marilyn became one of America's most famous sex symbols, in spite of both a difficult childhood and a short life. Defined by trauma in her youth, when an unknown father abandoned her and her mother's mental disease daily affected her, she shuttled through various foster homes and became a victim of both rape and attempted murder. After dropping out of high school at the age of fifteen, she believed marriage would help her escape the horror that had become her life. She interpreted her marriage, at sixteen to merchant mariner Jimmy Dougherty, as a signal of rescue. However, his work abroad in the South Pacific left her alone. Once again, Marilyn found herself faced with the demands of making a life for herself. She took up photography. Her teacher began photographing her, and encouraged her to apply to the Blue Book Modeling Agency. Soon, she embarked on a successful career. In 1946, at the age of twenty, she divorced her husband, changed her name to Marilyn Monroe, and set out on her own.

The first six years of her acting career consisted of bit parts and brief scenes. Though critics thought she had charm, they did not classify her in the gorgeous and gifted category of actresses defined by Jane Russell and Ava Gardner. Her break arrived in 1952, when she assumed the role of a sexy blonde in *Monkey Business*. The role provided her a reputation as an actress who could "suggest one moment that she is the naughtiest little thing," as Laurence Olivier once put it, "and the next that she's perfectly innocent."[5] Her appearance in 1953 as Lorelei Lee in *Gentlemen Prefer Blondes* made the movie a blockbuster. With the right look, disposition, and new husband Joe DiMaggio in tow, Marilyn Monroe became a star. While critics praised the acting of her costars, like Lauren Bacall and Betty Grable, when they turned to Marilyn, they raved about her body and her sex appeal.

Marilyn is not remembered for her acting, but rather for episodes like her standing over a subway grate while the breeze from passing trains flares her white dress. According to Susan Doll, "the shot of Marilyn's white dress billowing up to reveal her shapely legs is so identified with her image that it has become a virtual icon, at once celebrating her sexuality and encapsulating her legend."[6] The scene led to the dissolution of her marriage to DiMaggio, because he grew tired of her being typecast as the ditzy blonde and wanted her on his arm and at home. Marilyn, in a sense, rejected the role of Joe's domesticated blonde doll at home, and instead sought a career as doll for all.

Marilyn Monroe's tempestuous personal life only increased her reputation as a larger-than-life beauty icon and sex goddess. Later, married to playwright Arthur Miller, who offered an entry for her into the world of intellectuals and acclaimed artists, and rumored to be in an affair with President John F. Kennedy, her manufactured life threatened to overshadow her genuine professional triumphs. As her fame grew, so too did the need for others to possess her beauty, body, and sex appeal, and the need for her to escape the limits that such a desire placed on her. Decades after her death, she is still heralded as *Film's Sexiest Woman of All Time*.[7] Many in her wake have fantasized her life; they have taken on the form of Marilyn's sexuality, mimicking it in any way they could muster, without ever wrestling with the core of the bittersweet tragedy represented in her life's story. Perhaps this is all the more possible because of her early death. Her beauty is frozen in time eternally. Popular culture never had to watch Marilyn age in the same way it tracked the aging of Marlon Brando and Elizabeth Taylor, who both became fading caricatures of previous beauty.

As an American icon, Marilyn Monroe's life represented the feminine tragedy, the attempt to garner an image that would sustain the everlasting love of others. As Elton John expressed it in his tribute song, "Candle in the Wind," written in 1973, "Hollywood created a superstar and pain was the price you paid. Even when you died, oh the press still hounded you. All the papers had to say was that Marilyn was found in the nude."[8]

Vanity, no longer understood as a fruitlessness of human efforts in this world, has either become the forbidden fruit that we must taste or the fruit of one's labor that is ours for the picking. The woman who portrays beauty invites us to pay lip service, praise, or rebuke, attests Edwin Mullins, "while offering us full permission to drool over her. She admires herself in the glass, while we treat the picture that purports to incriminate her as another kind of glass—a window—through which we peer and secretly desire her."[9] While Mullins is correct with the vainglory of such representations of beauty, the analysis of our role in it is incomplete.

MYTHOLOGY

The clear myth surrounding body and sex is that "beauty is in the eye of the beholder." This phrase first appeared in print in 1878, when Margaret Wolfe Hungerford published a novel about a young irreverent Irish girl who flirted freely, arousing the jealousy of her lover.[10] The myth as adopted in the West reflects the reality that there is no objective, universal standard of beauty. Beauty can be connected with almost anything, including nature, architecture, animal life, the stars and sky, and even food. Since this chapter concerns itself with body and sex, we will focus on beauty in those connections.

What is considered beautiful can be as diverse as the ones who behold it. This leads all persons to suspect or hope that they are or will be beautiful in the eye of some beholder. It also means that while persons might think they are themselves beautiful, their beauty might not be affirmed in the eye of particular beholders. Yet across cultures, there appears to be some agreement regarding the qualities or features of beauty. This fact leads scholars to the conclusion that some aspects of beauty might, in some sense, be evolutionary. The linkages between physical attractiveness and reproductive potential make "such evolutionary adaptations . . . plausible."[11]

Beauty, and all that attends it, might be evolutionary in another sense as well. More often than not, for a mother, the most beautiful thing in the world is her newborn child. In the same manner, for a child, there is no better sight than his mother. Here, beauty is more than skin deep, for it reflects more than mere aesthetics (the complexion of the skin, the body mass index, the shape and proportion of eyes and nose, and so on). Beauty is that life the mother created, on the one hand, and the one who sustains the life of the newborn, on the other. Beauty, in other words, is connected both to the life we create for ourselves and to that which gives us life. In this sense, beauty becomes an indicator of something else. It often represents what the beholder needs to feel most alive.

The looking glass that Mullins describes with regard to vanity is akin to the long-held myth that beauty is in the eye of the beholder. Yet more needs to be said. The looking glass is not simply a mirror or a window through which we observe the object of our attraction. It is also a two-way mirror that illuminates how we need or want to imagine ourselves. Like the image of a nurturing mother, the images we define as beautiful help us to imagine a beautiful life for ourselves. In the final analysis, beauty becomes the "I" of the beholder. Beauty is not something merely to behold; it is something all beholders inevitably want to take hold of them, to internalize and own, so they can have life and have it more abundantly. Wherever beauty is encountered, desire is expressed not merely in the yearning for the beautiful but in the internalization of it as the ultimate delight. The obsession to fulfill the desire we crave becomes our central preoccupation, and the failure to fulfill it becomes our greatest torment.

The last century has turned the mythic axiom on its head. Beauty becomes the thing we *create* for others and expect them to behold in us so that we might find our *sustenance* for living. Beauty is the object of our desire, and when connected with our bodies, makes eros the core of the human spirit.

DOCTRINE

The doctrinal aspects of body and sex are connected to the importance of eros as, in the words of feminist Audre Lorde, "the life-force" and "creative energy" that affirms what is good about our embodiment and enables our celebration of it.[12] Carter Heyward expands its importance even further when she argues that "the erotic is our most fully embodied experience of the love of God . . . the source of our capacity for transcendence." By this, Heyward means to emphasize the Christian affirmation that proper love of God elevates the spirit, connects human beings with "the divine Spirit's yearning," and develops an empowering relationship with God. God's love is "agapic, philial, and erotic" and to the extent we are able to "embody and express it, it is ours."[13] The point for both Lourde and Heyward is to stress that our nature is bound up in some important way with the erotic. Those who worship at the altar of body and sex would agree; but, for them, eros is placed at the service of pleasure. Its purpose is to live comprehensively within the reality of *imago homo*; it is not rooted in any particular theological understanding of *imago dei*.

This erotic and pleasure-seeking activity produces a passion that, in its urgency and pervasiveness, takes on religious characteristics that make all other obligations pale by comparison. As one scholar describes it, it "is specifically disruptive in a similar sense to charisma; it uproots the individual from the mundane and generates a preparedness to consider radical options as well as sacrifices. For this reason, seen from the point of view of social order and duty, it is dangerous."[14] This powerful creative energy is the driving force of our primal nature as human beings. From the moment of birth, as a matter of human instinct and survival, we seek immediate gratification. We want our needs and urges met, and we want them met now. We don't understand when they are not met quickly; we cry and throw temper tantrums until we get them met. According to Plato, to be human is to "express those erotic longings for what we lack."[15] In essence, eros is ultimately connected to our primal needs. "We enter the world with eros," says scholar Jill Gordon, a philosopher at

Colby College. ("We cultivate it, and we follow it to our fates. In human life, it is eros coming and going."[16] We experience the erotic when we get what our souls most desire.

Freud describes this process as one connected to the "pleasure principle," where how we think and what we do are guided by the human desire to have our needs met. The pleasure principle impacts our basic humanity at the levels of being, thinking, and doing. In this sense, "being" is who one is or portrays the self to be (that is, one's aesthetic [style, tastes, dress, features, physicality] and culture [region, gender, generation, class]); "thinking" is how one strategizes or plots to meet desires; and "doing" is what one does to get needs met. This being, thinking, doing continuum provides purpose to our life and programs our actions to fulfill our desires for pleasure. Eros, as a primal need, should not ever be confused with perversion. The primal need itself is never inherently perverted; rather, how one seeks to meet primal needs could lead to a variety of both pleasures and perversions.

Freud emphasizes that the pleasure principle, in many ways, "decides the purpose of life." (Human beings literally program their lives to experience pleasure and to meet needs. For Freud, the instinctual always seeks pleasure without pain. As Freud points out, this understanding is "at loggerheads with the world." The world rarely delivers pleasure without accompanying pain. As the adage goes, "no pain, no gain." As Freud puts it, "What we call happiness in the strictest sense comes from the (preferably sudden) satisfaction of needs which have been dammed up to a high degree, and it is from its nature only possible as an episodic phenomenon."[17] The short-lived quality of happiness is probably a good thing, because as humans, "we can derive intense enjoyment only from a contrast and very little from a state of things." Freud concludes,

> Thus our possibilities of happiness are already restricted by our constitution. Unhappiness is much less difficult to experience. We are threatened with suffering from three directions: from our own body, which is doomed to decay and dissolution and which cannot even do without pain and anxiety as warning signals; from the external world, which may rage against us with overwhelming and merciless forces of destruction; and finally from our relations to [others].[18]

This is why, as humans mature from infancy through teen years to adults, our thinking adjusts normally from the pleasure principle to what Freud describes as the reality principle.[19] We have to learn to be more cautious about our being, thinking, and doing, so we can navigate ourselves around both desires and dangers, our pleasures and the pains that often accompany them.

ETHICS

The ethical question is always connected to how actions accord with beliefs. People who seek pleasure without pain must create an ethical framework to meet the desire. Ethics help us navigate the possibility of pleasure in order to avoid the pitfalls of pain. There are rules. There are goals. There are advantages and consequences. Society defines certain things as deviant (bestiality), perverted (pedophilia), socially irresponsible (polygamy), nonconsensual (rape), and aberrant (incest) by putting in place laws that curtail some desires we might have.

Ethics is about more than what is wrong. Ethics helps us to define the best means by which we can get what we believe we need or want. Notions of masculinity and femininity projected by society, expectations around age, profiles defining appropriateness for certain professions, one's marital status, and one's religious communities and commitments all contribute to an understanding of how one shapes the fitting response (doing) to who they are (being) and what they need (thinking). In other words, ethical behavior and eros always go hand in hand, in how we utilize our body, how we participate in sex, and how we choose to receive pleasure.

For Christian feminist ethicist Christine Gudorf, our ethical aim as erotic, embodied beings is to engender acceptance and appreciation of our bodies, our sexuality, and our pleasures, not denial and denigration of them or shame about them. Contending that body, sex, and pleasure are divine gifts, Gudorf interprets sexual desire as a positive, good, and life-giving force, whether or not it is attached to reproduction. Though not every form of sexuality is good, Gudorf believes sex "can function as an experience of divine reality." For scholars like Gudorf, the unity of body and sex, and the significance of the soul and body relationship, are embedded in the divine intention and ensconced in creation itself. Gudorf and many other scholars serve as a corrective to long-held neo-Platonic and theological notions that create a radical distinction between body (evil and material) and soul (good and spiritual). This dualism[20] has often resulted in particular sexist gender distinctions, including the notion that the body of women ensnares the soul of men. For contemporary feminists, the counterpoint is to acknowledge that both human experience and human wisdom are in fact inseparable from and grounded in the body.

Standing within the dualistic Neoplatonic tradition, Descartes assumed the human being was made up of both body and mind (soul). He understood the body as material, as an unthinking, unconscious machine subject to the laws of nature. The body, composed of nerves, muscles, and so forth, would be able to function without the mind at all, except for those functions imposed on it by the will, which depends on mind. He believed the mind was immaterial (was not at all visible), conscious, and not bound by nature. These "radically distinct substances," he understood, were connected by the pineal gland, which Descartes believed to be the location of the soul.[21]

Philosopher Maurice Merleau-Ponty challenges Cartesian thought, particularly the dualistic approach to mind and body. Where Descartes understood the body to be a material object completely subject to the mind, Merleau-Ponty sees the body as "a subject in itself, deriving its subjectivity from itself." He takes a thoroughly monistic approach to the relationship between mind and body. The fundamental essence of what it means to be human *is* embodied consciousness. There is a difference between "using a body" or "having a body" and "being a body." For Merleau-Ponty, rather than a human being possessing and using a living body (through the mind), the human being *is* the living body. Consciousness is embodied in all the motions and activities of the lived body. Every human being is a unity of the physical (doing), the biological (being), and the psychological (thinking). You can understand a human person only by analyzing the whole. The human being "in the world" can experience the world only through the body. Meaning is derived "by the interaction of the 'body-subject' and the world." As Merleau-Ponty puts it, "I have no means of knowing the human body other than that of living it, which means taking up on my own account the drama which is being played out in it, and losing myself in it. I am my body."[22]

Our bodies are the very substance of our moral conduct, providing the prime material for our ethical practices in society.[23] Morality is about how we act out our desires and treat the people we know. Ethics, however, is about how we treat the people we don't know. The relationship between the private morality and the public ethic drives everything about how we express our desires in life with those we know, how we preserve ourselves, how we perform as we experience pleasure, how we present ourselves, how we avoid pain, and how we persevere in the midst of our pursuits. When society is confronted with personal defective morality in the lives of public people who extol the ethics of family values, the messiness of all these connections becomes clear (such as, the Bill Cosby serial rape charges, teachers who bed their students, the Roman Catholic sex-abuse scandal, former President Bill Clinton and Monica Lewinsky). Thus, while the pleasure principle encapsulates our desires, ethics helps us know what to do with our bodies to gain through our pleasure and experience the full drama of who we are and what we hope to become.

RITUAL

Rituals represent that part of the drama that includes the routines people perform that help to prepare them for their religious practice. Or, as in the case of rites of passage, rituals actually provide transition to a new phase of life or transformation from the old to the new. When individuals and communities kneel, bow, stand up, pray, sing, shout, and dance to express reverence in worship, they engage in rituals that signify their experience as they face the mysteries of the universe in such a way as to bind themselves to their fellow human beings and to the Divine in a deeper and ongoing relationship. The relation of worshiper and the worshiped can be an act of praise, sacrifice, supplication, remembrance, celebration, or communication. As religious beings, our rituals testify to, and help us to maintain, our piety, express our religious ideals, and convey the depth of our commitments.

Personal and cultural rituals play a similar role in the area of body and sex. For many of us in America, cultural ideals from birth defined particular expectations for the bodies of men and women: "little girls bodies were judged by how they look, while little boys were judged on how they perform."[24] In the spirit of gender conformity, rituals help the beautiful woman to maintain her beauty, the strong man to keep his physique. Those who already embody the ideals must maintain them; those who do not yet embody these ideals must more fervently commit to the rituals that might produce the kind of body that faithfully represents the ideals.

We are going to spend some time in this section (more than we will in following chapters) in order to illustrate how Americans created, and imbedded in the making of a nation, normalized understandings—a definition of what constitutes normalcy—meant to assist in the assimilation of all who arrived on American shores. The efforts to assimilate helped to create rituals that have ever since become attached to bodies, sex, and pleasure. American rituals have everything to say about how we form our bodies and thus everything to say about who we are, and thus how our bodies represent a response to cultural ideals. While to be human is to have needs and desire pleasures, our bodies are the conduits through which we express them and the currency with which we obtain them. In this exchange between desire and fulfillment, our bodies are in fact formed.

As particular persons in natural form confront cultural ideals defining desirability, in most cases they find themselves lacking. Imagine for a moment the relationship between our private faces and our public faces. When a supermodel wakes up in the morning and gets a glimpse of herself in the mirror, no matter how beautiful her face without makeup, she must undergo the ritual of "putting on her face." Cultural ideals of beauty demand it. How much more is this the case for the average American? No matter who we are, what we see first in the mirror are the things we think we should mask. We undergo our beauty routines and physical regimens to help us cover up the reality. In the same way, society reflects back our bodily flaws, and we participate in rituals in order to mask them. Hollywood's Dinah Shore poignantly addresses this point: "One of the many things men don't understand about women is the extent to which our self-esteem depends on how we feel we look at any given moment—and how much we yearn for a compliment, at any age. If I had just won the Nobel Peace Prize but felt my hair looked awful, I would not be glowing with self-assurance when I entered the room."[25]

Caught within this aesthetic of existence, our value is determined by how we measure up to these ideals. Though no one, regardless of gender, escapes it, the bodies of women definitely carry the heaviest burdens. There are few areas in life where injustice is more blatant and failure more painful than the area of physical beauty for women. Women have still not learned how to ward off the dehumanizing slander that cultural ideals communicate about their bodies. Susan Friedman provides an exclamation point:

> You are ugly. You are fat. Your breasts are too small (or large). Your thighs are too fat, your calves are too thin. Your eyes are too small. Your hair is mousy-colored. Your nose has a bump. You are too skinny. You have hair on your face. Your hair is too curly. Your hair is too thin. You have midriff bulge. You have vaginal odor. You wear glasses. Your face is covered with pimples. You compare yourself to almost every woman you see, even ones you pass on the street . . . but no matter who you compare yourself with, you never really feel good about your body.[26]

Cultural perceptions of feminine beauty are dehumanizing, not only to the women who do not represent them, but also they become infuriating for those who do represent them and find the ground shifting beneath their feet. Cultural ideals of beauty often change faster than bodies themselves. We need only to look at a sampling of the top supermodels of all time to illustrate changing notions of the ideal woman: Twiggy and Verushka (1960s); Lauren Hutton and Iman (1970s); Cheryl Tiegs and Kalina Porizkova (1980s); Naomi Campbell and Kate Moss (1990s); Gisele Bündchen and Karen Elson (2000s); Kate Upton and Cara Delevingne (2010s). Hollywood's sampling of sexy celebrities makes the same point: Elizabeth Taylor and Marilyn Monroe (1960s); Linda Carter and Jamie Leigh Curtis (1970s); Bo Derek and Kim Bassinger (1980s); Uma Thurman and Demi Moore (1990s); Halle Berry and Angelina Jolie (2000s); Scarlett Johansson and Jennifer Lawrence (2010s). Linda Sanford and Mary Donovan stress the obvious when they point out, "There are usually many equally ridiculous and often diametrically opposed ideals operating simultaneously. . . . No woman can live up to—or even strive for—both these heavily promoted ideals at the same time."[27]

While the common experience of having desire is universal, the embodied experience of it is particular. Our bodies are not merely human in an abstract or homogenous sense; they are also raced, sexed, classed, and differently abled.[28] For each of these categories, American history has indelibly shaped us. American responses to aspects of its British past, in at least three respects, are specifically relevant here. First, Victorian ideals defined what it meant to be fully human and civilized.[29] They addressed how Americans carried their bodies both sexually and aesthetically. To be "civilized" translated into being enlightened, virtuous, industrious, and invested in the elevation of the race.

Second, America has had to deal with a notion of its own inferiority to Britain, ever defending itself as the container, in the words of Emma Lazarus, of "your tired, your poor, your huddled masses yearning to breathe free, the wretched refuse of your teeming shore. Send these, the homeless, tempest-tossed to me."[30] As a result, America has developed a robust understanding of its own identity, in part at least to portray a contrived and created sense of its own superiority. Early Americans, in rejecting their British identity, actually ended up reifying it as they attempted to prove their superiority to it and their independence from it.[31] The reputation of the "ugly American" who travels abroad is directly connected to this phenomenon. So much about being an American actually involves affirming ourselves as distinctly American.

Third, the African slave trade itself played a significant role in defining the ritualistic understanding and classification of American bodies. Shaped first by Enlightenment philosophies and later by Victorian principles, faced with the need to build an empire of its own, and marked by cultural capitalism, American identity became manifest through its ritual of colonizing darker bodies, which became one of the strongest forces shaping how we have classified or consumed bodies for our own use. We need to look no further than the plantation, where we see the genealogy of American bodies along a racial continuum, a caste system, an ageist structure, through a sexualized gaze, and based on physical ability.

When enslaved African men arrived on the good ship *Jesus* in 1619, they immediately became black, the color ascribed to evil, and thereby were stripped of land, ethnicity, and culture. Their enslavers bought them for an "average" price of $1,000 on the auction block. White masters valued them for their work as field hands and laborers. They described them as "work oxen" and bucks. In 1669, these masters bought black women for $50 to work as laborers and field hands, to serve as wet nurses for white children while breeding their own offspring to be enslaved. They described them as "brood sows" or "heifers."[32] For centuries, auction blocks displayed black bodies being sold and prodded alongside horses, cattle, bulls, and pigs. Enslavers routinely raped black women, often while their black male partners looked on, feeling impotent to stop it. White masters forbade black men and women to marry and routinely broke up their families and sold their loved ones and children. When black persons did not submit to their enslaver's demands, they were beaten, sold, or lynched. No black body could defy its white control.

Dowries, often a combination of money, land, livestock, and enslaved blacks, defined the value of the suitable (thus white and wealthy) wife. She served as mistress of the house and progenitor of the race.[33] White men described her as virginal and chaste, a prized possession, and put her on a pedestal. Her husband regarded her as an object to love and/or behold, rather than an object of lust and sexual longing. Thus, white husbands often regarded sex as procreation in the strictest sense in the white household, but acted out their sexual pleasures and fantasies on the bodies of black women. The sexual desires, needs, and longings of white wives often went unmet and unfulfilled.

Nobody bought and sold white men in the plantation system. The white man stood above all commodities; therefore, he was priceless. Instead, he attributed value to the people on his land. He served as the pioneer, the politician, and the patriarch. He was the mastermind: powerful in his reach, not bound by any body, yet able to manipulate bodies to fulfill whatever his mind could perceive. Based on this legacy, women and people of color were bodies that were available for fulfilling the needs and desires of white men. Whatever his heart desired and mind could conjure up, he subjected these bodies to, while his gaze and assessment of them became the mirror through which they assessed their social value and desirability. The ritual of making the American body beautiful is attributed to this master narrative and American ritual even today.[34] Political theorist Joan Cocks states this stridently,

> Male "myth-masters" and "enforcers" condition women to submit to male rule by implanting "false molds" in their minds, reinforced by "ego-depressing follow-up fixes," while the same myth-masters condition men to become the victimizers of women, giving them follow-up fixes that are "ego-inflating." Contemporary patriarchy takes on the monstrous form of a phallotechnocracy attracted to all that is "dead, robotized, [and] mechanical."[35]

The daily rituals devoted to the makeup women wear, to body modifications women and people of color undergo, and those rituals associated with whom we date or how we mate, are often driven by the larger narrative of the classification of American bodies since chattel slavery. According to Cornel West, the normative gaze of white men's social boundaries draws and sets the perimeters for categorizing American bodies as it informs the intelligibility and legitimacy of white supremacy.[36] Not all bodies are human. To be human is to inhabit realms of beauty, culture, and intelligence that only white bodies could possess and white men could affirm.

As mastermind, white men's roles in society established normative perimeters so as "to produce and prohibit, develop and delimit specific conceptions of truth, knowledge, beauty, character, aesthetic and cultural ideals."[37] The discourse of white, Anglo-Saxon, heteropatriarchal supremacy is comprehensible and intelligible only to those who share the classification, while incomprehensible and unintelligible to the bodies of others, even though they became subject to it. Everything is based on the gaze defined by normativity. Though the specifics or minutiae associated with the gaze might change from generation to generation, the overarching rigidity of white supremacy remains firmly in place.

Within that gaze, American cultural assumptions about what constitutes "the normal" create the rituals for everyone within the culture. No area within the American landscape is exempt from white supremacy. The prevailing mode of production in manufacturing cosmetics, fashion, and sex toys has white men in mind, even though women are buying the products. Additionally, national and local politics reflect the political interests of the ruling class through such practices as racial profiling, the design of the prison industrial complex, the exploitation of Mexican Americans, and the creation of a global economy. Darker bodies must cater to these local and political interests, or they become suspects. And to be a suspect and black is dangerous indeed.

Contemporary American events—including the acquittal of George Zimmerman in the shooting of Trayvon Martin and later the deaths of Michael Brown in Ferguson, Missouri, Freddie Gray in Baltimore, Sandra Bland in Hempstead, Texas, and Alton Sterling in Baton Rouge, Louisiana, among many others at that hands of police officers—reveal clearly that police tend to deal with black suspects (bodies) far more violently than suspects who happen to be white. These events ushered in the birth of a vital movement, known as Black Lives Matter, that gained national traction in the summer of 2015 with the Charleston Nine massacre and the heated debates surrounding placement of the Confederate flag.

Further, the psychological needs of white men create a culture where "men will be men." This means men sowing wild oats, having more than one woman, and even in extreme cases blaming the victims for what they wear in an attempt to rationalize rape. Finally, culture uses reason, science, and religion to legitimate the white normative gaze and the superiority of the aesthetic and cultural ideals associated with it in order to define the character of all American rituals.

In other words, writers, artists, and scholars promoted normative rules in "natural history" to govern the size of eyes, eyebrows, hair, forehead, collarbones, hands, feet, noses, complexion, and so on. Through the power of this cultural practice, they observe, compare, measure, and impose order on the visible characteristics of human bodies.[38] Rituals develop to respond to these definitions of the normal that correlate with the erotic (what our souls must have). As a result, both men and women will spend more than they can afford to put on a good face, flex their muscles, and dress for attention and success. Women undergo excessive dieting, working out, and even plastic surgery to become trophy wives and sex icons. Mothers train their daughters in the same path, perpetuating the notion that a woman's desirability (and thus self-worth) is connected to her outward bodily appearance and ability to land a man/husband. Plastic surgeons become the experts of a gaze that states how a woman's body ought to appear and be shaped.[39]

The housewife might undergo a "nip and tuck" to tighten abdominal muscles or flabby skin loosened by pregnancy or weight loss. The rich and famous often go to the extreme of repeated face-lifts, vaginal tightening, breast and cheekbone implants, collagen and Botox injections, and even the removal of ribs to whittle away their waists—all in the name of fulfilling their need to meet cultural standards of beauty and to be loved and admired.[40] This "feminine" ideal transforms women into objects and deprives them of any self-creativity not useful to the male scheme of things.[41]

This genealogy classifies bodies along a hierarchical scale based on race, ethnicity, class, gender, sexual orientation, and physical ability. This scale defines both beautiful and human in ways altogether comprehensible even to children. In this American context, the culture has historically defined normativity in creative and seemingly innocuous ways, through products like Aunt Jemima's syrup, children's stories like "Little Black Sambo," and nursery rhymes like "if you're black get back, if you're white you're alright."[42] This spectrum includes categories that might be described as honorary whiteness and dishonorable blackness. Many people of color attempt racial passing when possible or resort to skin bleaching, straightening hair, undergoing rhinoplasty, and changing eye color via contacts or eye shape via surgery, in an effort to brighten their chances of being considered attractive or beautiful.

Whether we are talking about the slanted eyes of Asians, broad noses and kinky hair of Africans, the swarthy color of Latinos, the protruding noses of Jews, the large ears of the Irish—the list could go on—the normative gaze of white, Anglo-Saxon, Protestant, heterosexual, propertied, enslaving men determined which bodies were beautiful, civilized, and human. Asian poet Nellie Wong recalls her pain of growing up in the gaze of white normativity, and asserts that racist and sexist standards of American beauty are unhealthy, unrealistic, and untenable:

> I know now that once I longed to be white.
> How? you ask.
> Let me tell you the ways. . . .
> when I was growing up, I read magazines
>   and saw movies, blond movie stars, white skin,
>   sensuous lips and to be elevated, to become
>   a woman, a desirable woman, I began to wear
>   imaginary pale skin . . .
> when I was growing up, I felt
>   dirty. I thought that god
>   made white people clean
>   and no matter how much I bathed,
>   I could not change, I could not shed
>   my skin in the gray water. . . .
> I know now that once I longed to be white.
> How many more ways? You ask.
> Haven't I told you enough?[43]

The normative gaze of the mastermind has been so successful that it has now become the mind of the bodies that are subject to it. This gaze continues to define American rituals associated with body, sex, and pleasure through those who took on the master's consciousness, so effectively that the mastermind is no longer needed to make this work. As W. E. B. DuBois put it, "It is a peculiar sensation . . . this sense of always looking at oneself through the eyes of others, of measuring one's soul through the tape of a world that looks on in amused contempt and pity. . . . One ever feels [this twoness] . . . two souls, two thoughts, two unreconciled strivings; two warring ideals in one dark body, whose dogged strength alone keeps it from being torn asunder."[44]

As a consequence, self-sacrificing women and people of color act out their rage and contempt, projecting these same classifications, and the inabilities of people to meet them, onto each other. According to Susan Parsons, this creates a perennial crisis of embodied identity for the individual objectified by this gaze:

> For in the look of others, I become an object through my body, so that my body becomes known by others, used by them, studied and examined, looked upon, and insofar as I exist in my body, I become frozen, stuck, fixed by this objectification. This knowledge of myself through the eyes of others begins for me a most difficult and tortuous journey of relationships with them, in which I face continual choices about how I am to be known to my body.[45]

Horizontal violence becomes a ritual of its own, as people size each other up and find one another lacking. Women, men, and people of color are often their own worst critics when it comes to their bodies. Although men in our society often take up license to inspect women from head to toe, pronouncing their approval in obscene catcalls or disdain in scolding and shaming insults, often from the mouths of fathers and husbands, women can pose an even greater threat to each other's self-esteem. Women become fashion police, as they "slut shame," or fall prey to the "mean girl syndrome." People of color will use colorism and pigmentocracy to belittle and "denigrate" each other. And black men, perhaps more subtly but still as demeaning, will "punk each other out," call each other "fat bastards," "pussies," and "bust each other's balls."[46]

On the plantation during the antebellum era, the mastermind lusted after black women and defined white women as virginal. Today, some also seek what the normative gaze grants naturally to others. Some women of color seek to be beautiful, human, and civilized, while some whites seek not merely to be beautiful but also to be sexy. Many women of color (blacks, Latinas, and Asians alike) attempt to meet white feminine notions of beauty through rituals of bleaching, excessive dieting, tucking in buttocks, downplaying full lips, changing hair texture, and donning wigs and weaves. White women seek exotic and erotic desirability by engaging in rituals that tan their skin, pad their butts, collagen their lips, and perm their hair. Just as their white male ancestors sought to find delight in enslaved women of color, so too might they want to be the subject of such erotic delight. Within current debates about race and beauty, desire and difference, cultural critic bell hooks writes,

> The commodification of Otherness has been so successful because it has been offered as a new delight, more intense, more satisfying than normal ways of doing and feeling. Within commodity culture, ethnicity becomes spice, seasoning that can liven up the main dish that is mainstream white culture. Cultural taboos around sexuality and desire are transgressed and made explicit as the media bombards folks with a message of difference no longer based on the white supremacist assumption that 'blondes have more fun.'[47]

One way or another, the normative gaze requires rituals that enhance bodies to increase pleasure, for to be both beautiful and desirable is to be more fully human.

EXPERIENCE

The sexual experience often becomes the central focus of body, sex, and pleasure. Intrinsic to one's desirability is the realization and embodied experience

of it. Experiences of sexual gratification or sexual attraction are social pro-
cesses that include not only specific actions (becoming desirable or getting
one's needs met) but also evaluations of how well one performs those actions.
Sexual experiences—ranging from "normal" sexual relationships, all the way
to the turn-ons experienced through the worship of celebrities; to cybersex
enjoyed by teenagers, married men, agoraphobics, differently abled, and the
elderly—are not merely reflective actions that involve social, economic, political, and cultural factors.

Sexual experiences also indicate communal aspects and personal yearnings
that are socially located, power defined, and interest laden. Sexual satisfaction is experienced alone or in groups through procreation, orgies, mastur-
bation, sadomasochism, voyeurism, virtual sex, intercourse, role play, felatio,
and cunnilingus (to name a few ways). It reveals and validates comprehensive ways of self-interpretation, of seeing and understanding the world, of
constructing one's self and society from an ever-expanding range of tastes,
appetites, abilities, means, contexts, and social locations. As varied as these
forms of experience are, the way people attend to their needs makes clear
that we cannot assume there exists a universal experience of sexual satisfaction. The normative gaze does not have the same stronghold in experience
that it maintains in ritual. In fact, since sexual satisfaction is a way of freeing
one's body to experience its most sacred delights and secret desires, many
regard sex between consenting parties as the ultimate experience of freedom.
At the same time, this notion of sexual satisfaction raises the issue of who is
being satisfied.

Without a doubt, if we asked a random sample of Americans to dream
up their wildest sexual fantasy and describe in detail what they considered
as awesome, earthshaking, mind-blowing, exhilarating sex, the fantasies
expressed would display considerable variety. When it comes to sexual satisfaction, there is no one-size-fits-all definition. For some, sexual fulfillment
includes feelings of trust, physical security, and bodily control—basically,
feeling as if you can really let go without being threatened or judged during sex. For others, gratification involves feelings of emotional closeness,
intimacy, and connection to a sexual partner. Interestingly enough, and
perhaps no surprise, men favored the first definition, while women favored
the second.[48]

So what do people experience when they are being sexually satisfied? It
is important to note that sexual satisfaction is not synonymous with orgasm.
For some, satisfaction requires experiencing orgasms; for others, it requires
faking them. For some, it involves taking off clothes; for others, merely imagining what lies underneath the other's clothes provides a measure of satisfaction. Asexual people are sexually satisfied when they achieve freedom from

the anxieties that come with sex. Those who abstain from sex, whether due to chastity, abstinence, or religious vows, may be sexually satisfied through pleasing their parents, saving themselves for a future mate, or understanding God as the lover of their souls.

(The experience of body, sex, and pleasure must resonate with the particularities of individuals whose very existence often depends on the ability to express and enjoy it. Nowhere is this fact more palpable than it is in the case of transsexual and transgendered peoples and their experience of sex reassignment. Trans people who experience mind-body dissonance live in a reality where their gender consciousness does not correspond to their physical sex. In this context, they are forced to pretend to be a member of a gender with which they do not identify. For many, their first experience of sexual satisfaction comes only when they have been able to integrate their consciousness with their bodies.)

According to biologist and transsexual woman Julia Serano, transgendered people and sexologists agree that often "the only thing that has ever been shown to successfully alleviate gender dissonance is allowing the trans person to live in their identified gender."[49] Such things are not easy to accomplish when laws in most cities across the nation prevent transgendered women from even entering women's restrooms. In the November 2015 election, the city of Houston rejected the Houston Equal Rights Ordinance (HERO) when those opposing it successfully used an ad campaign called "Any Man Anytime." The campaign stressed that HERO would allow any man anytime to enter women's restrooms with the intention to launch sexual assaults against women. The false claims of the ad seemed to be persuasive with a population that simply does not understand transgendered identities.

More than a ritual or idea to be considered, the experience of sexual activity and bodily pleasure is where many come to express themselves alone or in communion with others. An analysis of the practices of these experiences points not only to particularities and specificities, but also takes into consideration whatever power relationships are inherent in them. Much more than we have room to discuss, for some people, sexual satisfaction is felt only through power accompanied by the denigration or violation, and in some cases the dismemberment, of others. Rape culture—whether date rape, marital rape, stranger rape, pedophilia, or incest—and/or abusive or violent sexual acts— including sexual harassment, gay bashing, genital circumcision, necrophilia, or autoerotic asphyxiation—though extreme and perverse for most, has nonetheless become ubiquitous in popular cultural mediums. Some small percentage of people today can understand themselves as embodied, powerful, and experiential human beings only through the commission of such dehumanizing and life-threatening activities.

INSTITUTIONS

Social spaces are the consecrated places where one can practice the rituals of body and sex, or find the experiences that lead to satisfaction. In these spaces and institutions, people's actions are organized to suggest that their rituals and experiences are altogether sacred and vital to how their world should be ordered. As sociologist Anthony Giddens has stated, "Institutions by definition are the more enduring features of [our] social life."[50] In the same way that nation-states create regimes not only to discipline, manage, and provide for citizens, but also to differentiate between their citizens and citizens of other cultures, so also do American social relations, holidays, and institutions create and consecrate the social spaces that serve cultural notions and needs related to body and sex. Pierre Bourdieu writes,

> That is exactly what the ritual of institution does. It says: this man is a man—implying that he is a real man, which is not always immediately obvious. . . . The act of institution is an act of social magic. . . . The act of institution is thus an act of communication, but of a particular kind: it *signifies* to someone what his identity is, but in a way that both expresses it to him and imposes it on him by expressing it in front of everyone . . . and thus informing him in an authoritative manner of what he is and what he must be.[51]

No social relationship maintains more power in American society than the heteropatriarchal family. The makeup of the classic American family (man + wife + 2.5 children + pet + white picket fence) is the site where American identity has been historically normalized.[52] Heterosexuality is legitimated as the fixed sexual orientation, gender construction is rationalized, middle-class status is assumed, sexual reproduction is expected, and children's identities are socialized.[53] The typical American family remains powerful as a social aspiration, even though the 2010 census revealed such homes are disappearing at a rapid rate. Many marriages end in divorce, nobody can have 2.5 children, and a growing number of children (approximately 40 percent) are born to unwed mothers. Only 48 percent of households have married couples, and only 20 percent have both married couples and children who live with them. America is "in the midst of a major change in the way families and marriage are organized," says historian Stephanie Coontz, so much so that "[i]t's distressing, because all of the rules we grew up with no longer work and so we're having to learn new ways of thinking about families."[54]

Media is today beginning to celebrate alternative families, from the multigenerational family, to the blended family, to the gay family. A black and Christian president has publicly affirmed marriage equality for gays and lesbians. Though some states and politicians continue to drag their traditional feet, in June 2015 the Supreme Court ruled that no state can deny marriage licenses or recognition to same-sex couples without violating the Constitution. Some white male government leaders, formerly heads of traditional families, have come out of the closet as gay men and continue to hold office. These significant victories sit alongside remaining losses for women, whose reproductive rights and equal pay for equal work remain a subject of debate.

The sex trade in America is one of the biggest industries in the country. Legal only in parts of Nevada, its extent is not easy to nail down. Prostitution, as an institution that traded sex for pay, has been often regarded as the oldest profession of women.[55] As always has been true, prostitution comes in a variety of forms. Though illegal, few people who take advantage of its services need worry about prosecution.[56]

Sex trafficking is a global phenomenon that preys on the vulnerabilities of its victims by enslaving women and young girls for the purposes of servicing johns. It represents the "walmartization" of the sex trade because it adapts to every form of technology and tries to provide a product to meet every demand. Likewise, the Internet has provided a burgeoning social space where people can anonymously ply the sex trade and access its services. Cybersex and the income produced from it represent one of the largest new economies in the country. For those who see themselves as morally above prostitution or those who see themselves lacking in sexual prowess, the web allows them to bring its sexual possibilities into their own homes. The red-light district has moved online, where both men and women are performing sex acts using live cams for tips, processed on their behalf by administrators of websites. In addition, pornographers have found an entirely new clientele, and strengthened their ties to long-term users, on the Internet. A strong market has also been developed for softer porn, movies not quite as graphic as porn itself, or that included in the literature of romance novels that appeal especially to women.

An entire industry has developed around the *Fifty Shades of Gray* phenomenon. British author E. L. James created new characters in Anastasia Steel and Christian Grey and has written a series of books to track their relationship, known for an explicit treatment of the sexual relationship, including some BDSM activities. In the wake of the book hitting it big, Trojan noted that its sales of women's vibrators rose 14 percent in one quarter. Babeland, an adult-toy store chain with stores in New York and Seattle and with a website presence, reports a sales boost of 40 percent and a particular increase in bondage toys. Another wholesaler to around four hundred sex shops across the country, and co-owner of Bootyparlor.com, reported 26–32 percent increases in the wake of *Fifty* popularity. An album of classical music, selected by the author and released under the title *Fifty Shades of Grey: The Classical Album*, reached number four on the Billboard charts in 2012. A major motion picture appeared in 2015.[57] The books themselves have spawned many imitators, not surprisingly spawning a new line of Harlequin romance novels featuring explicit erotic fiction.

Eroticism has entered the mainstream. Some married couples are engaging in videotaping, and even sharing, their own sexual trysts.[58] For others, the potential release of a private video constitutes one of their largest fears. Columbia Pictures in 2014 released a movie titled *Sex Tape*, starring Jason Segel and Cameron Diaz, that explored these anxieties in comedic fashion. Today's erotic practices also take the form of sexual liaisons, without the exchange of money, between total strangers. These casual hookups were once accomplished through the art of advertising in places like Craigslist. Now new apps and websites (Tinder for heterosexuals, Grindr for gay men, and Parlez for lesbians) are emerging to make them even more accessible and, in some cases, immediate. There remain actual social spaces provided by strip joints, swinger clubs, fetish dens, and a variety of assorted sex clubs.

Other social spaces are defined by activities associated with the beauty industry. It provides products, advice, and treatments for people who want to improve their appearance. The beauty industry supposedly gives its consumers, most often women, the tools to make themselves beautiful.[59] Traditionally cosmetic and fashion, the two pillars of the industry's strength together defined beauty, even as they created careers for cover girls and fashion models. Girls donned makeup for the likes of Max Factor, L'Oreal, or Estee Lauder or became models for Calvin Klein, Chanel, or Yves St. Laurent and graced the covers of *Vogue* and *Cosmopolitan*.

Major makeup companies like L'Oreal or Estee Lauder refined the nature of beauty itself. According to feminist Sandra Bartky, "In the language of fashion magazines and cosmetic ads, making up is typically portrayed as an aesthetic activity in which a woman can express her individuality. In reality . . . it is, in fact, a high stylized activity that gives little rein to self-expression."[60] Trends, fads, and styles established by cosmetics, clothing lines, and magazines encouraged women, and also men but to a lesser degree, to go into debt, undergo treatments, or purchase new wardrobes to match or identify with the colors, clothes, and styles sold by the industry's various brands.[61] While this is often attributed to the vanity of consumers, it actually is proof of our insecurities and our belief that without these resources we are somehow deficient. The market is controlled by the industry, not the consumer.

The truth is the fashion industry dictates many more of our choices than most of us realize or would care to admit. If the color, style, or fashion one wants is not included in existing industry lines, it simply is not available. There are people, of course, who actively seek to dress according to fashion-industry choices. For example, some who do not even like pastels will buy and wear them, if they are this year's colors, in order to be in style for spring. These fashion-conscious consumers believe they somehow vicariously participate in the levels of prestige associated with their favorite designer labels. Like moths to the flame, we are drawn in by the beauty and fashion industries and as consumers, more often than not, we end up being consumed.

Sanford and Donovan write,

> Advertising, television and fashion magazines are not only promoters of the cultural ideals, but often in the absence of other sources of information, the entertainment and advertising media become our teacher of what a normal and healthy woman's body should look like. But the point is the woman who sees herself in severed parts. In advertisements, male models are usually shown from head to toe, or at the very least, from the waist up. Women are *cut up* with the same consistency. Only her legs are shown to sell the panty-hose, when a whole woman could sell the product just as well. Female models' hands, breasts, mouths, hips and genital regions, eyes, etc. are severed from their entire selves. The same mentality carries over into daily discourse. We hear statements such as, 'He's a leg man' or 'I'm a breast man' or 'I like 'em with small waists and curvy hips.' . . . Certainly some women have preferences for certain body characteristics in men, but they tend to value the man for his entire self as opposed to one severed part of himself.[62]

The beauty industry promotes its products to create a lasting impression on the minds and bodies of girls and women nationwide. To be sure, "ideals of beauty were important, for without them one was unable to detect those cases deviating from the perfect norm."[63] Beauty pageants emerged as an industry that has contributed to that endeavor since at least the first quarter of the last century. On the website for the long-running Miss America pageant, one finds the claim that "Miss America represents the highest ideals" and is the "type which the American Girl might well emulate."

Begun in the summer of 1921, the pageant has long embodied the normative gaze regarding beauty for women in American culture. Contestants show off their womanly forms in bathing suits and formal gowns, with their faces "dolled up" and their hair teased, sprayed, pinned, and/or extended. Although pageants incorporate personality, talent, and responses to the questions of judges as criteria for determining a winner, physical appearance is most valued. Beauty pageants reinforce the beauty industry's emphasis that young girls and women should conform to conventional beauty standards. These days, pageants have sought to engage younger and younger audiences, even creating pageants for toddlers sporting their tiaras. This pursuit of physical beauty, nurtured by the beauty industry, also feeds the coffers of other industries affecting body and sex.

Gone are the days when you had to be wealthy to buy a membership into an athletic facility, or when you had only family-based options, like those associated with the local YMCA. The fitness industry has arrived. A haven, the industry serves a variety of constituencies. For some, gays and straights alike, the local facility enables casual hookups or new romantic possibilities. Others, particularly women, like to use it for the quick workout routine, perhaps thirty minutes of cardio and aerobics, yoga, circuit training, or Pilates. Men usually prefer to engage in both body conditioning and muscle building. Today's fitness industry actually creates a rather democratic social space. As one blogger put it: "The gym brings people together [romantically and otherwise] that simply wouldn't meet in the real world. Something about the atmosphere makes the invisible borders that guide our real life interactions— class, status, *gulp*, race—nonexistent in the gym."[64]

Some women and men, colloquially known as "gym rats," engage in intense excessive workouts (Insanity, PX90, CrossFit, Tough Mudders, Spartan Race, and so on), often combined with various supplements or, at the most extreme pole, with performance-enhancing drugs, where all is sacrificed on the altar of fitness. Some even engage in the practice of biohacking. Much as the name suggests, people try to short-circuit or reverse engineer the essence of their genetic structure in hopes of enhancing physical prowess and longevity. They surgically implant cybernetic devices in their bodies, whether insulin meters to determine glucose levels or hardware specially designed to transport them to the "transhuman" experience, the hope of uncovering paths to a superior, perhaps posthuman existence. Much as some women have turned to plastic surgery as their fountain of youth, some men biohack to accomplish the same result.

MATERIALITY

The industries surrounding sex are instrumental in producing materials that create or alter idealized notions of body and sex. These materials include the gamut of objects from children's dolls to adults' sex toys; from drugs designed to strengthen muscles to those that aid and sustain erections; from tattoos and piercings that adorn the body to teen jelly bracelets that communicate willingness to perform sexual favors; from clothing that nurtures sexual appetites or creates a world of role play to books, websites, and/or videos that instruct us how to perform sex or invite us to do so, in real space or in virtual space; from prophylactics, like condoms and dental dams, to genital accessories, like women's merkins and vagazzlings or men's penis rings and Tucknits, each in its own way showing how sex is accessorized by an ever-widening market of material goods.

While cultural icons, institutions, and rituals focus on real-life, flesh-and-blood people, the notion that "beauty fades" necessitates that certain lifeless objects, eternally young, never fat, always beautiful, replicate what flesh and blood eventually lose.[65] This inanimate object serves as a model, an idol that serves culture by representing the real, although we know it is not. These two dimensional icons allow us imaginatively to internalize and emulate their beauty. Probably no other material item can match the longevity of the cultural influence of Mattel's Barbie and all the marketing machinery that Mattel has created around her. She is that archetypical prototype, modeling cultural ideals about beauty, body, and sex. Aligned with ideas about the eternally young, never-fat body, along with the buxom, pouty, and usually blond Marilyn Monroeish sex appeal, but able eternally to sustain what Marilyn could not, a straight man's mini model of a blow-up sex doll to a drag queen's muse, Barbie inspires as she shapes "*consumer* markets, fantastic desires, and new technologies of the flesh." To be sure, Mattel has gone to great lengths to diversify its Barbies line, with brunette Barbies, African American Barbies, Asian Barbies, and so forth, but the core Barbie body and features remained ever the same until early 2016, when Mattel announced new sizes of "petite," "tall," and "curvy" to accompany the "original."[66] The move came in the midst of slumping sales. Yet, within the "special edition" Barbies, the Marilyn Monroe Barbie remains the number one selling doll. As Mary F. Rogers in her text *Barbie Culture* writes,

> She symbolizes how today's bodies defy boundaries once deemed constants of nature. Barbie is thus an icon of an emergent, consumerist "somatics"—a technology of the body driven by the idea that our bodies can be whatever we like if we devote enough money and attention to them. This development makes the body an aerobic instrument, a surgical object, a dietary experiment, a fleshy clay capable of endless remolding. Tanning parlors, "fat farms," nail salons, day spas, therapeutic massage centers, and medical practices built around liposuction and other cosmetic procedures thus join upscale, unisex health clubs and fitness centers as the body increasingly serves as the site of individuals' greatest control.[67]

How does Barbie, a mere girlhood toy, mediate the veritable key aspects of American cultural meanings around body, sex, and pleasure? Actually, regardless of her anatomical impossibilities, she often models how America's women's bodies should look—the body little girls dream about, the one women die to possess, the body the dieting programs advertise and fashion designers want to clothe, the body men want on their arms as trophy wives, the body that stereotypical straight men want to bed and many drag queens want to be, the body upon which plastic surgeons market their craft. Barbie models how sexual categorizing works. She reproduces in material form the hierarchy of race, ethnicity, and gender. As she affixes gender roles, she nonetheless makes sexuality more ambiguous. Her gender is clear, but her sexual identity is not. The market confirms that her staying power is sure, and her enormous reach makes a mere plastic toy a lifestyle accessory that guides consumers more dramatically than even they or their parents might realize.

Most of today's religious communities remain entrenched in their dualism; the separation of body from soul remains a given. The altar of body and sex unites them and intentionally ministers to both. Since many traditional expressions of religion seek to save souls, often ignoring or losing bodies in the process, congregants as consumers are today tending to look elsewhere to address their human cravings or to come to grips with understanding the meaning associated with embodied sexuality. Purveyors of body and sex promise an overflowing wellspring of pleasure and desire: "whoever drinks of the water that [we] will give . . . shall never thirst."[68] While churches and other religious communities may be in a crisis over mind-body dualism, gender roles, sex in general, and sexual orientation in particular, this altar of body and sex communicates a clear message. Whosoever will, may come:

> Till our body and soul
> [We] doth fully control,
> And our all on the altar is laid.[69]

2

Big Business

As the notoriously taciturn President Calvin Coolidge once declared, "The chief business of the American people is business."[1] Nightmares of financial hardship and economic inequality, on the one hand, and dreams of success and comfort, on the other, drive most Americans to view making money as a matter of ultimate concern, as Paul Tillich might have phrased it. No American can make money without encountering the power of big business. Over time, big business has proven to be the prime mover in the nation. Stated another way, big businesses influence what Americans eat, where they live, how they work, what they do for leisure, what they wear, and often what they think. As Harvey Cox put it in an essay for *The Atlantic Monthly* in 1999, we are living in a new dispensation with the "market as God."[2]

Over the past several decades, cultural interest in economics has increased considerably. Economists Alan Greenspan, Bruce Bartlett, Paul Krugman, David Stockman, and Larry Summers have found themselves not only studying the generators and indicators of prosperity but also enjoying a fair share of it themselves. Today the world's political and corporate leaders routinely use economists as veritable fortune-tellers, in the same style as the fabled oracle of Delphi. In the words of English philosopher Thomas Carlyle, economics as a field of informed study is "the dismal science."[3] Virtually every political leader or business executive finds a favorite economist to predict outcomes to bolster their own views. Achieving mastery over the seemingly uncontrollable, unpredictable, and even unintelligible aspects of economic activity is the mark of true success, and it drives big business.

Of the figures most identified as paragons of the American economy and business world, industrialist Andrew Carnegie stands above most others as the patron saint of Gilded Age capitalism. A towering business leader during the late nineteenth century, he helped define the modern economic reality in the United States. As biographer Harold Livesay notes, "Andrew Carnegie's rise from poor Scottish immigrant boy to 'the richest man in the world' seemed to his contemporaries and to succeeding generations irrefutable evidence of the [American Dream's] validity."[4] Carnegie's life began in Dunfermline, a small mill town in Scotland, on November 25, 1835. Faced with financial ruin as the practitioner of an anachronistic trade, William Carnegie, Andrew's father, had to sell off his looms. Out of work and luck, the Carnegie clan made their way from Scotland to New York in 1848 and then settled in the Pittsburgh area. Like millions of other immigrants, the Carnegie family hoped to escape devastating poverty and spiritual brokenness with a fresh start in the New World. At thirteen, young Andrew took on several jobs to contribute and do his part to help keep his family afloat financially.

Through the experience of hard work, education, and persistence, Carnegie met his mentor, Thomas Scott, while working as a telegraph operator. As head of the Pennsylvania Railroad, Scott offered Carnegie work as his personal secretary and right-hand man. From 1853 to 1865 Carnegie rose in power and prominence within the Pennsylvania Railroad. He proved himself integral to the success of the company. Carnegie's annual income exploded from $2,400 in 1859 to $50,000 in 1863. In 1865 Carnegie resigned from the Pennsylvania Railroad at the age of thirty to devote himself fully to his own financial interests. By the early 1870s, he had made up his mind to "put all of his eggs into one basket and then watch the basket grow," a decision that eventually led him to steel. In the post–Civil War era, the newly reunited nation needed rebuilding. Carnegie rightly perceived that given enough money, time, ruthlessness, and ingenuity, he could become the sovereign lord of the most essential material in the known world.

Andrew Carnegie believed he and other industrialists of his era served the national interests of America by building their enterprises. By their reckoning, the bigger their businesses became, the greater America also became. Carnegie's "actions continuously manifested an ambivalence rooted in his double exposure to the old world among the cottages, glens, and firths of Scotland and the new world of smoky factories in America." He "demonstrated mastery" over everything "that formed the core of modern industrial practice." But in "his attitudes toward politics, society, culture, and . . . even [the] ownership structure of his business," he "exhibited the Old World ideas he had absorbed as a boy in Scotland."[5]

Self-taught, yet perhaps the most articulate and literate of his ilk, Carnegie demonstrated some characteristics that were quite atypical. He routinely memorized and quoted long segments of William Shakespeare and Robert

Burns by heart. He devoted more of his resources and energy to philanthropy than many of his contemporaries. But he also typified one characteristic that many people shared, namely, the belief that the creation of wealth represented the noblest human endeavor imaginable. "All his life," Harold Livesay notes, "Carnegie adhered to this theme of the interdependence between political equality and economic superiority."[6]

Carnegie's favorite motto, "All is well since all grows better," originated in his reading of the English philosophy of Herbert Spencer. The motto generally reflected his steadfast belief that the accumulation of vast wealth would result in human progress as an outgrowth of God's divine will for humankind, the nation, and the world.[7] He brought this viewpoint most sharply into focus in his wildly popular book *The Gospel of Wealth and Other Essays* (1888). Written at the height of his career, the book argued that individual capitalists were bound by a supreme duty to improve society. Carnegie encouraged people of wealth to support building parks, libraries, museums, and schools in order to contribute to the "lasting good."[8] On February 5, 1915, at age seventy-nine, Carnegie testified before Congress: "My business is to do as much good in the world as I can; I have retired from all other business."[9]

Carnegie maintained a visceral hatred of inherited wealth. He believed that the offspring of prosperous businesspersons were rarely as talented as their forebears.[10] In keeping with the struggles of his impoverished upbringing in Scotland, Carnegie believed that America's future leaders would arise from the nation's poorest members.[11] He believed children living in poverty had the advantage of developing a stronger work ethic by learning from parents attempting to alleviate their own poverty.[12] Demonstrating his own conflicted morality about the significance of accumulated wealth by individuals, Carnegie argued that the person who dies rich "dies disgraced."[13] By 1900, Carnegie produced one fourth of the steel in the nation. As evidence of his company's massive success, $25 million of the company's $40 million in profits went directly to Carnegie himself. He had made a number of philanthropic bequests, but now he wanted to devote himself entirely to this end for the remainder of his life. In order to do so, he had to convert his industrial wealth into liquid capital so he could commence pursuing his charitable works.

Witnessing the ways that sectarianism had characterized religion during his youth, Carnegie deliberately kept his distance from Christianity.[14] Biographer David Nasaw observes that, in matters of religion and theology, young Andrew Carnegie became a spiritual seeker who was deeply uncertain about matters of faith. Not long after his family's arrival in the United States, Carnegie's father and aunts introduced him to Swedenborgianism, a marginal Christian spiritualist sect founded by Emanuel Swedenborg in the eighteenth century. While Carnegie managed to keep the more arcane Swedenborgian beliefs at arm's length, he ultimately found the tradition attractive for a variety of reasons. Carnegie found in Swedenborgianism, in contrast to the stern Presbyterianism of his youth, "a gentle religion, with no infant damnation, no authoritarian ministers, and lots of wonderful music . . . a tolerance, gentleness, and openness to discussion, which he cherished."[15]

However, his Presbyterian church connections during his formative years also nurtured his intellectual aspirations, literary appetites, and democratic impulses in the presence of family, friends, and fellow believers in ways that would last a lifetime. Although Carnegie rejected the core tenets of Calvinist orthodoxy in an outright fashion, and later separated from the Swedenborgians, Nasaw asserts that Carnegie "tried hard . . . to hold on to some kernel of religious belief. He wanted desperately to believe that there was some moral order to the universe, but refused to put his faith in a divine being whose existence and omnipotence he found entirely unreasonable."[16]

Instead of entering into this spiritual fray, Carnegie preferred to view matters related to human affairs through a naturalistic and scientific framework. At one point in his life, Carnegie noted, "Not only had I got rid of the theology and the supernatural, but I had found the truth of evolution."[17] Late in his life, his staunch resistance to traditional religion gradually softened. From 1905 until his death on August 11, 1919, the membership roster of Madison Avenue Presbyterian Church in New York City included his name.[18] The pastor, the Rev. Henry Sloane Coffin, enjoyed a reputation as a leading proponent of the social gospel movement.

While traditional religious principles informed his moral sensibilities, the basis of Carnegie's foundational religious belief came from another source. Many business leaders applied Darwin's understanding of evolution to human society in a grossly oversimplified fashion. Social Darwinism emphasized that "survival of fittest" would lead naturally to the greater civilization of society. Business tycoons, who saw themselves as among the fittest and who believed their own accomplishments elevated all humanity, naturally found social Darwinism attractive. Herbert Spencer provided the mind behind its original formulation. Upon reading Spencer, Carnegie concluded that "light came in as a flood and all was clear." Carnegie accepted Spencer's conclusion that "man was not created with an instinct for his own degradation but from the lower he had risen to the higher forms. Nor is there any conceivable end to his march to perfection. His face is turned to the light; he stands in the sun and looks upward."[19]

Social Darwinism suggested that people succeeded because they are virtuous, thus enabling the wealthy to forget the grotesque side of their success. (Carnegie's own perpetual ruthlessness was legendary.) With all his energy, he routinely drove his managers and workers to their limits, frequently pitting partners and plant managers against one another. When any proved ineffective or inefficient, he forced them out. Carnegie took even a tougher approach to his competitors. In accordance with his social Darwinist outlook, Carnegie knew that little of value came easily. His attention to ruthless rigor provided him a way to overcome his meager beginnings and transformed him into a man of steel.[20] Ardent supporters of big business and free-market capitalism often have reframed the story of Carnegie's financial ascent from wretchedness to wealth as a narrative of personal redemption. He was a prime example of the self-made man. The exemplary nature of Carnegie's transformation presaged the great allure of the gospel of prosperity within the American cultural psyche and theological imagination for generations to come.

MYTHOLOGY

The "self-made" man or woman looms large as a quintessential American myth. The idea popularly depicts "a person who was born poor or otherwise disadvantaged, but who achieved great economic success thanks to their own hard work and ingenuity rather than to any inherited fortune, family connections or other privilege."[21] Henry Clay coined the phrase "self-made man" in the early nineteenth century as the mythic example of how successful businesspeople tap into a homespun American gospel of success by overcoming risk and adversity through hard work and determination.[22] In the nineteenth century, Horatio Alger Jr. wrote more than one hundred novels containing plots that variously described how children of poverty created middle-class lives through hard work and integrity. Critics, however, emphasize that the protagonist is more often than not rescued more by mentors than by their own hard work. In these cases, Alger's characters, in contrast to others who worked hard in the nineteenth century, usually benefited from the paternalistic "old boy's network" in action. The "rags-to-riches" narrative characterized his work, even though it did not appropriately characterize the author himself. Nonetheless, Alger's work both defined and described realities during the Gilded Age so much that it practically became a literary genre unto itself.[23]

While Horatio Alger popularized the myth of rugged individualism, Ayn Rand, the novelist, playwright, and screenwriter, provided the philosophical understanding of the "self-made person" in American life. Born in 1905 in Russia, Rand arrived in America in 1926. After a couple of rather unsuccessful novels, she achieved fame with *The Fountainhead* (1943) and *Atlas Shrugged* (1957). Eventually, she published nonfiction and her own magazines, because, according to the Ayn Rand website, she wanted "to elaborate on the philosophy set forth in her own novels and to use her philosophy, which she named 'Objectivism,' to explain crucial cultural events and fight the negative trends she observed."[24]

Rand moved fluidly from novels to deeply metaphysical texts. In her view, reason always trumped any dependence on religion. The Objectivist movement continues to spread her ideas.[25] Libertarians and American conservatives have been among her most ardent followers. Present-day conservative pundits often cite Rand as an influence, despite the reality that many of her positions, including her pro-choice activism and her avowed atheism, were diametrically opposed to their own ideologies.[26] A 1987 *New York Times* article referred to her as the Reagan administration's "novelist laureate." Leading Republicans including Ron Paul, Paul Ryan, Rand Paul, Ted Cruz, Sarah Palin, and Glenn Beck have proclaimed themselves her disciples, acknowledging her influence and referring to her writings as if they were sacred texts.

The Great Recession of 2008-2009 sparked renewed interest in Rand's work, and particularly in *Atlas Shrugged*. Some have argued the novel foreshadowed the crisis. Op-ed essays have compared real-world events with the novel's plot. T-shirts, banners, and signs mentioning John Galt, fictional hero of the novel, have shown up at Tea Party protests.[27] Meanwhile, members of the political left have criticized her ideas. According to *Mother Jones*, "Rand's particular genius has always been her ability to turn upside down traditional hierarchies and recast the wealthy, the talented, and the powerful as the oppressed."[28] *The Nation* magazine alleged that similarities exist between the "moral syntax of Randianism" and fascism.[29] There can be no doubt that, for Rand, the free reign of markets enables the best of all possible worlds to develop. The market becomes the invisible hand of God, where private enterprise and personal initiative, unhinged from any control by government, create a world where all can prosper.

According to Geoffrey James, for many in big business and politics, Ayn Rand's philosophy creates a religious worldview. Her vision of the "self-made individual" quite literally exists as counterpoint to that of the biblical witness: "It is [God] who has made us, and not we ourselves" (Ps. 100:3). CEOs of major corporations have glommed on to Rand's canon "with evangelical intensity." They use her work to advocate principles that represent "the antithesis of Judeo-Christian teaching." Where Jesus says, "Blessed are the poor;" Rand would say, "Damn the moochers."[30] Money is the ultimate good, not the root of all evil. As James puts it, "Rand practically worshipped the almighty dollar, seeing the acquisition of wealth as a goal worthy in and of itself." For Rand, the ultimate good is a person's own happiness.[31] The myths associated with the rags-to-riches stories of Horatio Alger, and the dependence on self-reliance found in the work of Ayn Rand, provide historical understanding for why so many contemporary Americans invest both their trust and hope in the activities of big business.

President Herbert Hoover embedded the power of these myths in his version of the American way of life. In his legendary "Rugged Individualism" speech of October 1928, used to close his successful presidential campaign, Hoover claimed that America has been built upon both "rugged individualism" and "self-reliance." Government had gathered too much economic power during wartime and needed to shed that power and avoid any interference with the activity of big business. Governmental interference only injured "the initiative and enterprise of the American people."[32] Government need not involve itself in relieving the people's burdens. Following World War I, Hoover's vision of rugged individualism clearly appealed to leaders of big business, dismayed by the regulatory bureaucracy built up by the Wilson administration.

When the Great Depression started, Hoover insisted that the market would right itself. However, as the economy spiraled further downward, he concluded he had to "[do] something, but not too much!" Unfortunately, he intervened with such ineffectiveness that his actions were the equivalent of doing nothing. Even though Hoover launched the largest, most ambitious federal works project to date, he doubted the action would provide long-term solutions and believed relief programs would make people overly dependent on government. Despite bearing witness to widespread misery and panic nationwide, he deemed government action in the form of public assistance as a cardinal violation of his orthodox belief in self-reliance. For Hoover, the only genuine success stories depended on self-reliance. In his examination of failure in the United States, Scott Sandage contends that "the American who fails is a prophet without honor in [his/her] own country. Our creed is that hard work earns prosperity and prestige. When talk turns to failure, people change the subject with an uneasy laugh and a cliché. Quitters never win. Failure builds character. And yet, everyone knows a modern Job, a salt-of-the-earth type who tries and tries but meets only disaster. We mention [that person] with sympathy and disgust."[33]

Hoover sought to solve problems by relying on private dollars to make the public project work. Never too successful in this regard, Hoover's activities call to mind the phrase "much too little, much too late."[34] Despite his own impoverished and underprivileged background, Hoover failed to recognize that the structural nature of the nation's economic problems had taken a psychological as well as a spiritual toll on the people. For millions of Americans who were unable, when left to their own devices, to deal with the extent of their hardships, the Great Depression was quite literally a crisis of faith that nullified any significance attached to "rugged individualism."

ETHICS

Although intended as a full-throated denouncement of the Reagan-Bush era's corporate excess, Oliver Stone's 1987 film *Wall Street* is most memorable for Michael Douglas's iconic portrayal of the wealthy, unscrupulous corporate raider Gordon Gekko, who professes to a room full of shareholders that "greed, for lack of a better word, is good." Stone envisioned the film to be a cautionary tale about the cynical, get-rich-quick culture of the 1980s. However, he could not have anticipated that countless viewers would revere both Gekko's wanton materialism and reckless financial exuberance as if they were moral virtues. Gekko's story inspired a generation of stockbrokers and investment bankers to enter the business and actually increased applications to business school. Political commentator Kevin Phillips cogently argues that twenty-first-century American capitalism,

> at a pivotal period in the nation's history, cavalierly ventured a multiple gamble: first, financializing a hitherto more diversified U.S. economy; second, using massive quantities of debt and leverage to do so; third, following up a stock market bubble with an even larger housing and mortgage credit bubble; fourth, roughly quadrupling U.S. credit-market debt between 1987 and 2007, a scale of excess that historically unwinds; and fifth, consummating these events with a mixed performance of dishonesty, incompetence, and quantitative negligence.[35]

Huck Gutman points out that the "current spate of bad news" on Wall Street clearly began with the corporate bankruptcy of Enron. Enron executives under the leadership of its late CEO Ken Lay were "propelled by greed" and unsatisfied "with immense salaries." They established "all sorts of spin-off partnerships to enrich themselves at the expense of stockholders and the corporation's bottom line." Yet "in a little more than a decade Enron soared from obscurity to become the nation's seventh largest company, with over 20,000 employees in forty countries." Corrupt machinations to increase profits and

> its off-the-books energy deals, abetted by fiscal accounting that was erroneous, misleading, and downright dishonest, eventually caused an implosion of gigantic proportions. . . . On December 28, 2000, Enron stock sold at over $84 a share. Eleven months later, to the day, Enron shares plummeted to less than a dollar in the heaviest trading volume ever recorded by a major stock exchange. . . . Two months later, Enron stock was delisted by the New York Stock Exchange, and today its stock is just that, worthless.

The government pursued a much-publicized "criminal investigation of the energy-trading company, but the damage to shareholders and pensioners" had already been done.[36]

Since Enron, many examples "of corporate greed and accounting malfeasance" have surfaced. Gutman's essay examines several of them. Qwest, at one time the nation's fourth largest telephone company, provided basic service to fourteen states, had "revenues of over $18 billion a year, and handled over 240 million phone calls and 600 million e-mails each day." Under criminal investigation, "indications of likely fiscal impropriety have caused its stock to crash from a high of $67 to less than $2 a share."

Meanwhile, in the early 2000s, criminal investigations led to the resignation of Dennis Kozlowski, Tyco International's CEO. Tyco operated in "over 80 countries with revenues of 36 billion." In the wake of investigations, stock fell from a high of $60 a share to just over $10 a share. The company rebounded and by 2007 had split into three publicly independent companies. During the same period, the Securities and Exchange Commission investigated for fraudulent accounting Global Crossing, a company that helped develop fiber-optic cable networks nationwide. "The corporation, it appears, arranged 'deals' in which no goods or services were exchanged but which nonetheless made it appear that profit was being generated."[37] Global Crossing declared bankruptcy in 2002, and its stock plummeted from $60 a share to less than 10 cents per share. Then there was WorldCom, a 103-billion-dollar company that declared bankruptcy in July 2002, again the result of fraudulent accounting practices. Stock fell from $64 per share to around 20 cents per share. Markets across the world were shaken profoundly by these developments.[38] In strict adherence to the gospel according to Gordon Gekko— "Greed . . . is good"—these and many other of the nation's leading businesses repeatedly made moral decisions to pursue corporate interests of maximum profitability, as ultimate concern, no matter the costs.

Previously one of the Big Five international accounting firms, Arthur Andersen LLP, had been involved in several of these widely publicized corporate debacles. The government indicted and convicted Andersen for its role in destroying Enron-related documents. The company had also served as the accounting firm for WorldCom, Qwest, and Halliburton. Though the Supreme Court vacated the conviction in 2005, due to inadequacy of jury instructions, the company has not been able to regain its former reputation. In 1996, Dick Cheney, an executive with Halliburton before he became vice president, made a promotional videotape for the ill-fated accounting firm. "One of the things I like that they do for us is that, in effect, I get good advice, if you will, from their people based upon how we're doing business and how we're operating, over and above," Mr. Cheney said, "just sort of the normal by-the-books audit arrangement."[39] Halliburton itself later pled guilty July 26, 2013, to destroying evidence related to its role in the Deepwater Horizon oil spill of 2010. Such examples of corporate malfeasance and mendacity have become so rampant that much of American society has become largely inured to the revelation of these acts. Nonetheless, the moral schema that desires huge profits over human possibility provides some understanding of the nature of corporate America's soul.

When it comes to the ruinous and devastating effects perpetrated on American life by corporate greed, virtually no malefactor has left more chaos in his wake than Bernie Madoff. Liaquat Ahamed tells the story:

> As a side business he began managing money for other people, at first informally, for friends and family. His results were good but not spectacular. . . . Through word of mouth he soon began attracting outside investors, spawning a cottage industry of various types of feeder funds that channeled assets his way. At some point (no one is quite certain when; Madoff claims it was not until the early 1990s . . .), after losing money, rather than come clean to his clients, he fudged the numbers, hoping to recoup the losses later and get back on track. Instead he ended up digging himself into an ever deeper hole. After a while, the chasm between what he claimed to investors and what was actually in their accounts became so deep that he stopped even bothering to invest the cash, relying on money from new clients to pay out fictitious returns to older clients—the classic Ponzi scheme.[40]

Like all Ponzi schemes, his investment fund came tumbling down because he could not grow it fast enough to keep up.

During Madoff's sentencing on June 28, 2009, the victims who spoke in the courtroom united "in their demand for a maximum sentence, saying that Madoff had forfeited his right to live in society."[41] Yet they had all found Madoff's greed appealing. As long as Madoff satisfied their own greed for returns, they were happy. Perhaps Madoff was not all wrong when he claimed that his investors were complicit in his actions. "They had to know," Madoff said, "but the attitude was sort of, 'if you are doing something wrong, we don't want to know.' "[42]

The promise of quick returns attracted a wide variety of investors. While "Mr. Madoff's luxurious lifestyle, including a penthouse, yachts and French villa, all quickly became fuel for public outrage,"[43] all his investors had originally been attracted to him due to these very characteristics. Sentenced to 150 years, Bernard L. Madoff received maximum time for his crimes. The saga of Madoff's criminal exploits actually puts an entire era of rampant greed and unfettered corruption on trial. Fed by competitive deregulation and globalized finance, and marked by deception, fear, betrayal, panic, and loss, the greed continues. Faith in endless returns remains a characteristic of our current economic order.

RITUAL

Americans exercise their faith in big business by consuming goods. Even in bleak times, the remedy in America is dictated by the idea of "economic stimulus," producing an environment where Americans are expected to bring their offerings to the altar by performing their civic duty to buy. In a society completely overrun by the phenomenon of "conspicuous consumption," it is hard to imagine that someone ever had to invent the phrase. American sociologist Thorstein Veblen first coined it in his classic text, *The Theory of the Leisure Class* (1899). Veblen offered a somewhat scathing critique of the newly emergent consumer society at the end of the nineteenth century in America: "Closely related to the requirement that the gentleman must consume freely and of the right kind of goods, there is the requirement that he must know how to consume them in a seemly manner. His life of leisure must be conducted in due form. Hence arise good manners . . . conformity to the norm of conspicuous leisure and conspicuous consumption."[44]

No person remains untouched by the connection between consumption and a personal understanding of American identity. Society connects manhood with the right kind of car or the ability to "dress for success." The phrase "diamonds are a girl's best friend" is tied to the cultural expectation that retail therapy will cure whatever ails any woman. As historically marginalized and oppressed racial and ethnic groups in America, African Americans and Latino/as are nonetheless included among the nation's most faithful and conspicuous consumers. According to Nikolai Roussanov, a professor at Wharton, blacks and Hispanics, typically people who find status hard to come by, spend 30 percent more than whites who earn comparable incomes.[45] The benefits associated with this form of racial redemption suggest that the price of these social symbols is worth the cost. People, regardless of race or class, often go into debt as various holidays turn into opportunities to "shop 'til you drop." Technology has now enabled a "one-click" variation to the whole phenomenon.[46]

To make matters worse, Americans are driven by the demands of their ego rather than the dictates of their reason. Most folks channel surplus income into seeking immediate gratification rather than into productive investments or savings. People will invest a personal windfall or inheritance in new high-tech gadgets, name-brand clothes, or exotic vacation getaways instead of investing it in the education of family members or setting it aside for a rainy day.[47]

Showing off with ostentatious symbols of status, wealth, and power, however, is not sufficient on its own. As Veblen contends, conspicuous consumption is intended to assert one's superiority to others.[48] Thus, the ritual of consumption thrives on envy and generates competition, not only to keep up with the Joneses but to overtake them. Consuming well can provide a sense of something akin to spiritual fulfillment. Yet, as Karl Marx reminds us, the production of too many useful things results in too many useless people.[49] The wealthiest in America play the game at higher levels. Whether by intention or not, they are able to purchase some form of immortality when they place their names on hospital wings and public buildings.

Ultimately, none of this would make much of a difference if the ritualistic appetite for consumption were restricted to the richest members of society. For better or worse, conspicuous consumption has become the prime mover of the present-day economy. An illustration comes from the immediate aftermath of the 9/11 terror attacks. For a salient moment, the entire nation was united; people, regardless of background, were ready to contribute whatever they could to the common good. So President George W. Bush urged Americans to go out and spend, lest the economy falter. In spite of his administration's professed "compassionate conservatism" grounded in evangelical roots, the Bush White House, in the wake of our greatest and most recent national trauma, suggested that the best sacrifice Americans could offer each other and the world involved unfettered, unrepentant mass consumption.

Even the middle class and poor are drawn into this high-stakes poker game of competitive envy and anxious acquisition. Those in a consumer-oriented culture find themselves either dying to keep up or suffering a slow death due to utter humiliation because they cannot.

MATERIALITY

Money is the license to become fully American. In our culture, money, like the accumulation of consumer goods (also a material dimension of our economy), shows that you matter. In 1973, the Philadelphia soul group the O'Jays performed and recorded their classic hit song "For the Love of Money." Written and produced by Kenny Gamble and Leon Huff for their label, Philadelphia International Records, the first verse includes lyrics that emphasize "For the love of money, people will steal from their mother . . . will rob their own brother . . . for that lean, mean, mean green Almighty dollar, money . . ." The song's title comes from a well-known biblical verse: "For the love of money is the root of all evil) which while some coveted after, they have erred from the faith, and pierced themselves through with many sorrows" (1 Tim. 6:10

KJV). The Bible does not denounce money in and of itself as the root of evil, but rather the love of money.

As a visible, tangible manifestation of the economy in action, money captures the human spirit on a daily basis. "In eighteenth- and nineteenth-century novels," economist Thomas Piketty observes, "money was everywhere, not only as an abstract force but above all as a palpable, concrete magnitude. Writers frequently described the income and wealth of their characters . . . not to overwhelm us with numbers but because these quantities established a character's social status in the mind of the reader. Everyone knew what standard of living these numbers represented."[50] Even though some may think this emphasis on the love of cash might seem a bit overblown, the exploration of the popular fascination with money is actually meaningful.

Money is our main means of exchange. In his classic economic treatise *The Wealth of Nations* (1776), Adam Smith wrote that "money is the exact measure of the real exchangeable value of all commodities . . . at the same time and place only."[51] It compensates us for our work and enables us to purchase things we need. Without it, rewarding work or purchasing and selling goods would be difficult, left to one's ability to barter with whatever one might have to offer. In that case, there would be no guarantee that what one can offer is truly what the other side of your barter really needs. But everybody can use money. Therefore, money provides the ability to move in and out of various spaces without having to barter.

Without money, anyone has difficulty functioning in American culture. All manner of legislation protects it, because, in the eyes of government, money *is* sacred. While some may feel they have money to burn, actually burning it is a crime. Americans can cremate people and burn crosses, but turning cash into ashes is strictly forbidden in Title 18, Section 333 of the United States Code: "whoever mutilates, cuts, disfigures, perforates, unites or cements together, or does any other thing to any bank bill, draft, note, or other evidence of debt issued by any national banking association, Federal Reserve Bank, or Federal Reserve System, with intent to render such item(s) unfit to be reissued, shall be fined . . . or imprisoned . . . or both." The Secret Service is responsible for enforcing this law.

The images on American money help to underscore the religious understanding of an America that somehow serves divine purposes in the world. Look particularly at the two symbols on the back of the dollar bill. The images in the two circles represent the front and back of the Great Seal of the United States: On the right side of the bill, an eagle appears with the olive branch (for peace) in one talon and thirteen arrows (representing willingness to fight) in the other, with the words *E Pluribus Unum* ("Out of Many, One"). On the other side is the image of the incomplete pyramid (all other considerations aside, this may be a particularly good image for a government project). Just above the pyramid appears a triangle containing the eye of God. Above it all is a Latin motto: *Annuit Coeptis*, meaning "God has favored our undertakings," a roundabout way of saying, "God Bless America." On the bottom runs another Latin phrase, *Novus Ordo Seclorum*, meaning "A New Order for the Ages."

The Great Seal and these mottoes imprinted on our currency seem to signify a spiritual meaning for America as a nation chosen by God to fulfill divine purposes. American money, both coins and bills, carries the phrase "In God We Trust," a phrase designated as the motto for the nation by a joint resolution of Congress in 1956.[52] The sacred is woven into even the design features of American money. Yet the design begs the question, how do we identify the god in whom "we trust"?

In his book *Greenback*, British journalist Jason Goodwin tells the story of the dollar, the world's dominant currency. "America's theology was a secular one," Goodwin comments. "It revolved around money and liberty, promise and return, profit and loss. It revolved, in fact, around the miracle of money."[53] Few could deny that this sentiment has blossomed significantly. To this point, he observes,

> the money religion is the worship of Mammon, and the Almighty Dollar is the supreme being. . . . In the last fifty years several countries have converted en masse to the dollar, while in others, where the process has been officially discouraged, individuals have enthusiastically converted their pesos, pounds, or rubles; wild scenes ensue around the globe as people scramble to buy dollars as a hedge against inflation, deflation, devaluation, or the bitterness of persistent poverty.[54]

For better or worse, there is a mass cultural perception that the acquisition and accumulation of money is a very present help in times of trouble and need. Many believe the free reign of money is the key to salvation, not only for the economic system, but for people as well.

Monetarism emphasizes that the slow and stable growth in the money supply, free of governmental intervention, is the best way to ensure lasting economic growth. Championed by Milton Friedman, the late Nobel Prize–winning economist who established the Chicago school of economics, monetarism zealously defends a laissez-faire approach to all economic matters. Monetarists typically renounce "price supports for agriculture; restrictions on international trade; rent controls; legal minimum wage rates; detailed regulation of industries such as banking or transportation; control of radio and television by the Federal Communications Commission; Social Security (which [Friedman] called a Ponzi scheme); licensing restrictions on any enterprise, occupation or profession; public housing programs; the military draft;" and virtually every other form of governmental intervention.[55] Under Friedman's leadership, monetarism became an integral part of a global resurgence of conservative political ideology illustrated by President Ronald Reagan's fiscal policies.

The most revolutionary aspect of Friedman's theories harkened back to the antiquated arguments about laissez-faire around the late eighteenth century. Friedman argued that income, prices, and employment were far more dependent upon money supply and the rate at which currency changes hands than any level of investment by the public sector. Given Friedman's utter disdain for any level of government intervention, he and his followers would be perfectly content to leave every aspect of human welfare up to the market, with the Federal Reserve monitoring money supply over time but remaining wholly indifferent to the triumphs or tragedies faced by ordinary people.

In reality, there are billions of U.S. dollars floating around the globe outside the banking system and certainly beyond the control of the Fed (in far-flung places such as Russia, China, and the Middle East). Moreover, in the worst-case scenario, when the Fed lowers its prime interest rate to zero and opens the floodgates of money supply by pumping cash onto the streets, it does not possess the magical power to correct accompanying deleterious effects. Finally, the skyrocketing levels of credit and subsequent debt arising in the past few decades, due to credit cards and other financial service instruments, have created a parallel economic universe over which the Fed has little or no control. All in all, the monetarists' slavish love of cold hard cash, the trust they have placed in it, and the policies they have created to govern it, translate into the fact that most Americans have chosen to place their supreme trust in about the most lackluster and contextually limited godhead available.[56]

DOCTRINE

Literally from French translated as "let do," laissez-faire has been regarded as a catchall economic doctrine in American life since the 1700s. Since that time, the term refers to a noninterventionist macroeconomic policy that many conservative scholars and politicians have construed as the economic partner to American philosopher Henry David Thoreau's adage in his classic text *Walden*, "That government is best that governs least." Interestingly enough, although the concept of a hands-off approach to the state's role in the economy has still never been fully defined, much less tested, in live market conditions, its staunchest advocates and ardent political proponents tout a laissez-faire market in much the same fashion as fundamentalists describe their inerrant and infallible Bible.

To trace the original roots of this idea, one has to revisit the seminal work of a group of French protoeconomists dubbed "physiocrats" (from the Greek term meaning "the rule of nature"). Under the leadership of François Quesnay, the physiocrats constructed an abstract theoretical model of a market economy that sharply differentiated urban work from rural, artisan from farmer. Essentially, they believed that "the closer one was to nature, the more likely it was that one would divine the natural laws that govern the physical and moral order of the universe."[57] The economy could depend on nature, but not on governments, most of which tended to create stupid policies and restrictions. The monarchies ruling Europe at the time micromanaged almost everything of an economic nature. In response, the physiocrats supported a laissez-faire approach so that nature could pursue a natural course, creating, in their view, an economy much more efficient and dependable.

The question of who actually coined the phrase "laissez-faire" has been subject to great historical debate. Some sources credit Quesnay with the rise of the laissez-faire doctrine, while others acknowledge his contemporary Vincent de Gournay, a convert to physiocratic doctrine. Whatever the case might be, the physiocrats were ultimately better at coining catchphrases than establishing economic policies. Louis XVI's government entertained a brief fascination with the concept of laissez-faire as a slogan, although that did not last long. In the aftermath of the French Revolution, economists and philosophers reintroduced the concept (in a somewhat diminished and deformed fashion). The idea eventually found a safe haven in England.

While the signers of the Declaration of Independence were laying the foundation for the American Revolution as the biggest tax protest in world history, the Scottish moral philosopher and groundbreaking economist Adam Smith published the work that both popularized and propagated laissez-faire on both sides of the Atlantic. During the span of more than two centuries since the appearance of *An Inquiry into the Nature and Causes of the Wealth of Nations* (1776), Smith has assumed the role of patron saint for every conservative politician, pundit, and power broker opposed to taxation in any form. Drawing heavily upon the formative ideas of the French physiocrats, as well as English intellectual forebears such as Sir Dudley North and Sir William Petty, Smith's text gathered together a series of arguments that dealt a veritable deathblow to the absolutist notion of managed economy. *The Wealth of Nations* is likely the most venerated and widely celebrated economic treatise in history. In truth, much of its claim to fame may have more to do with its rhetorical prowess and clear prose than with its originality of thought or direct applicability to social problems.

In keeping with the tenets of the physiocratic tradition, Smith believed that nature was humanity's greatest guiding influence. In this fashion, God ("Providence") has so arranged and ordained the universe that if men and women are left free to pursue their own interests, they will instinctively act in ways that are best for society. "Every individual," Smith argues, "necessarily labours to render annual revenue of the society as great as he can."

> He generally, indeed, neither intends to promote the public interest, nor knows how much he is promoting it. By preferring the support of domestic to that of foreign industry, he intends only his own security; and by directing that industry in such a manner as its produce may be of the greatest value, he intends only his own gain, and he is in this, as in many other cases, led by an invisible hand to promote an end which was no part of his intention.[58]

Whether they intend to or not—and mostly they do not—people help each other by helping themselves; even the basest of ulterior motives by the greediest person supposedly leads to the happiest results for all. According to Smith, this is the work of Providence's "invisible hand." Smith introduced the concept of "the invisible hand" in his earlier book *Theory of Moral Sentiments* (1759) but brought it into full bloom in *The Wealth of Nations*, where he proposed the harmony of self-interests and societal aims. If each person looks out for herself, the end result will be a perpetually rising tide of economic bliss that lifts all boats.

Following this logic, society should allow people to enrich themselves as much as possible. All people will do what they do best to realize the greatest profit, producing goods or providing services that other members of society can buy more cheaply than they could make for themselves. If anyone within the economy gets too greedy, benefiting at society's expense by driving up prices, this invisible hand will prompt others to join the fray and compete against the bad actor. Since the invisible hand does its job so well, it is pure folly for governments to intrude upon macroeconomic activity. Moreover, Smith argues, "kings and ministers . . . are themselves always, and without any exception, the greatest spendthrifts in the society."

The classic doctrine of laissez-faire works fairly well in a relatively free, strong, and expanding economy such as eighteenth-century England. However, as history has proven, laissez-faire as an economic principle does not work so well in a contracting or volatile economy, or in developing nations, or contexts with high unemployment. More than anything, it is doubtful that Smith would be able to explain why the invisible hand occasionally allows the business cycle to spiral downward or why the supposed neutrality of the boom periods brought forth by free trade is almost always followed by the punishing reality of inevitable busts.

Economists and historians credit another physiocrat, Anne Robert Jacques Turgot, with devising the economic doctrine known as the "law of diminishing returns." The doctrine states that, after a certain point, continued effort or constant expenditure only produces lesser results. Turgot devised the notion around 1767, in terms of piling weight on a tight spring. Some significant weight, he reasoned, is required to overcome the spring's internal resistance. However, Turgot wrote, "after yielding a certain amount it will again begin to resist the extra force put upon it, and weights that formerly would have caused a depression of an inch or more will now scarcely move it by hair's breadth. And so the effects of additional weights will gradually diminish."[59] A contemporary illustration might describe the discovery of a massive oil deposit underneath the backyard of your family home. No matter how much the crude oil might be worth, it will profit you nothing unless you sink a huge sum of money into clearing the yard and setting up an oil rig to extract the commodity. Since the oil itself is a limited commodity, over time each dollar spent yields far less profit.

Englishman John Maynard Keynes, possibly one of the most influential economists of the last century, once praised by the left, is now routinely condemned by the right for the theory known as "deficit spending." Published in 1936 and an ambitious and unprecedented work for its day, Keynes's *The General Theory of Employment, Interest, and Money* introduced to the world the concept of microeconomics.[60] Keynes advocated governmental funding of public works. This Keynesian doctrine flew in the face of laissez-faire economics by defying the conventional wisdom that the free market would run itself and that such negative economic conditions as unemployment should be deemed temporary inconveniences at worst. This conventional wisdom stood until the Great Depression shook the ironclad orthodoxy of laissez-faire ideology to its very roots.[61]

Essentially Keynes argued that we might better be able to comprehend and maintain national economies if leaders accepted one simple truth: a nation's income equals the sum of investment and consumption. Moreover, the level of employment nationwide is directly proportional to the national income. Therefore, according to Keynes, there is a very simple yet profound correlation related to the stimulation of the national economy: every dollar invested in the economy generates more than a dollar in national income, which in turn generates more than a dollar's worth of new jobs. Thus Keynes concluded that when the market cannot achieve the necessary equilibrium on its own accord, public investment via government spending is always in the best interests of society.[62] This remains true even if the government cannot recoup the expenditure by means of income tax or other revenue, and even if the state must experience a period of short-term debt (hence the term "deficit spending").[63] Keynes recognized that habits of consumption change more slowly than income does. Yet he believed both are necessary to see a rising tide of employment. An infusion of public investment can at times be vital to the well-being of the nation as a whole.[64]

Like most economists, Keynes opposed the idea of debt, but he was even more appalled when governments maintained fiscal frugality simply for the sake of tradition. More importantly, Keynes had virtually no faith that free-market capitalism, when left to its own devises, would ever result in full employment, fairness for all society's members, and the best use of a society's resources. To the contrary, Keynes's observation led him to conclude that unfettered capitalism always favored the greedy, the wealthy, the unscrupulous, and the cunning, to the extent that it only resulted in greater inequality of wealth and soaring rates of unemployment.[65] Ironically, it took an economic upheaval like the Great Depression to provide the perfect living laboratory for liberal politicians. Franklin Delano Roosevelt's New Deal brain trust applied Keynesian theories to the gravely wounded U.S. economy and effectively overturned the dogmatic stronghold of laissez-faire as conventional wisdom in American life for more than a generation.[66]

The backlash against Keynesian economics began in earnest during the Reagan administration, particularly through the process of governmental deregulation. This was due to the increasing influence of Milton Friedman and the more rigid tone of modern political conservatism, which created a climate generally opposed to both taxation and government spending.[67] Over the course of the next thirty years, this neoliberal economic policy hearkened back to Smith's laissez-faire ideals.[68] In twenty-first-century America, the era of unfettered big business has returned in earnest, as exemplified by hedge funds and "dark pools" of equity and capital. For Tertullian, who a little more than eighteen hundred years ago first gave us the notion of the economy, God was the source of all things and guaranteed the resources necessary for life. Today, advocates of big business are guided instead by the doctrine that the invisible hand of the market, if left to its own devices, more effectively provides this service.

INSTITUTIONS

For many people today, the classic Frank Capra film *It's A Wonderful Life* (1946) is a staple of Christmas television viewing. Though the movie offers enjoyable entertainment, it also offers a deeper social critique than most viewers tend to recognize. The film's protagonist, George Bailey, has used his life to work tirelessly for the citizens of his small hometown of Bedford Falls. The modest family-run Bailey Brothers Building and Loan Company stands as the only institution in the community that stands between the unscrupulous Mr. Potter, owner of the local bank, and the welfare of Bedford Falls. Early in the film, George Bailey remarks, "This town needs this measly, one-horse institution if only to have some place where people can come without crawling to Potter."

However, on Christmas Eve, while en route to make a crucial deposit of a large sum of cash in the nearby bank, George's Uncle Billy loses the money and places the entire business in jeopardy. The ruthless millionaire, Mr. Potter, finds the money and hides it from the absent-minded uncle. A bank examiner uncovers the shortage, and George knows he could be charged with fiscal mismanagement. Burdened by family obligations, communal responsibility, and an intense sense of personal failure, Bailey is so financially drained and spiritually devastated that he thinks about ending his life.

Although the movie ultimately has a typical Hollywood happy ending, occasioned when townspeople come to George's aid, the lost money is recovered, and George Bailey is able to rediscover both his faith and his love of life, the film's embedded social critique remains very much intact. The film deliberately contrasts the virtues of a small community-oriented financial institution with the cruel and callous actions of the all-powerful profit-minded bank. In one interesting development, the evil banker Mr. Potter remains both unpunished and unrepentant at the end of the movie. While filmmakers of that generation may have felt any additional focus on Mr. Potter's despicable behavior would dilute the film's more positive messages, modern viewers might think Potter got away with his dastardly deeds because he and his bank were "too big to fail."

The phrase "too big to fail" describes a protection of financial institutions that are so large that their financial collapse would bring devastating effects to the American or global economy. Thus the federal government is forced to protect them. Stewart McKinney, Republican congressman from Connecticut, popularized the phrase during a congressional hearing conducted in 1984. By 1984, the Continental Illinois National Bank had failed, the largest such failure in American history. Once the seventh-largest bank in the United States, the bank, with deposits worth approximately $40 billion, had become deeply involved in speculative oil and gas loans associated with the Penn Square Bank in Oklahoma. When Penn Square failed in mid-1982, its failure combined with other factors, including a tight money supply, Mexico's default on international loans, plummeting oil prices, and press rumors of Continental's own impending difficulties, to create an eventual run on Continental in early 1984.[69]

The measures taken by the Fed did not stop the run. Simply put, a considerable hue and cry arose when it became common knowledge that the nation's seventh-largest bank faced financial commitments it could not satisfy. Regulators could not consider selling all assets as a resolution because, even in the case of small banks, the disruptions caused by such an action were too large to overcome. Given the financial realities, no suitors seeking to buy the bank existed.[70] Regulators feared failure would significantly disrupt the entirety of national payment and settlement systems. Essentially, regulators deemed the bank "too big to fail," concluding that the only option involved full provision of governmental assistance.

Oddly enough—as noted by dissenting voices from the left such as Sen. Bernie Sanders, Sen. Elizabeth Warren, Cornel West, Jim Wallis, and the Occupy movement—in 2008 such examples of governmental grace, mercy, and forgiveness were not extended to America's struggling middle class and working poor.

Although the phrase "too big to fail" had previously been used sporadically in the news media, the financial meltdown of 2008 thrust it into the national lexicon.[71] Faced with the potential calamity wrought by the implosion of a sizable portion of America's economic sector, Princeton economist and Federal Reserve chair Ben Bernanke revisited the definition of the term in 2010. "A too-big-to-fail firm," Bernanke said, "is one whose size, complexity, interconnectedness, and critical functions are such that, should the firm go unexpectedly into liquidation, the rest of the financial system and the economy would face severe adverse consequences." He continued:

> Governments provide support to too-big-to-fail firms in a crisis not out of favoritism or particular concern for the management, owners, or creditors of the firm, but because they recognize that the consequences for the broader economy of allowing a disorderly failure greatly outweigh the costs of avoiding the failure in some way. Common means of avoiding failure include facilitating a merger, providing credit, or injecting government capital, all of which protect at least some creditors who otherwise would have suffered losses. . . . If the crisis has a single lesson, it is that the too-big-to-fail problem must be solved.[72]

In addition, Bernanke worried about the competitive edge that this mentality provided for the bigger banks. As Sheila Bair, former chairperson of the Federal Deposit Insurance Corporation, put it in October 2009, "'Too big to fail' has become worse. It's become explicit when it was implicit before. It creates competitive disparities between large and small institutions, because everybody knows small institutions can fail. So it's more expensive for them to raise capital and secure funding."[73]

Should larger banks be broken up into smaller banks? Alan Greenspan said, "If they're too big to fail, they're too big." He added, "I don't think merely raising the fees or capital on large institutions or taxing them is enough. . . . They'll absorb that, they'll work with that, and it's totally inefficient and they'll still be using the savings." Paul Volcker, former Federal Reserve chair, has suggested that the government must "limit how much money big institutions can wager trading." As Eric Dash of the *New York Times* put it, "the way things are now, banks reap profits if their trades pan out, but taxpayers can be stuck picking up the tab if their big bets sink the company."[74] Additionally, as discussed by Vermont Senator Bernie Sanders, who mounted a robust Democratic presidential campaign in 2015–16, if taxpayers are contributing to save these companies from bankruptcy, they "should be rewarded for assuming the risk by sharing in the gains that result from this government bailout."[75]

Echoing trailblazing economist Joseph Schumpeter's principle of creative destruction, former Federal Reserve chair Alan Greenspan has stated that "failure is an integral part, a necessary part of a market system."[76] By this reasoning, when large institutions take unacceptable risks in order to reap huge profits, they deserve to fail. Failure, in fact, could provide the deterrence that prevents others from taking the same risks in the future. Yet the prevailing wisdom in today's world of big business still maintains that our major financial institutions are simply too big to fail, thus creating an environment that continues to encourage irresponsible and unstable activities benefiting the wealthy and the privileged few, while placing everybody else at a considerable disadvantage.[77]

Because many Americans live with their noses pressed to the grindstone, dealing with their own daily economic struggles, rarely do they understand the full reach of the devastation wrought by big institutions, not only in their own lives, but also in the lives of others, and the effect across the globe itself.[78] Most Americans live in a bubble that keeps them from internalizing the realities of global sweatshops, privatized water markets, obliterated rain forests, and the realities existing in war-torn nations. These institutional realities associated with "free-market fundamentalism," according to labor strategist Peter Laarman, have worked to our benefit. What we don't know does not seem to hurt us:

> To be sure, we could see the enormous wealth beginning to concentrate at the top of our own society. But as long as enough trickled down to us plebeians (and as long as we could get easy credit to keep up with those Joneses) we were okay with it. It is only now that the latest and largest *financial* bubble has burst that we are beginning to break through our perceptual bubble to wonder whether entrusting

our fates to self-interested and unregulated moneymen was really such a great idea.[79]

But Laarman warns that catching a glimpse of the truth will not likely deliver us from the evil of big business. Escaping its seemingly omniscient, omnipotent reach is unfathomable in the American context, because institutional wealth is omnipresent, not merely in the financial sector, but throughout the entirety of American society.

EXPERIENCE

Recorded history cannot recall exactly who devised the notion of a division of labor, the parceling out of varying tasks and assigning work to different persons or groups within a society, as a core principle of social organization. Early in human history, the division of complex tasks and indiscriminate use of a vast supply of human laborers by elites contributed to constructing great Egyptian pyramids, the Great Wall of China, and the Intercontinental Railroad. Moreover, as demonstrated by the rise of the transatlantic slave trade, the exploitation of colonized populations served as the backbone of developing capitalism in the modern world. Yet, before the industrial revolution, workplaces did not necessarily view the division of labor as standard operating procedure. By most accounts, philosophical interventions and scientific innovation, along with a growing need for modern mass production during the nineteenth century, suddenly created a greater need for specialization.

Once again, Adam Smith stands out as an important contributor to the eventual dominance of division of labor within modern economic theory. In fact, Smith thought the situation so vital to any discussion of a functioning modern economy that he made it the first topic in his magnum opus: "The greatest improvement in the productive powers of labour, and the greater part of skill, dexterity, and judgment with which it is any where directed, or applied, seem to have been the effects of the division of labour."[80]

In order to illustrate his point, he cited the manufacturing of pins as an example of a seemingly simple yet slow and tedious task for one person to perform alone. When industry divided the procedure of making pins among ten to twenty workers, each highly skilled at one specific operation in the process, it became possible to churn out about twelve pounds—an estimated 48,000 pins—per day. Smith found this discovery to be particularly exciting for various reasons. First, the division of labor allowed each worker to focus on one and only one task, at which a person could become both proficient and dexterous. Second, it saved time, since workers would not have to switch tasks. Most importantly, the division of labor into a series of limited precise tasks made it possible to operate in at least a quasi-mechanical fashion, thus enabling "one man to [do] the work of many."[81]

His enthusiasm did not prevent him from acknowledging that the division of labor also created setbacks as well. Even though Smith did not envision a time when mechanization and other forms of automated production would cost human beings jobs on an immense scale, he did worry about coercing laborers to spend all day in simple repetitive tasks. He believed long-term repetition could deaden the spirit of workers. If a person is not daily called upon to either "exert his understanding, or to exercise his invention" in facing new challenges, then the worker "generally becomes as stupid and ignorant as it is possible for a human creature to become."[82] Interestingly enough, Smith's rather radical solution to this impending dilemma involved the establishment of free and possibly compulsory education.

Today, the severity of class divisions has taken center stage. As both a trilogy of young adult novels and a subsequent series of blockbuster films, *The Hunger Games* features class warfare in a dystopian American society where the decadent and privileged elite keep the rest of society (let's say the 99 percent) distracted and oppressed by staging elaborate brutal competitions using their best and brightest teenagers as the unwitting fodder for grisly televised spectacles. In the similar *Divergent* series of books and films, those unable to fit neatly into the postapocalyptic class distinctions defined by such "faction" names as Candor (honest), Dauntless (brave), Erudite (wise), Abnegation (selfless), or Amity (peaceful) become Factionless, those with no standing or status within the society. Some of the Factionless are "Divergent," those who seem to possess the ability to connect with multiple factions. The Divergent are fighting for the right to be independent from class distinctions and expectations. These books and films each top their respective charts and are raking in millions of dollars.

One of the most vital distinctions in the definition of class identities between the wealthy and the working class has to do with the notion of dialectical materialism. In the wake of the Occupy Wall Street movement, there has been a considerable resurgence of rhetoric concerning the differences between the elite (1 percent) of society and the poorest (the remaining 99 percent).[83] Yet the kind of sloganeering heard today is much too simplistic to address the complex matter of class divisions.

When Karl Marx infused G. W. F. Hegel's dialectic with his own observations of the material world over and above the idealistic realm, he articulated a truly provocative idea: rather than eliminate capitalism, Marx argued for its evolution. The materialist dialectic, as such, is about the gradual and consistent progression of civil society from oppression to freedom, from agrarian feudalism to a hyperindustrialized revolutionary workers state (communism). Marx clearly identified capitalism as a necessary phase of this societal journey.

Many critics of Marxist thought have the wrong idea about his definition of materialism. Rather than describing a lust for acquiring and hoarding costly possessions, he emphasized that material circumstances shaped human aspirations, attitudes, and activities. As for the dialectical dimension of the paradigm, Hegel imagined history as an ongoing and progressive struggle in which theses were in direct conflict with antitheses to produce better syntheses. While enthralled with the Hegelian model, Marx utterly rejected Hegel's assumption that God (i.e., "Ideas" or the "Spirit") guided the historical dialectic.[84] By asserting his atheistic perspective and his belief that history does indeed progress through a series of reversals and upheavals, Marx asserted that these shifts are inspired by the material circumstances of life, whose "base" is the economic foundation of the time. Absent the dictates of a divine being, economic arrangements determine every form of cultural expression and social change, whether in the areas of politics, labor, art, or even religion. At a given point in time, the dialectic emerges out of conflicts inherent within capitalism itself as an economic system.

To cite the best-known example, conflict is inevitable and necessary between those who control the means of production (the bourgeoisie) and those who actually do the producing (the proletariat). The rise of capitalism brought into existence the natural and internal conflict between worker and capitalist. This conflict leads inevitably to class struggle, where, in dialectical terms, the thesis of capitalism runs headlong into the antithesis of an organized and politicized workforce. The resulting struggle manifests itself in the synthesis of a new social state. Marx imagined in the midst of the transformation that class distinctions would be dismantled, private property would be abolished, and society would become inherently fair and just. Eventually a new synthesis would rise from the ashes of the old, producing a classless democratic society.

Marx opposed religion's role in human affairs because he judged it an impediment to the process of remaking the political economy. Most famously, Marx stated that "religious suffering is at one and the same time the expression of real suffering and a protest against real suffering. Religion is the sigh of the oppressed creature, the heart of a heartless world and the soul of soulless conditions. [Religion] is the opium of the people."[85]

Although typically used to demonstrate Marx's animosity toward religion in its many forms, this statement actually conveys an alternate, deeper significance. Depicting religious faith as a painkilling drug can be quite shocking and appalling for many fervent believers, both in Marx's time and now. Yet, more than simply denouncing religion, Marx intended actually to criticize the conditions of a cruel society that led people to escape to a dependence on the sacred. The public condemnation of "godless communists" throughout much of the twentieth century acted as shorthand for implying that Marxism lacks any morality or redeeming social values. This, however, is not necessarily the case.[86] Marx understood that religion functions as a means of social control and is often used to pacify the oppressed, something both his critics and devotees have often misconstrued. Marx defined oppression as a moral wrong. For Marx, therefore, religion reflected what is lacking in society. For the poor and oppressed, religion offered an idealization of what they aspired to in the afterlife only, because they could not have it in the world.

Marx did not dismiss religion as superstition or illusion. Instead, he regarded it as a social function employed to keep the poor from comprehending the fact of their oppression. So long as the exploited and marginalized believe their sufferings will earn them happiness and freedom in the hereafter, they will define their oppression as part of the natural order of things. The poor then come to perceive poverty as a necessary burden associated with their lowly existence, rather than an affliction imposed upon them. Religion, as "the opium of the people," may dull their pain, but over time it makes them sluggish and apathetic by clouding their perception of reality. Ultimately, religion robs them of their will to demand change.

So what on earth did Marx want, and why did it matter? He wanted the poor and exploited to wake up from their delusional stupor in order to resist the capitalists' efforts to extract more and more profitability from their labor without either restitution or accountability. He wanted the poor to develop their own sense of self-realization. To that end, Marx called for the "abolition of religion as the illusory happiness of the people." He wanted workers and the poor to demand "real happiness," crystallized by his materialist philosophy focused upon attaining fulfillment and freedom in this world and not the next. Marx believed workers should have control over their own productivity and possession of the values they created through their own labor. These things would create a newfound sense of self-esteem, freedom, and power. Since the wealthy are not going to hand these things over of their own volition, and because no divine being exists who can step in to reconcile such egregious inequality, workers will have to take what they desire on their own terms.

Given the reality of the power of big business in twenty-first-century America, the experience of American families is considerably disparate. Those experiencing the upside of laissez-faire economics are quite content. Yet, for many others, perhaps not for 99 percent, but certainly for a vast majority of American families, the collapse of the middle class means a downward spiral, rather than any kind of genuine advancement up the social ladder. In our context, perhaps it is helpful to reframe the class strife described by Marx as a question of theodicy: why does the market allow the wealthy to live so well and enjoy so much luxury while the poor work so hard and suffer so much? When viewed against the backdrop of rampant exploitation and abuse by big business, many of Marx's allegations seem quite valid. One has to ask whether the rags-to-riches narrative or the ideal of conspicuous consumerism is actually operating as a new form of religious opium for many of America's poor. Perhaps it is time for those on the downside of laissez-faire economics once again to pay some heed to Marx.

3

Entertainment

Americans invest a great deal of their sacred energy in kneeling before the altar of entertainment. This is due, in large part, not only to their attempt to escape the stresses and strains of everyday life, but also to their desire to experience hopes and dreams that will enable them to transcend it. Human beings often seek an escape from things as they are, to a place where things are as they should be. Few people have more successfully transformed both the scope and scale of the human capacity to hope and dream than Walter Elias "Walt" Disney during his brief yet productive lifetime.

According to Steven Watts, the creative output and commercial success achieved by Walt Disney from the 1930s onward resulted from his genius to be able "as a moralist [to combine] the role of the educator, the child psychologist, and even the theologian. . . . No mere maker of amusing films, . . . Walt Disney was a major purveyor of moral values."[1] Gary Laderman argues that the allure within much of Disney's seminal animated films exists because they explicitly and implicitly articulate an innate desire of his audience to triumph over the power of death itself.[2] Disney established a global corporate empire devoted mostly to the ingrained desire within all people to find some place in the world that would simultaneously enable them to escape the mundane and experience the miraculous.

Disney and those around him are responsible for some of the most beloved cartoon characters, including the iconic Mickey Mouse, for whom Disney provided the original voice. His studio subsequently launched an entire cadre of supporting characters, including Donald Duck, Minnie Mouse, Goofy, and Pluto. Following the unprecedented success of his first feature film, *Snow White and the Seven Dwarfs*, Disney received an Oscar, along with seven Oscar statuettes. *Snow White* ushered in a nearly-twenty-year period characterized as the Golden Age of Animation, as Disney redefined the industry through films like *Pinocchio, Fantasia, Bambi, Alice in Wonderland, Peter Pan, Dumbo, Lady and the Tramp, Sleeping Beauty, 101 Dalmatians*, and *The Sword in the Stone*.

Meanwhile, Disney turned to live-action family features, with *Treasure Island* (1950), followed by *20,000 Leagues under the Sea* (1954), *Old Yeller* (1957), *The Shaggy Dog* (1959), *Pollyanna* (1960), *Swiss Family Robinson* (1960), *The Absent-Minded Professor* (1961), *The Parent Trap* (1961), and *Mary Poppins* (1964). "The 'golden age' Disney Studio," Steven Watts contends, "was a very attractive place to work. Almost without fail, Disney employees believed they were part of something special, and many of them provided testaments to the magic of the Disney workplace."[3]

As Disney's films gained in both commercial success and critical acclaim, his company expanded its entertainment operations, including a concerted effort to gain a foothold in television. Disney's studio produced a television special in 1950, *One Hour in Wonderland*. Soon after, Disney hosted a weekly series called *Disneyland*. The show featured clips from past Disney productions, provided tours of the Disney studio, and introduced the public to a new theme park the company was building in Anaheim, California. In 1955, the studio created its first daily television show, the *Mickey Mouse Club*, for children, on ABC. Under Disney's tutelage, this groundbreaking comedy and variety show succeeded well into the 1990s.[4]

The company underwent an almost incomprehensible evolutionary process from a humble animation studio to a multibillion-dollar empire that became the dominant force in the realm of leisure activities and escapist fare. Disney's career garnered him twenty-two Academy Awards (among fifty-nine nominations), including four in one year and four honorary Academy Awards. No individual in Hollywood entertainment comes even close to matching this total. Disney also won seven Emmy Awards. Renowned not only as a filmmaker and animator, Disney became a trailblazer in theme-park design. He provided both the vision and his name to the two major theme parks in the United States (Disneyland in Anaheim, California, and Walt Disney World Resort in Orlando, Florida), to international resort properties in Tokyo, Paris, and Hong Kong, as well as to a growing fleet of luxury cruise ships designed to serve entertainment needs of families.

During the first decade of the twenty-first century, the Walt Disney Company's acquisitions of ABC, the Jim Henson Company, Pixar Animation Studios, Marvel Entertainment, and Lucasfilm reaped huge profits and also enabled it to cultivate "a treasure trove of intellectual property"[5] that dominated the world's imagination. By 2015, the Disney corporation had remade itself into a global multimedia conglomerate with annual revenue in excess of

$48 billion and an estimated market capitalization (total value of outstanding shares of a publicly traded stock) of more than $202 billion. In his endeavor to capitalize on the hunger for whimsy and magic that exists in all people, Disney quite literally made a fortune out of child's play.[6] Neal Gabler writes that "Walt Disney's influence cannot be measured by numbers or encomia. It can only be measured by how thoroughly he reshaped the culture and the American consciousness. Disney was protean."[7]

Using his visionary imagination, Disney tapped into the almost-sacred belief shared by many Americans that virtually anything is possible if one asserts his sheer will with dogged determination over and against adversity. According to Disney biographer Gabler:

> If one source of Disney's magic was his ability to mediate between past and future, tradition and iconoclasm, the rural and the urban, the individual and the community, even between conservatism and liberalism, the most powerful source of his appeal as well as his greatest legacy may be that Walt Disney, more than any other American artist, defined the terms of wish fulfillment and demonstrated . . . how one could be empowered by fantasy—how one could learn, in effect, to live within one's own illusions and even to transform the world into those illusions. . . . In numerous ways Disney struck what may be the very fundament of entertainment: the promise of a perfect world that conforms to our wishes.[8]

Steven Watts has argued that Disney's magic kingdom expressed a mythical, idealized version of the values and aspirations of the modern United States. Watts quotes a close associate of Disney's who said that Disney unfolded for his audience "a dream of the way the world ought to be."[9] In retrospect, the life and legacy of Walt Disney had been fully realized in the fact that "Walt Disney had been not so much a master of fun or irreverence or innocence or even wholesomeness. He had been a master of order."[10]

For a good number of people in North American culture, entertainment such as that offered by Disney provides an avenue to imagining a better life. For some, the experience actually reshapes their everyday lives according to values and beliefs defined largely by the entertainment industry. Movies, for example, often speak to the meaning of life. At the dawn of the twentieth century, the Hollywood studio system established the fundamental template for the narrative style of filmmaking that has dominated the modern film industry. American moviemaking is not merely the merger of creative and commercial interests to produce films; it also exerts considerable influence on our cultural ethos. "To think of classical Hollywood cinema," Thomas Doherty suggests, "is to think not solely of a means of production and film style, silent or sound, but to conjure a moral universe, with known visual and ethical outlines. . . . What makes Hollywood's classic age 'classical' is not the film style or studio system but the moral stakes."[11]

The ironclad control that Hollywood studios wielded over a huge array of film images and cinematic storytelling tropes had a profound impact on box-office revenues and broader socioeconomic concerns. Hollywood also served as a fertile seedbed for shaping and projecting visions of race, gender, class, sexuality, nationality, ethnicity, and religion within both collective consciousness and popular imagination. Or, as James Baldwin contended in his own inimitable fashion, "the language of the camera is the language of our dreams."[12]

Much like Binx Bolling, the protagonist of Walker Percy's classic novel *The Moviegoer*, many people find themselves going to movie theaters in order to escape "living the most ordinary life imaginable," in order to find what he affectionately referred to as "treasurable moments." For millions of us, regardless of our specific backgrounds, the world of film often serves as a realm of imaginary refuge and vicarious escape from the pains of our relatively mundane existences, no matter how temporary it might be. "Most of us," bell hooks argues,

> go to movies to enter a world that is different from the one we know and are most comfortable with. And even though most folks will say that they go to the movies to be entertained, if the truth be told lots of us . . . go to movies to learn stuff. . . . As cultural critics proclaim this postmodern era the age of nomadism, the time when fixed identities and boundaries lose their meaning and everything is in flux, when border crossing is the order of the day, . . . popular culture, particularly the world of movies, constitutes a new frontier providing a sense of movement, of pulling away from the familiar and journeying into and beyond the world of the other.[13]

Hollywood conveys even the dreams of the traditionally religious. No story is too sacred to escape Hollywood's imprint or a filmmaker's editorial hand.[14] Though Hollywood occasionally takes on the films of other religions, mainly when the subject involves historical significance, along the lines of someone like Mohandas Gandhi, the evolution of Hollywood films involving religious themes has been rooted largely in the biblical epic.[15] Key examples of religious films, a popular genre during the 1950s and 1960s, are *The Robe* (1953), *The Ten Commandments* (1956), *Ben-Hur* (1959), *King of Kings* (1961), and *The Greatest Story Ever Told* (1965). These films boasted of huge cinematic scale, massive production budgets, and box-office celebrities like Richard Burton, Jean Simmons, Max von Sydow, Charlton Heston, Deborah Kerr, and Yul Brynner.

Hollywood has become so pervasive in dominating the American imagination that a good many confessing Christians cannot imagine a Moses who does not look like the buff and polished Charlton Heston, who stood well over six feet and was barely recognizable as the hesitant biblical prophet. A younger generation of Christians will likely picture Christian Bale, who assumed the role in *The Exodus: Gods and Kings* (2014). Contemporary moviegoers have also discovered a strong, determined, and dominating role model in Noah, through Russell Crowe's performance for the 2014 movie by that name. In some respects, given both historical and contemporary treatments of biblical narratives, the Hollywood version influences Christian understandings of these stories more than any church's interpretation.

Jesus is the most depicted character on the silver screen, with more than a hundred treatments. These films have portrayed Jesus in ways that speak specifically to both the historical moments and the particular contexts of their time. In 1961, MGM's release of *King of Kings* (a remake of Cecil B. DeMille's 1927 film of the same title) represented the first attempt by a major film studio to produce a religious epic in which the Christ event served as the central focus. Other cinematic renditions of Jesus soon appeared, including *The Greatest Story Ever Told* (1965), the musical *Jesus Christ Superstar* (1973), *The Last Temptation of Christ* (1988), *The Passion of the Christ* (2004), *The Color of the Cross* (2006), and most recently *Son of God* (2014), a 20th-Century-Fox epic covering Jesus's entire life, starring Portuguese actor Diogo Morgado.[16]

Adele Reinhartz begins the conclusion of her book on the *Jesus of Hollywood* with a tantalizing statement: "If the historical Jesus of Nazareth was the unique and only Son of God, as the Gospels proclaim, then Jesus of Hollywood is his opposite—multiple, diverse, and born of many parents."[17] Reinhartz argues that the "Jesus of the biopics reflects our own societies and cultures more than he illuminates the historical Jesus whose story these movies purport to tell."[18] The story of Jesus, as is the case with so many other religious figures, is not immune to cultural tendencies to define longstanding stories so they are in tune with prevailing myths active in the storytellers' contemporary milieu.

MYTHOLOGY

In recent years, a spate of superhero movies, based on comic books, have garnered both considerable commercial success and critical recognition.[19] Comic books as a medium function in a manner analogous to myths. They reveal our core ideals, critical foibles, and communal realities in ways that speak directly to the fundamental essence of our everyday lives, and they do so on a grand and mythical scale.[20] For instance, Marvel Studios has become a major force in Hollywood by forging interconnected movies and television series into a sprawling, hugely successful shared narrative continuity referred to as the Marvel Cinematic Universe.[21]

When examining the hero's journey in the context of the world's religious tradition, Joseph Campbell offers a definition (which he defines as "classic monomyth"): "A hero ventures forth from the world of common day into a region of supernatural wonder (x): fabulous forces are there encountered and a decisive victory is won (y): the hero comes back from this mysterious adventure with the power to bestow boons on his fellow man (z)."[22]

Philosopher Marco Arnaudo contends that "the similarities between the superhero genre and classical myth are truly remarkable—and most important, more remarkable than they are between myth and any other popular contemporary genre. Whenever [he or she] dons a mask and costume and travels to another planet or even just to the tops of skyscrapers to defeat supercriminals, the superhero symbolically retraces the traditional journey of the mythical hero."[23]

Over various iterations, the dual identity Clark Kent/Superman has been used to portray everything from the Americanized immigrant to the superhuman paragon of virtue to the alien messianic figure working to save humanity while always remaining set apart from it. *Superman* (DC Comics), created in 1938, provided comfort to anxious Americans during World War II and later during the height of the cold war, when he appeared in film (1948) and in a television series (1950s). He illustrates the belief that there is always an answer to the evils that beset us ("Faster than a speeding bullet, more powerful than a locomotive, able to leap tall buildings in a single bound . . . to best be in a position to use his amazing powers in a never-ending battle for truth and justice. . . . This looks like a job for Superman!").[24] In similar manner, Terrytown produced eighty animated films featuring Mighty Mouse between 1942 and 1961. Television showed the films between 1955 and 1967 ("Here I come to save the day!").

As a prime example of the correlation between superheroes and classical mythology, one need look no further than DC Comics's landmark *Death of Superman* story arc (circa 1992–93), which featured the death and resurrection of the iconic comic-book character. Even those who are only casually aware of the classic origin story of Superman, an extraterrestrial superhuman infant sent to Earth eventually to become the protector of the planet and savior of humanity, generally recognize its Judeo-Christian overtones. But Superman's demise at the hands of his superpowered nemesis Doomsday proved to be a creative game changer. Contrary to the fairly ubiquitous practice of having a superhero narrowly escape death by some outlandish means (such as time travel, alternate universes, psychic transference, cloning), this story arc depicts the ultimate sacrifice of Superman as the supervillain succeeds in killing him during his attempt to save Earth. Advanced alien technology nestled in Superman's Fortress of Solitude resurrects the superhero. The connection between Superman and Jesus reaches completion in this infamous story line that shocked millions of comic-book fans as well as the mainstream media.[25]

The world of comic books provides other mythic examples. Despite his life as a wealthy playboy, Bruce Wayne's deep-seated pain and rage at the murder of his parents drives him compulsively to hone his mind and body with ruthless precision until he becomes Batman (DC Comics, 1939). This story line also emerged during the anxious days of World War II. In yet another example, Peter Parker, a science nerd, becomes the wall-crawling, web-slinging superhero in *Spider-Man* (Marvel Comics, 1962). As the first teenage comic-book crime fighter with a starring role, his dedication to foiling criminal activity emerges from his late Uncle Ben's sage advice: "With great power comes great responsibility."

Other superheroes seem to adhere to this maxim as well. For example, Marvel's Captain America is a scientifically enhanced supersoldier intended to be a symbolic embodiment of the U.S. military. Designed to promote the military's good name, he is probably the noblest and most virtuous of the comic-book superheroes. Another proxy for the U.S. military-industrial complex, *Iron Man* alter ego Tony Stark is a brilliant and noble weapons developer. Although a devil-may-care wealthy playboy, he largely maintains a collaborative relationship with the U.S. military and serves as a force for good against rogue weapons manufacturers as well as rival nations. As a cold war–era update of Dr. Jekyll and Mr. Hyde, *The Incredible Hulk* is the accidental product of top-secret military experiments gone wrong. Scientist Bruce Banner, the character's alter ego, is both the beast's creator and his most consistent victim. Haunted by this tragic irony, he spends all his time in pursuit of a cure to his problem. In an ironic conundrum, Banner eludes the military in order to keep Hulk from being co-opted into a weapon, while the latter relishes fighting for fighting's sake, utterly devoid of ideology and intentionality.

Not all comic books are about white males. Mythologies associated with the entertainment industry have also developed feminist and ethnic sensibilities. In the world of comic books, *Wonder Woman* (DC Comics, 1941), though scantily clad and heavily sexualized, hailed the advent of a strong and independent woman who also fights for freedom, justice, and the American way.[26] Storm (aka Ororo Monroe) is a particularly notable example of a black female superhero in the Marvel pantheon of characters from the *X-Men* series. She is an East African hailed as a demigoddess because of her mutant ability to control the weather. Her battle seeks mythical justice and reconciliation by seeking harmony between "mutantkind" and humanity.

While these are certainly not the only characters of diverse backgrounds, there has been a more concerted effort to acknowledge changing identity politics in innovative and interesting ways in the comic-book industry. Writing stories and characters that illustrate greater multicultural worldviews and global concerns, Marvel has remade its most revered superheroes in the hopes of more accurately reflecting the demographic diversity and democratic possibilities of American society. In 2011, the Afro-Latino character Miles Morales assumed the mantle of Spider-Man. On the heels of Morales' Spider-Man, Kamala Khan became the first Muslim American superhero by assuming the role of Ms. Marvel. Sam Wilson, an African American character formerly known as the Falcon, replaces his friend and partner Steve Rogers as Captain America while a brilliant Korean-American teenage scientist named Amadeus Cho becomes the new alter-ego of the Incredible Hulk following the death of Bruce Banner. Similarly, female versions of classic white male heroes like Thor (Jane Foster), Wolverine / X-23 (Laura Kinney), and Iron Man (Riri Williams) have become more commonplace. In 2015, Ice Man (Bobby Drake), a core character of the various X-Men comic book series, also came out as gay, helping to make the superhero genre more inclusive to LGBTQ characters as well. On the whole, Marvel's social experiment seeks to use the comic book medium to explode cultural stereotypes while also expanding racial, ethnic, gender, and sexual diversity within its pantheon of superheroes.

Originally published in 1986–87, Alan Moore and David Gibbon's *The Watchmen* limited series is among the most influential and revered comic books of all time. Its narrative is multilayered and fairly complex. In a version of America drawn from its past, a group of superheroes find themselves ignored as they solve basically insignificant crimes. The world has more significant problems, including the escalating nuclear arms race between the United States and Russia during the height of the Cold War. The series inverts central themes of the comic-book format, particularly around the uses and abuses of power in its myriad forms. One of the themes of *Watchmen* focuses on how all idealism and noble intentions are eventually corrupted, as demonstrated by the ulterior motives of this eponymous group of aging, jaded superheroes themselves.[27]

Myths in entertainment generally reinforce existing cultural norms. Regardless of their abilities, attitudes, and motivations, all the heroic figures discussed here represent qualities that society finds admirable and inspiring. Ultimately, their accomplishments inspire the rest of us by implying that every one of us is capable of pushing ourselves to be better than we otherwise might be. These characters are popular because they represent values connected to self-reliant and rugged individualism. They continue to reinforce specific cultural and mythical notions of the ideal person, the ideal life, and a better world, a world where evil is always defeated by good.[28]

In the late 1960s and early 1970s, there were numerous horror films with religious themes, particularly dealing with evil. These included, most notably,

Rosemary's Baby (1968), *The Exorcist* (1973), and *The Omen* (1976). In *Rosemary's Baby*, a coven of witches deceives a young Manhattan housewife into giving birth to a child who is actually the son of Satan. *The Exorcist* deals with a young girl's demonic possession and her wealthy mother's desperate attempts to rescue her by recruiting two Catholic priests to perform an exorcism. Serving as the pinnacle of the "demon child" movies of the era, *The Omen* is the story of a wealthy diplomat's family unknowingly adopting a child who is actually the Antichrist foretold in the book of Revelation. These films have had an enduring resonance with American popular culture, most evident by the numerous sequels and remakes for these movies over the years.

These films dealing with personified evil and demonic possession provide their own contribution to doctrinal understanding in the category of entertainment. They depict an evil that is palpably present, in ways the viewer would rarely if ever personally experience. These films encourage the American tendency to lack subtlety when dealing with evil. Evil is bold and obvious and attempts to take over everything good. It is all around us, even within us. But it gets within us only if we do something terribly wrong that invites it in. It is possible that our children, the most innocent among us, can be consumed by it. You can't miss it when it appears. As long as your head is not turning circles on the axis of your neck (*The Exorcist*) or walls are not bleeding (*Amityville Horror*), you are likely, at the moment, not under the purview of its influence.

People love watching the grotesque treatments of evil; they can even munch contentedly on their popcorn while doing it. Yet they don't often reflect critically about their own participation in evil. These movies encourage us to ignore subtler forms of evil in life. The evil force from the outside, the one that inevitably threatens our own tranquility and welfare, is much easier to imagine than the subtle ways we might facilitate the presence of evil by our own activities.

The capacity for human nastiness is even more fully depicted in "slasher films," a subgenre of horror films in which the villain, although humanoid in form is no longer recognizable as humane. In these kinds of movies, evil simply prevails. There is no salvation or happy ending. Yet these monstrous creatures—most vividly rendered in the *Nightmare on Elm Street, Halloween,* and *Friday the 13th* film franchises—attack only those who, arguably, have done something wrong themselves and thus have invited evil into the house. There is a logic provided both for how Freddie Krueger, Michael Myers, and Jason Voorhees became evil, and for why certain people are attacked by them. Evil is explained. Ambiguity has no place. As long as viewers of the movie can personally understand how and why they are exempt from this recognizable and explainable evil, they can rest assured they will not suffer from it. One contains this kind of unresolved evil by living according to the rules of the road—if you don't do those kinds of things to invite evil into your life, then you will not suffer because of it.

In an eschatological sense, godless creatures like Michael Myers and Freddy Krueger play a role in the larger endgame of the Hollywood narrative. They dispense a sort of divine retribution upon those who have chosen illicit behavior in this or that life circumstance. The audience can believe that when evil is inflicted on those who are innocent, righteousness can and will prevail; but when evil is inflicted on those who deserve it, it is part of the grand scheme of life and contributes to the ebb and flow that ultimately results in a victory of good over evil.

Movies convey assurance that good overcomes evil in a variety of ways. As depicted in movies, heroes and heroines are men and women who typically embody the most important ideals and values of our culture. They can be ordinary or extraordinary. Ordinary people from humble origins often rise to greatness by accessing some measure of extraordinary courage, exceptional cunning, a particularly disciplined knowledge or honed skill that enables them to accomplish remarkable feats in the face of some imminent danger. Action-adventure film characters like Indiana Jones, John McClane, and Jason Bourne are mere mortals who, when faced with intense crises and insurmountable odds, somehow manage to rise above the fray and fulfill self-appointed missions to defeat various and evil threats decisively.

What role do these movies play when evil is obviously evident in everyday life, as it was when planes flew into the Twin Towers in New York City? How do they help us to cope? An escape into fictional depictions of evil that is overcome by good can be cathartic, for a time at least, by turning evil into something that is manageable and controllable. These movies reinforce a mythical belief that every instance of evil on the stage of human history can actually be defeated, even though, in reality, evil wins as often as it loses. These movies provide a sense of hope that the evil that directs planes into towers can be effectively dealt with once and for all. Hollywood echoes the long historical drumbeat of the entertainment industry in America that portrays the mythological belief that America represents all that is good in the world and stands as the world's last best hope against all that threatens human life.

Over time, these types of films helped to create a ready-made audience for George W. Bush's response to 9/11. Multitudes of people were ready to believe his argument that righteousness will prevail against evil. People did not merely recognize that there might be some resolution to the mess of evil that brought down the Twin Towers. Rather, they breathed life into the mythical belief that we, the righteous ones, could bring the resolution into being. Bush's response fit the doctrinal schema defined by Hollywood that has subtly shaped the religious understandings of many Americans. They could quickly rise to support a president who declared that two conventional wars (Afghanistan and Iraq) and an unconventional one (the Global War on Terrorism) offered an ultimate solution to the evil faced by the country.

Television, as a medium that tells longer and more intricate stories than the movie industry, has begun to offer more sophisticated treatments of evil, and hence is subtly transforming the myth. At the dawn of the twenty-first century, television enjoyed such a vibrant visual and narrative renaissance that it easily became the dominant cultural medium of the era. Although elite cultural naysayers often dismissed television entirely as "the idiot box," the heightened quality and variety of television programming has inundated millions of viewers with television shows qua works of art that contained great resonance with, and relevance in, contemporary popular culture. Our era has increasingly witnessed watercooler conversation, dinner-table chats, and incessant fan obsessions hovering around serialized television programs.

The increased popularity of contemporary television has emerged thanks largely to a massive influx into television of innovative and brilliant creative talent, best exemplified by the television showrunner[29] as auteur. The power and glory of the modern-day auteur has increased with the seemingly endless proliferation of media outlets (running the gamut from broadcast TV networks to basic and premium cable offerings to Internet-based media streaming venues like Netflix, Hulu, Amazon, and Yahoo) that relished the opportunity for dark, visceral, complex, and compelling storytelling. As Brett Martin notes, the emergence of antiheroes is noteworthy because

> these were characters whom, conventional wisdom had once insisted, Americans would never allow into their living rooms: unhappy, morally compromised, complicated, deeply human. They played a seductive game with the viewer, daring them to emotionally invest in, even root for, even love, a gamut of criminals whose offenses would come to include everything from adultery and polygamy (*Mad Men* and *Big Love*) to vampirism and serial murder (*True Blood* and *Dexter*).[30]

For better or worse, contemporary television showrunners like David Chase (*The Sopranos*), David Simon (*The Wire* and *Treme*), David Milch (*Deadwood*), Joss Whedon (*Buffy the Vampire Slayer, Angel,* and *Firefly*), Alan Ball (*Six Feet Under* and *True Blood*), Matthew Weiner (*Mad Men*), Jenji Kohan (*Weeds* and *Orange Is the New Black*), Vince Gilligan (*Breaking Bad* and *Better Call Saul*), Shonda Rhimes (*Grey's Anatomy, Scandal,* and *How to Get Away with Murder*), David Benihoff and D. B. Weiss (*Game of Thrones*), and Beau Willimon (*House of Cards*) have been hailed as imaginative storytellers and innovative geniuses.

Thanks to them and their peers, we currently have a pop cultural landscape awash with central male and female characters who can be categorized only as antiheroes in the most classical sense.[31]

Writing for the *New York Times* in 2013, A. O. Scott points out that there are three principal antiheroes of the twenty-first-century television universe that inhabit different regions in the "kingdom of modern capitalism." As the central character of *The Sopranos*, Tony Soprano inherits the "family business"; he is the head of a New Jersey organized-crime family masquerading as the owner/operator of a waste-management company. His daily decision-making process is constantly challenged by complicated family dynamics, seething self-loathing, middle-aged angst, and quasi-tribal customs of his fellow gangsters. On *Mad Men*, advertising executive and picturesque family man Don Draper inhabits "a high-rise corporate zone of corner offices, mergers, and expense accounts" but can never seem to find any lasting vestige of personal satisfaction in either his personal or his professional life. In *Breaking Bad*, high-school-chemistry teacher Walter White begins the saga as a disconsolate, cancer-stricken "sad-sack" who stumbles upon his life's vocation by manufacturing the finest crystal methamphetamine in the world and ultimately transforming himself in a chameleon-like fashion by shifting his appearance and attitude based on whoever is around.

While *The Sopranos* and *Mad Men* may be original, "they also knowingly draw on a rich reservoir of popular-cultural meanings attached to their chosen worlds." As Scott puts it, "They look at familiar material from a fresh perspective, without letting go of the inherited romance of the Mafia and the advertising industry." By contrast, the central conceit of *Breaking Bad*'s Walter White is the one he wanted his friends and loved ones to believe—"and may, at moments, have convinced himself—that he was a decent man driven by desperate circumstances to do terrible things." Yet what viewers surely realize by the end of the series is that this "notion was either wishful thinking or tactical deceit."[32]

Arguably the pinnacle of the antihero narrative trope within contemporary televisual storytelling has to be *Breaking Bad*. During the entire lifespan of this series, the faithful audience witnessed Walter White evolve (or, more accurately, devolve) into a complex portrait of the slippery moral slope incumbent to the contemporary moral psyche that is both imminent and immanent. In the words of series creator/showrunner Vince Gilligan, millions of devoted viewers have been transfixed by the main character's transformation from "Mr. Chips to Scarface." However, the show taken as a whole offered its viewers a deeply nuanced and engrossing exploration not only of morality (or the lack thereof) but also of mortality, mendacity, masculinity, mutability, mutuality, middle-class angst, and mediocrity as particularly contentious issues in our contemporary lives.[33] We are always already aware in a visceral fashion of the causes and consequences of his actions, as well as how they affect others. To this point, Walter White's chosen nom de guerre, "Heisenberg," becomes quite illustrative. The name is derived from "the physicist whose uncertainty principle is popularly understood to express the idea that the presence of an observer changes the nature of what is observed." "In truth," A. O. Scott observes, "the development over five seasons has been less a shocking transformation than a series of confirmations" about the inherent flaws of his character as they unexpectedly come into view.

Much of the profound success of *Breaking Bad* rests in the show's actors giving masterfully human portrayals of their characters while nestled in Vince Gilligan's frenetically dynamic narrative. The entire plot of the show, with all of its twists and turns, unfolded over the course of five seasons, according to Scott, "to reveal the Walter White who was there all along." In the final analysis, the mythological construct of the show forced viewers to wrestle with the fractured sides of Walt's broken being—"sociopath and family man, scientist and killer, rational being and creature of impulse, entrepreneur and loser"—to discover that his fragmented selfhood is "not necessarily as contradictory as we might have supposed."[34] Without question, through superb acting and excellent storytelling, the darkly comic yet morally fragile world of *Breaking Bad* has exposed the sort of morality tale that turns out to be best suited to our times.

In his classic treatise *Beyond Good and Evil*, Friedrich Nietzsche advances the theory that the "will to truth" is present in all of us. Truth may be uncovered in the web of human circumstances only when we learn to question those things we all tend to take for granted. This questioning posture must include not only those things we take for granted about ourselves or our social order, but also those things we believe in the area of religion. Questioning ourselves, our social order, and even our religious beliefs takes some moxie. Nietzsche had little time for those who did not possess the will or the ambition to question their own self-assured answers and to seek answers to the world's unanswerable questions. Nietzsche also doubts whether opposites exist, especially the opposites of good and evil. They are more likely somehow related to one another. Nietzsche's core argument is that "it might even be possible that what constitutes the value of these good and revered things is precisely that they are insidiously related, tied to, and involved with these wicked, seemingly opposite things—maybe even one with them in essence."[35] The stories of antiheroes might actually illustrate Nietzsche's argument.

DOCTRINE

Most Hollywood movies display doctrinal confidence that everything comes out right in the end. Hollywood, above all else, believes in the happy ending, even though it also can relate stories with endings much more ambiguous or even messy.[36] Hollywood's happy ending is defined or accomplished in any number of ways. It can come through the agency of the superhero or super-heroine who triumphs over incredibly evil power, or through the struggles of the everyday man or woman who, with meager resources, outsmarts or out-wits an enormously powerful malevolent force. In other cases, self-realization is all-important to reaching the happy ending.

The happy ending can be accomplished only when you first see yourself for who and what you are. In an altogether different genre, the romantic comedy, the happy ending is not about saving the world or reaching self-realization but, rather, about two people who have found love and are now able to "live happily ever after." Hollywood offers escape, a way to experience the happy ending, even when real life seems dismal or downright depressing. These happy endings, of course, often end up reinforcing cultural stereotypes as well.

Renowned filmmakers Joel Coen and Ethan Coen have also wrestled with stereotypical issues through film. *Barton Fink* (1991) and *The Big Lebowski* (1998) were especially noteworthy for their diverse abundance of overtly, albeit offbeat, Jewish characters. The Coen brothers have been accused of depicting in their numerous films anti-Jewish ethnic stereotypes, such as Ber-nie the Shmatte, a cravenly duplicitous hustler, in their third feature film, *Miller's Crossing* (1990). However, their film *A Serious Man* (2009) provides a remarkably provocative and poignant portrayal of Jewish American experi-ence during the 1960s, culled from their own childhood memories of grow-ing up in St. Louis Park, a suburban Jewish community west of Minneapolis, Minnesota. Drawing heavily from the cultural tradition of Ashkenazic Juda-ism, the film centers on the Job-like professional and private plights of Larry Gopnik, a physics professor undergoing a crisis of faith. Struggling to make sense of his ruined life, Gopnik desperately seeks metaphysical advice and spiritual guidance from three rabbis to become a person of substance. The film grapples with theological issues pertaining to human suffering in ways that strive to reconcile the spiritual and the absurd.

Much like the entirety of the Coen Brothers' film canon, *A Serious Man* ultimately upholds a doctrinal belief that life is filled with a haphazard and unpredictable mixture of good and bad. While not quite falling fully into a doctrine of "you reap what you sow," the film encourages people not to break covenant and not to do the things they know that they should not do, in spite of all obstacles they might face. However, when you do break the covenant, or the ties that bind us together, you are likely to reap some measure of unpleasantness. Every person has to figure this truth out for herself or himself. Yet in Hollywood, this doctrinal certainty is usually connected to another belief, as depicted in *True Grit* (whether the original 1969 movie or the 2010 Coen brothers remake): that people, no matter how far "beyond the pale," can find redemption, if only they become attuned to the signs around them that point to a better way to live. Hollywood often presents the doctrinal belief that we are left to our own devices to resolve the struggle between destiny and human free will in order to discover the path to our own salvation.

Salvation as happy ending meets you where you are. When you are lonely, or newly divorced, or unhappy in a relationship, the doctrinal form of the "happy ending" is communicated most through the idea that love will win out. Romantic comedies (referred to as "rom-coms") constitute another key genre of movies defining doctrine in Hollywood filmmaking. These films are typically light-hearted cinematic fare with humorous plotlines focused on two protagonists who are exemplars of romantic ideals, like the notion that true love is able to surmount almost any obstacles.

When Harry Met Sally (1989), directed by Rob Reiner and written by Nora Ephron, starring Billy Crystal and Meg Ryan, has become the gold standard of this genre. The story follows the title characters from the time they meet in 1977, shortly after college graduation, through the next twelve years of emerging friendship while living in New York City. The film's central theme explores Harry's and Sally's divergent ideas about relationships. Harry offers the view that "men and women can't be friends because the sex part always gets in the way" . . . even with ones he "finds unattractive." Sally, of course, makes the argument that men and women can develop meaningful friendships without sex. One of the cleverest elements of this film rests in its narrative structure. The movie frames its story by using several elderly couples to tell stories about their relationships and then culminates with the film's main characters joining the procession.

The movie sits in a long history of similar films, including such classics as *His Girl Friday* and *The Philadelphia Story*. *When Harry Met Sally* has become "the quintessential contemporary feel-good-relationship movie that somehow still rings true."[37] The story is told over and over again in films like *Sleepless in Seattle* and *You've Got Mail* or *As Good as it Gets* and *It's Complicated*. Every film season usually has one or two of these movies.

In her reflections on the film's enduring success, screenwriter Nora Ephron indicated she received letters for years from people obsessed with the film who would describe a relationship by indicating something along the lines of, "I was having a Harry-and-Sally relationship with him or her."[38] This sort of identification with not only the film's characters but also its outcome has been instrumental to the staying power of the film and of the entire genre. Hollywood provides reassurance that, no matter how tumultuous and desultory romance might be, a sustained and substantial loving relationship is awaiting everyone. It will happen if you can simply persevere in the face of a certain level of hardship and heartbreak. Out of the messiness of our lives, love wins in the end. Our universe provides preferential treatment for love. Love is the norm. There is somebody for everybody.

Movies like *I Love You, Man*, a depiction of the "bromantic" love existing between two male lead characters, or *Bridesmaids*, a movie exploring the theme of the enduring love between female characters as best friends, provide a variety of ways to understand how love plays itself out in the world. All of them play on the widespread doctrinal belief that "love makes the world go round." Television reinforces this message and even expands it. Situation comedies like *Will and Grace* and *Modern Family* show how real love plays out between gay characters, while managing both to maintain and to make a bit more complex the long-held belief that "family matters," a longstanding though far less complicated doctrinal message contained in television classics like *Father Knows Best* and *Ozzie and Harriet*.

ETHICS

An appropriate religious response is concerned with not only what you believe but what you do and how you do it. Entertainment gives us rules for the road and prescribes action based on the models that it provides. With respect to the family, for instance, entertainment historically modeled the conventional nuclear family, with one woman, one man, and at least two children. We learn through entertainment what a family is by watching them function effectively or struggle through some measure of dysfunction. Entertainment not only defines the nature of the family, but tells us how to be a man, in some cases "a man's man," and explains how to be a woman—and in some cases defines what makes for "an attractive woman." In like manner, the very nature of the toy industry thrives on a gender-specific approach.

Toys enter a child's life early and contribute to defining gender roles. Boys play with cars, trucks, robots, and soldiers like Power Rangers, Transformers, and G.I. Joe action figures, through which they plot troop movements and guard bridges. They learn how to build things, to make things go faster, and to be efficiently violent. On the other hand, girls learn motherhood as they enter childhood. They take care of dolls, tend to dollhouses, and cook on play kitchen stoves. Play continues to engender particular ideas about how one should be male and how one should be female, even when significant portions of our culture have moved well beyond them.

Children's shows as diverse as *Dinosaur Train, Doc McStuffins, Sesame Street*, and *Daniel Tiger's Neighborhood* explain to children how to be a citizen, what a job is, how to be a neighbor, how to live in community, how to play, how to imagine, and how to understand the nature of sex and sexual relations. One might even argue that, since the 1970s and the creation of the latchkey generation of children, today's youth form their ethical values more from these kinds of shows than from their parents. For some families, entertainment does the parenting. A study conducted by the University of Michigan health system and published in 2010 has concluded that, on average, children ages two to five spend thirty-two hours per week watching television, DVDs, and DVRs and playing video games, while kids six to eleven spend twenty-eight hours a week, 97 percent of that time in front of live television. Among eighteen-year-olds, 71 percent have a television of their own in the bedroom (54 percent have a VCR and DVD player, 37 percent have either cable or satellite, and 20 percent have premium channels). The study concludes, "Children learn to accept the stereotypes represented on television. After all, they see them over and over."[39] The study mentions some specific stereotypes:

> A review of the research on gender bias shows that the gender-biased and gender-stereotyped behaviors and attitudes that kids see on television do affect how they see male and female roles in our society. . . . In 1990s' commercials, white men more often were depicted as strong, while white women were shown as sex objects. African American men more often were portrayed as aggressive and African American women, as inconsequential. . . . [In] G-rated movies . . . , whether live action or animated, males are shown more than females, by three to one, they are not often shown in relationships, and do not solve problems peacefully. In G-movies, characters of color are underrepresented, and are usually shown as sidekicks, comic relief, or bad guys. Male characters of color are more aggressive and isolated.[40]

Children's television, like the entertainment industry generally, reflects the beliefs and the ethics taken for granted in the culture. More dangerously, however, entertainment concretizes what is actually in flux within the culture. Entertainment makes stereotypes the norm. Movies and children's programming provide an ethical framework within which children understand the other, and also guide young lives by providing stereotypical categories into which they can fit themselves.

One category of entertainment that, at its best, challenges cultural values and norms from an ethical perspective is the comedic. While comedy can and often does reflect the same kinds of cultural values and ethics affirmed by entertainment generally, it can also transcend them effectively. Comedy is among the oldest, most enduring, and most deeply significant forms of social critique and cultural commentary in human history. Dating back at least to the ancient era, when the philosopher Socrates would subversively interrogate students and fellow citizens with rhetorical musings that were at once witty and whip-smart, comedy has provided a way to expose, deconstruct, and lambaste flaws and foibles of human thought and behavior. The voice and vision of a contemporary comedian can provide sage warnings to people about inherent shortcomings and blind spots. Anyone seeking to understand more fully the true disposition of a culture and society really ought to take seriously what makes people laugh.[41]

A comedian's jokes or narratives represent not only proper preparation on the performer's part but also a distinct point of view. What endears an audience member to the comedic stylings of Jerry Seinfeld, Chris Rock, Roseanne Barr, Aziz Ansari, George Lopez, Louis C.K., Amy Schuler, or Wanda Sykes, for instance, is the sense that theirs is a unique perspective and frame of reference not found elsewhere. For some comedians, that perspective is essential to maintaining a personal sense of hope. In the midst of increased Islamophobia and cultural intolerance nationwide, comedian and political commentator Dean Obeidallah noted that while most comics "have always used jokes as a means of entertainment, catharsis and social change," he and his fellow Muslim American comics "see their art as a tool for survival."[42]

Finally, we should say a word about the experience of an audience (regardless of size or demographics) enjoying shared laughter publicly. As anthropologist Victor Turner suggests, there is something not just transformative but actually liberating about community laughter in response to a comedian's treatment of things deserving ridicule, while the comedian also affirms an emerging sense of community and shared values.[43] Even though some may readily dismiss what is said in the midst of a comedic performance as "just kidding," "acting silly," or doing "mere comedy," the experience nonetheless promulgates clearer understandings of both community and culture—who we are and what we hold dear—and establishes common standards of mutual understanding and expectation that last long after the laughter stops.

EXPERIENCE

When people contemplate the transcendent truths of human existence and the ways their consciousness is permeated by deeply held feelings, they often do so in the categories born of their personal experiences. They reflect about first love, yearn for a better life, mourn for a deceased loved one, or remember particular joys or sorrows. In the entertainment world, music often invokes such experiences.

In Rudolf Otto's *The Idea of the Holy*, the concept of the numinous is used to explain the sacred as the heart of religion. His definition describes the numinous as a *mysterium tremendum et fascinans*—a mystery that is awesome to the point of inducing fear and at the same time fascinating in its allure. When considering the numinous within music, one might describe the way music connects with the depths of human emotion within a listener, allowing for a measure of vulnerability while creating an almost irresistible mood of introspection. Music offers a rich cultural production and complex phenomenon that seems to have a profound impact upon us as human beings, both individually and collectively.

Over a century ago, the average person could listen to only a few musical works, most of them from a specific genre typical to their social class and cultural milieu. Today, people listen to myriad types of music from all around the world. In 1900, people seldom heard a piece of music more than once, with the possible exception of hymns, and rarely heard it repeatedly in a short period of time. Thanks to audio recording (both analog and digital) and other related technologies, musical compositions from around the world can be repeated whenever and wherever one may wish. The number of new music types we can hear grows daily. The sights, sounds, and sensations of music, especially in cities, have become an integral part of our everyday environment. Faced with such an embarrassment of sonic riches, one's conscious choice of music becomes ever more important.[44]

By selecting a particular type of music, one also selects a group of people with whom this music is shared and a recognizable identity. The best example is undoubtedly hip hop music, a genre that largely emanates from inner-city African American youth culture. To be considered rappers, these young people—typically black but increasingly white, Latino/a, and Asian—must identify with experiences that define and demarcate psychosocially what it means to be connected with hip hop, as a musical art form but also as a culture. To make this identification part of who they are, these youngsters have created their own code of conduct, attitudes, vernacular, clothing, dance moves, gestures, and so on that aid them in identifying the true lovers of hip hop music without ironic detachment or outright cultural appropriation.[45]

Our tastes nowadays are based primarily on the social and spiritual meanings and values our choice of music conveys. Music speaks to us; it speaks the language of experience we are most likely to understand and value. Whether moshing at an all-ages punk-rock show, line dancing at a honky-tonk bar, dancing to electronica at a late-night rave, listening to classical music at an upscale symphony hall, nodding heads in rhythm to a hip-hop cipher, or singing hymns in a church sanctuary, music for both the artist and the audience has the power not only to transfix people but to transform their immediate context and even to help them transcend their reality (if only for a brief time).[46] Addressing the religious roots of music, psychologist Anthony Storr notes: "The origins of music may be lost in obscurity but, from its earliest beginnings, it seems to have played an essential part in social interaction. Music habitually accompanies religious and other ceremonies. Some anthropologists have speculated that vocal music may have begun as a special way of communicating with the supernatural."[47]

Popular music gives utterance to the things people feel most deeply. Music is much like a spirit that abides in us. It wakes us up, accompanies us in both the shower and the subway. Music creates feelings in us and provides meaning for them. It is written on our hearts and burned in our minds. In Rogers and Hammerstein's famous musical *The King and I*, the schoolteacher Anna sings, "Whenever I feel afraid, I whistle a happy tune." Music is a divine experience to the extent that, within Western culture, it is omnipresent. It exists everywhere, in the background of movies dictating emotions and moods, on the elevator to fill the space of social awkwardness and ward off claustrophobia, in the operating and birthing rooms to provide pacing and comfort. Music sits with romantic diners and accompanies shoppers in malls. Like the Holy Spirit, music is always there.

A song immediately places you somewhere; it can transport you to a distant memory ("The Way We Were" by Barbra Streisand) that is suddenly brought to mind (the backseat of that car when you were sixteen) or can propel you to a place you may have never been but you often visit through the experience of music ("We are the Champions" by Queen, for the team who has never taken first place in anything) or teleport you to a place you could never be ("I'll Take You There" by the Staple Singers).

Music begs to be embodied. It compels us to move. Dancing becomes the embodiment of our religious experience of music and provides proof that this mode of entertainment has meaning and validity. Feelings and music and body become one. Few can avoid embodying music in one fashion or another: humming with it, working out to it, making love to its rhythms, swaying one's head to it, being in concert with it, dancing to it. Some music begs for community embodiment. Virtual strangers become a communion of saints, if only for a moment. Beyond the directive line-dancing songs like the "Cotton-Eyed Joe" in Texas, the "Macarena," and the "Electric Slide," there are other songs that create their own active communal participation, like "I Will Survive," "YMCA," "We Will Rock You," and "Shout." Few can hear these songs and remain passive.

Music takes us outside ourselves. There are genres that specialize in it, like jazz or the blues or country and western music. Individual songs can also shift our mood instantaneously: moving us into melancholy ("Ode to Billy Joe" by Bobbie Gentry); infusing an uncritical patriotic sensibility ("I'm Proud to Be an American" by Lee Greenwood); putting us in the mood for a breakup ("Fifty Ways to Leave Your Lover" by Paul Simon or "I Can't Make You Love Me" by Bonnie Raitt); inspiring courage ("The Coward of the County" by Kenny Rogers); providing an inspirational philosophy for life ("The Gambler" by Kenny Rogers); responding to the feeling of exploitation in a powerful way ("RESPECT" by Aretha Franklin or "Say It Loud" by James Brown); or cheering us up ("Don't Worry, Be Happy" by Bobby McFerrin).

The experiences driven by music provide meaning for large numbers of Americans. Yet, if we are honest, music tends to become a quick fix. It lulls us into a belief that we are dealing lastingly with the effects of human life by giving proper attention to the mix of melody and lyrics. We actually begin to believe that within the timeframe of a musical track, we can effectively deal with real-life experiences. We can lament losses, create milestones, and overcome obstacles, even though the music that helps us do it is fully separated from our experiences. How can we fulfill our lives through music?

Many of us derive greater emotional benefit from music than from social interaction or church or an actual community of faith. Music fills in the gaps of our lives; it encourages and consoles and heals us. Where music is the experience, it enables us to be introspective, to analyze our inmost yearnings and our social successes and mistakes. In these cases, it is predictable and provides what we need without the risks of additional human interaction. Yet music can also drive us to both action and interaction; music can make us believe it prepares us for an encounter of some kind, whether combative, romantic, or retributive. For some, music powerfully shapes the actual experiences of human life. For this reason alone, when music is driven by the ethos and values of the entertainment industry, perhaps we should become a bit more self-critical about how the industry itself impacts our self-understanding or affects our very souls.

Take, for example, the way that entertainment, particularly through film and television, has desensitized us to the experience of violence. We are often entertained by what otherwise (outside of a fictional story line) would be abhorrent. We enjoy Coca-Cola while we watch people being blown away in *Pulp Fiction*, *Saw*, *Reservoir Dogs*, *Man of Steel*, and *Deadpool*. Such desensitization enables the current generation of viewers to stomach watching a news event like the three-minute-thirty-six-second video of journalist

Daniel Pearl being beheaded on a live broadcast by the Taliban on February 1, 2002.[48]

Luka Rocco Magnotta, a Canadian gay pornography actor, sought thirty minutes of fame by filming his murder and dismemberment of Lin Jin, a thirty-three-year-old Chinese international student, in May 2012. The video graphically showed the enslavement, torture, dismemberment of genitals and limbs, necrophiliac acts, decapitation, feeding of body parts to animals, and acts of cannibalism. Posted on a website called "Best Gore," the video received more than 300,000 hits in a four-hour stint before it was removed. A Montreal high-school teacher even showed the video to his class of sixteen- and seventeen-year-olds after they begged him to see it.[49] Magnotta regularly sought fame, constantly seeking auditions for a reality-television show, posting "pouty glamour shots" on Facebook, and starring in pornographic films. When arrested in Germany at an Internet cafe, after nine days on the run, authorities discovered him "googling news stories about himself and looking at porn videos he starred in." As the *Toronto Sun* put it, his "thirst for fame has turned to grubby infamy."[50] One has to wonder, however, in what ways we have actually created the culture that motivates people to seek fame in this way. Is our thirst for graphic and realistic entertainment a coproducer in this kind of quest?

RITUAL

Entertainment's effect on our souls, in addition to the values and beliefs we imbibe through movies and television, is also accomplished through the power of cultural rituals associated with it. Americans worship regularly at the altar of celebrity and have created significant rituals to enable worship there. For almost all of us, the fascination with celebrity is something ingrained in our daily routines. Most of us engage in some variety of celebrity worship: glancing at salacious headlines on tabloid magazines; listening to some tidbits of gossip offered by a drive-time morning radio show; being caught up in reality-television programs featuring both actual and aspiring celebrities who expose every aspect of their private lives for public consumption; scouring the Internet using sites like YouTube, Facebook, Twitter, MySpace, Tumblr, and TMZ to learn the latest about celebrity lifestyles; watching late-night talk-show hosts skewer famous folks in their opening while, minutes later, fawning over famous people hawking their latest book, film, play, or whatever; and watching the annual cavalcade of award ceremonies and red-carpet galas dedicated to honoring those who are already celebrated and adored.

Film critic Ty Burr argues that

> as the twenty-first century settles into its second decade, we are more
> than ever a culture that worships images and shrinks from realities.
> Once those images were graven; now they are projected, broadcast,
> podcast, blogged, and streamed. There is not a public space that
> doesn't have a screen to distract us from our lives, nor is there a cor-
> ner of our private existence that doesn't offer an interface, wireless or
> not, with the Omniverse, that roiling sea of infotainment we jack into
> from multiple access points a hundred times a day. The Omniverse
> isn't real, but it's never turned off.[51]

In these and so many other ways, American society has surrendered itself
wholeheartedly to rituals designed to serve entertainment.

Not all celebrity is deserved. In his classic text *The Image*, historian Daniel Boorstin argues that the celebrity of the early 1960s was famous for being
famous, a "celebutante," in the current terminology of popular culture. This
depiction refers to someone who attains celebrity status for no identifiable
reason—the Lindsay Lohans, Justin Biebers, and Paris Hiltons of our day.
In the words of Boorstin writing in 1961, "our age has produced a new kind
of eminence." The very practice of our rituals as everyday Americans creates
celebrities as much as it worships them. These manufactured celebrities represent the "human pseudo-event"[52] (defined by Boorstin as an event "manufactured solely to be reported"). Over the past half-century, Americans have
become enamored with the human pseudo-event and have included regular
attention to it in daily rituals and routines. Yet this is juxtaposed with the fact
that notoriety becomes a value in itself, especially when, as cultural critic Christopher Lasch argues, "success in our society has to be ratified by publicity."[53]

As a glaring (if not garish) example of celebrity as a quasi-cultish enterprise,
one need look no further than the meteoric rise of reality-television star Kim
Kardashian. Following the release of her infamous sex video with R&B singer
Ray J Norwood in 2007, Kim and her family—including her husband, hip-hop
superstar Kanye West, and their children, daughter North West and son Saint
West—realized a new level of fame. Under the direction of her mother and
manager, Kris Jenner, Kim used her fame to land numerous magazine covers, product endorsements, book deals, and several reality-television series. In
addition to her successful stint in television shows, Kardashian and her family
have developed clothing and fragrance lines. By 2014, her estimated annual
earnings exceeded $28 million, according to *Forbes* magazine and her celebrity
brand pervades along all avenues of social media.[54] The American love affair
with ritualistic following of celebrity keeps the human pseudo-event vibrant.

We are fed a steady diet of details of superstars' lifestyles as a testament of what
it means to be fearlessly and wonderfully human. For many, rituals connected

with celebrity worship offer those who engage in them the ways and means to be fearlessly and wonderfully human by emulating (if not imitating) the object of their veneration. We style ourselves after them by wearing their T-shirts, jewelry, hairstyles, and designer clothes and by paying attention to whatever trends they have set. There are heretics. Some in this ritualistic community—like John Lennon's killer, Mark David Chapman, or star-crazed groupies who present the body at the celebrity's altar as a living sacrifice, like Pamela Des Barres—become murderous stalkers who take their devotion too seriously.[55]

MATERIALITY

Much of the materiality of entertainment is issued by the industry itself or the byproducts associated with it. There are Oscars and Emmys and Tonys and Golden Globes and People's Choice Awards and the Grammys and the American Music Awards, all revered material items sitting in hallowed spots on shelves or enclosed cases, designating a successful career for an elite number of entertainers. In fact, people in the entertainment industry have dubbed the period from September to February "award season" for the glut of award shows that proliferate on the annual calendar.

There are many hallowed shrines of the entertainment world, such as Graceland, the Rock and Roll Hall of Fame, and the Hollywood Walk of Fame, as well as renowned performance halls like the Grand Ole Opry in Nashville, Radio City Music Hall in Manhattan, the Hollywood Bowl in Los Angeles, Red Rocks Amphitheatre near Denver, Colorado, and the Apollo Theater in Harlem.

Fan memorabilia also contribute to the materiality associated with the religious experience of entertainment—things like autographs, tickets, coasters, pictures taken with stars, old programs and playbills, and scrapbooks of various kinds. These tangible items become spiritual touchstones enabling us to recover and recall our own personal meaningful encounters with entertainment, or ushering us into a sense of connection with celebrities we revere who once physically inhabited these now sacred spaces (Elvis slept in that bed).

INSTITUTIONS

Everything that operates as religion needs an institutional framework where religious commitments can be expressed. On one side, on the business side of the entertainment industry, multinational corporations with global reach control everything related to film, television, literature, music, gaming, toys, and merchandising/branding. As an industry, entertainment falls into the classification of big business as religion (treated in a different chapter), which is second only to the military-industrial complex as the largest economic engine in North America. Yet the big-business side reaches each of us personally in a wide variety of ways. We attend theatres, play video games, go to rock clubs and concerts, join book clubs, and buy digital media. Hardly a day passes for any of us when we do not personally encounter an institutional incarnation of the entertainment industry. Sales and income associated with virtual institutions are skyrocketing, changing the cost of doing business considerably, as digital music and movies replace older methods of distribution of recorded media, like CDs and DVDs.

There is the institutional side of award ceremonies. The year 2016 was the eighty-eighth year the Academy of Motion Picture Arts and Sciences presented Oscars. The Emmy Awards celebrated their sixty-seventh award ceremony in September 2015, and the National Academy of Recording Arts and Sciences celebrated its fifty-seventh Grammys ceremony in February 2015. All these awards were created in the twentieth century, saying something in itself about the developing importance of entertainment for American culture in that century. Although the limitations of time and space do not permit a fuller, more robust exploration of this matter, it is important to address briefly the widespread public outcry against the lack of diversity within the entertainment industry, reflected in the controversy surrounding the 2016 Oscar ceremony.

A groundswell of complaints surfaced once the Academy of Motion Picture Arts and Sciences announced an all-white list of nominees in all acting and best picture categories for the second consecutive year, ignoring the fact that some of the year's most critically acclaimed and commercially successful films—namely, *Straight Outta Compton*, *Creed*, and *Star Wars: The Force Awakens*—had black talent both in front of the camera and behind it. Despite the allegations of reactionary critics and ill-informed opponents of the #OscarSoWhite boycott, the outrage over racial discrimination and exclusionary practices is not just a bunch of ballyhoo about a couple of bad years for people of color in the film industry. Rather, this is a dilemma that can actually be traced to the genesis of modern American cinema.

The Birth of a Nation (1915), pioneering filmmaker D. W. Griffith's filmic adaptation of Thomas Dixon's racist novel *The Clansman*, is a sordid legacy in the history of Hollywood. On the one hand, the film has been an influential touchstone of cinematic techniques and storytelling tropes for subsequent generations for an amazing array of filmmakers ranging from John Ford and Akira Kurosawa to George Lucas and Quentin Tarantino. On the other hand, the movie has become equally infamous as a revisionist work of

Confederate history that viewed the arrival—but not the enslavement—of African people on American soil as the nation's "original sin," which, according to the source material, could be redeemed only by the salvific heroism of the Ku Klux Klan.

Historian John Hope Franklin examined *Birth of a Nation* as a propagandistic tool for endorsing white supremacy and justifying the sociopolitical subordination of African Americans. He argued that, if one could somehow overlook the virulently racist agenda at the core of the movie, it "would be celebrated—and properly so—as the instrument that ushered the world into the era of the modern motion picture, a truly revolutionary medium of communication."[56] Despite becoming the reigning box-office sensation of its era, the movie also galvanized protests and boycotts by coalitions of black educational, religious, and civil rights organizations—most notably the NAACP—as well as like-minded white progressive allies, not only to ban the film itself but also to transform the nascent entertainment industry into a more respectful and representative enterprise regarding racial and ethnic diversity. As we clearly see, however, more than a century later, that work still remains unfinished.

Chris Rock hosted the 2016 Oscars awards ceremony and used humor to expose the industry's racism. "If they nominated hosts, I wouldn't even get this job," he said in his opening monologue. "Ya'll would be watching Neal Patrick Harris right now." Rock's comedy took Hollywood to task for its blatant racism, and even effectively called out "the liberals" of Hollywood for being "the nicest white people on earth," in spite of the fact that they just "don't hire black people." He handled a tough task with considerable humor and aplomb. Given the renowned activism of George Clooney, Susan Sarandon, Sean Penn, Angelina Jolie, Matt Damon, and Leonardo DiCaprio, among other contemporary Hollywood luminaries, many Americans have taken for granted that movie stars are outspoken advocates for social and political causes. However, when African American counterparts such as Spike Lee, Danny Glover, Harry Belafonte, Will Smith, and Jada Pinkett Smith take defiant stances against institutionalized racism in the so-called liberal world of Hollywood, mainstream America treats such protests as a novelty at best and a nuisance at worst.

Contrary to comedian Chris Rock's wisecrack that African Americans did not protest exclusion from being nominated for the Oscar categories in the 1950s and 1960s "because we had real things to protest . . . too busy being raped and lynched to care about who won best cinematographer," a handful of celebrities—both black and white—risked their careers and even their lives boldly crusading for racial equality, and ironically forged the role of the politically active celebrity within American popular culture.[57] Despite that and other missteps, Rock's stint as host of the Oscars during the height of the #OscarSoWhite controversy offered an unwavering and often scathing rebuke of an institution that excludes people of color from Academy Award nominations. Aside from Rock's unrelenting comedic performance, the producers of the Oscar ceremony tried desperately to make the show appear as inclusive as humanly possible, by including presenters from a variety of racial and ethnic groups to reflect the fact that they welcomed and celebrated diversity everywhere—except, of course, when it comes to honoring people of color with nominations and awards.

Yet his comedy missed the mark in several places. Writing for *The Guardian* online, Steven Thrasher, a film blogger, noted that Rock sold $65,000 worth of his daughter's Girl Scout cookies, but unwittingly proved "how much more Hollywood cares about Girl Scout cookies than it does about drinking water for black people." Here Thrasher raises a reference to events in Flint, Michigan, to emphasize that another black comedian, Hannibal Burress, hosted a "Justice for Flint" fundraiser intentionally set by several black Academy members for the same night. Thrasher also notes that Rock too easily dismissed sexism and the #AskHerMore campaign, which pushes media to ask women filmmakers about more than what they wear, by simply saying, "Everything's not sexism, everything's not racism." This, Thrasher concludes, in an industry where "93 percent of top films are directed by men."[58]

Another criticism of Rock's humor comes from an Asian theologian, Grace Ji-Sun Kim, who emphasized for *Time* readers the morning after the Oscars that Chris Rock should have known better than to describe racism in such black and white terms. Ignoring the plight in Hollywood of Hispanics, Asians, Native Americans, and other people of color only serves "to further white supremacy and white privilege."[59] In response to these criticisms, #notyourmule was a Twitter hashtag created by Mikki Kendall that began trending in defense of Rock's performance. Referring to a metaphor found in Zora Neale Hurston's venerable novel *Their Eyes Were Watching God*, referring to black women bearing the burdens of the world, Rock's supporters used this hashtag to argue against presumption that Rock's obligation included the need to tackle the racism confronting all other minority groups.[60] The Academy of Motion Picture Arts and Sciences, perhaps more publicly than other powerful institutions in American life, clearly illustrates the racism and sexism that remain deeply embedded within American culture.

Even though brick-and-mortar institutions are of supreme importance for human beings as social creatures with religious longings, our contemporary era increasingly finds people drawn into institutions existing only in the realm of virtual reality. Gaming, with the virtual reality that accompanies it, has created a new growth industry in institutional culture. Online casinos, particularly poker sites like PokerStars, which sold recently for $4.9 billion, attract hundreds of thousands of players at any given time. The online market across the world is worth around $37 billion per year and is growing at a clip of 11 percent per year, as eighty-five nations have legalized this form of online gaming.[61] Millions of dollars change hands daily online.

Over the past twenty to thirty years, the technologies of simulation and visualization have developed exponentially. Today's average person sees more mediated and manufactured images in one day than a person one hundred years ago saw in an entire lifetime. Asserting that video games should be considered "semiotic domains," educator James Paul Gee notes video-game players are learning a new literacy predicated by a "set of practices that recruits one or more modalities (e.g., oral or written language, images, equations, symbols, sounds, gestures, graphs, artifacts) to communicate distinctive types of meanings."[62] From real-time strategy games, first-person shooters, simulation games, fantasy role-playing games, and other genres of video games, the players find various ways to inhabit and navigate these various realms that possess their own distinct rules, languages, and logic. The thirst for excitement and escape generated by these technological developments has resulted in the raging success of gaming. With an estimated 183 million gamers in the United States alone (the United States has a population of more than 315 million), Jane McGonigal estimates we spend three billion hours per week on our planet playing games.[63]

McGonigal questions whether video games should be considered merely as escapist entertainment. Through her groundbreaking research, McGonigal "shows how we can leverage the power of games to fix what is wrong with the real world, from social problems like depression and obesity to global issues like poverty and climate change." She envisions innovative games that can positively impact the spheres of "business, education, and nonprofit worlds."[64] According to McGonigal,

> the truth is this: in today's society, computer and video games are fulfilling *genuine human needs* that the real world is currently unable to satisfy. Games are providing rewards that reality is not. They are teaching and inspiring and engaging us in ways that reality is not. They are bringing us together in ways that reality is not. . . . And unless something dramatic happens to reverse the resulting exodus, we're fast on our way to becoming a society in which a substantial portion of our population devotes its greatest efforts to playing games.[65]

The allure is certainly compelling.

As Steven Johnson emphasizes, gaming actually teaches life skills:

> Most video games differ from traditional games like chess or Monopoly in the way they withhold information about the underlying rules

of the system. . . . In the video game world . . . the rules are rarely established in their entirety before you sit down to play. You're given a few basic instructions about how to manipulate objects or characters on the screen, and a sense of some kind of immediate objective. But many of the rules—the identity of your ultimate goal and the techniques available for reaching that goal—become apparent only through exploring the world. You literally learn by playing.[66]

Games of all sorts have been an elemental dimension of human civilization for thousands of years. For example, Herodotus wrote in the opening book of *The Histories*:

When Atys was king of Lydia in Asia Minor some three thousand years ago, a great scarcity threatened his realm. For a while people accepted their lot without complaining, in the hope that times of plenty would return. But things failed to get better, the Lydians devised a strange remedy for their problem. The plan adopted against the famine was to engage in games one day so entirely as not to feel any craving for food . . . and the next day to eat and abstain from games. In this way they passed eighteen years, and along the way they invented the dice, knuckle-bones, the ball and all the games which are common.[67]

Whether the story is true or not, in his commentary about an eighteen-year famine overcome through gameplay, Herodotus reveals the fundamental truth associated with gaming. Rather than merely being escapist, games serve a purpose where the experience is thoughtful, active, and deliberate. Playing games together in the midst of a severe crisis made life bearable. The games effectively empowered the starving Lydians and enabled them to bring order out of supreme chaos. Although separated by thousands of years, we and the ancient Lydians are alike in seeking a better way. Odd as it may seem, gaming, especially when more than half of our population is doing it, can affect the world either for better or for worse.

In a contemporary sense, the world of gaming operates very much as a facsimile of everyday reality. One way in which we see the overlapping nature between the real world and the game world is in the form of gratification and rewards. According to Johnson,

in the gameworld, reward is everywhere. The universe is literally teeming with objects that deliver very clearly articulated rewards: more life, access to new levels, new equipment, new spells. Game rewards are fractal; each scale contains its own reward network, whether you're just learning to use the controllers, or attempting to complete the game's ultimate mission. Most of the crucial work in game interface design revolves around keeping players notified of potential rewards available to them, and how much those rewards are currently needed.[68]

Once you figure out the game, you know how to "game the system." The end result of the education of a gaming generation is that they believe they can also learn how to "game the system" of real life. Rules matter less than manipulating the system to one's personal advantage. You go from gaming the system to controlling it. Once you learn how to do that, essentially you become a god within the system.

In most games, the player actually enters a "god mode," a state usually afforded the player through use of cheat codes, or as a built-in reward unlocked after an extraordinary level of play. In this mode, the player-character is granted invincibility, invulnerability, or both. A new genre of games has also emerged known as "god games." In this particular form of role-playing game (RPG), as *Wikipedia* puts it, players control "the game on a large scale, as an entity with divine/supernatural powers, as a great leader, or with no specified character" (as in *Black & White*, *Afterlife*, and *Spore* video games and the *SIMs* series). The player transcends the semiautonomous characters of the game, safeguards them from harm, and influences their motives and behaviors. "The player's power comes from simulated worshippers, who are usually simple or tribal in nature."[69] Games like *Spore* emphasize the act of creation and monitoring how your creatures develop, while others such as *Afterlife* and *The Sims* place the process of playing god fully within a human idiom.

The religious lesson contained within contemporary forms of gaming is rather obvious. Not only can you rescue yourself from the problems that beset you with no help from others, but once you master the skills of manipulation and crack the code of the game of life, you can recreate the world you inhabit. The others who live alongside of you within your sphere will have to play according to your rules. Gaming does not lend itself well to understanding what it means to live in a community where values like compassion, teamwork, and justice must be taken seriously.

In this chapter we have addressed the contours of entertainment in our time as an altar largely obsessed with disposable amusements and diversions offering instant gratification. We know that attempting to capture and distill the essence of entertainment as escapist fare is not a static affair. The task is like trying to hit a moving target while riding atop a runaway train headed in the opposite direction. Much of what makes the works of entertainment so enjoyable is connected to the same attributes that make them ephemeral. Nevertheless, those songs, films, stories, games, and celebrities that seize mass appeal in one moment inevitably wax and wane over time. Yet, no matter how dated the references in this chapter might become, or perhaps because of that inevitability, we do wonder about the lasting efficacy of happy endings, mostly connected to venues as temporary and fleeting as most things tend to be in the world of entertainment.

4

Politics

Politics encourages an individual to be a part of something greater than the self. In fact, politics has a natural connection to the notion of transcending the self. The art of politics emphasizes a sense of community and citizenship, something that is always comprised of more than just one person. By definition, it always involves others. Politics brings us into connection with others and enables us to hold things in common with a sympathetic community. The community itself is, of course, anonymous as much as it is intimate. Our personal opinions, when they connect to the resonance of the opinions of anonymous others, enable us to transcend our isolated experiences. We become part of a public platform that mandates change. We create new laws and policies, or generate funding that can be used to transform our personal experiences. Throughout American history, individuals have taken their personal anxieties seriously enough to find ways to connect with one another to fight oppressive or more powerful entities and to bring about change—in effect, to create "a more perfect union." If there is anything specific about what it means to be an American, this might in fact describe it.

To take politics seriously, one must have a sense of the constituency that makes up the public and consider the things that exist beyond a concern for merely personal, private, or individual desires. Politics actually originates in the term *polis*. Originally, *polis*, in ancient Greek, indicated a city-state. In practice, however, the word had a fuller meaning. It indicated citizenship itself or, in a broad sense, a body of citizens. *Polis*, therefore, came to mean the role of the people in governing the affairs of the city. Plato in *The Republic* emphasized the connection between *polis* and the notion of the common good.[1] His notion of the "philosopher king" indicated that the best leader of the *polis* knew well, as Plato has Socrates state it, the "idea of the good." The good makes sense of everything else. Knowledge of the good makes the idea of justice possible. All great human ideas—whether one is talking about justice, beauty, truth, or equality—originate from the idea of the good.

The philosopher king, in Plato's view, took seriously the notion of *forms*, those things that lay beneath any one example of the good. For example, the best governor understands the nature of equality, that thing that lies beneath all instances of equality, and would never define equality itself by any singular instance of its appearance. The philosopher king, in other words, loves true knowledge and does not confuse it with, or define it by, the pursuit of that which is petty and trivial. Plato also knew, however, that philosopher kings had to be practical; they had to steer the ship of state. Thus he emphasized the "king" part of this term as much as he emphasized the "philosopher" part.

Reason and reflection for its own sake, as Socrates practiced it, due to Plato's approach, created a practical reason that actually worked to persuade people and to order society. As Plato established the academy, he also connected reason and practice in such a way that he lent credibility to the old adage that "knowledge is power." Plato transformed philosophy into politics. With politics, he created a mechanism designed to transform the personal pursuit for the good life into a systematic process meant to govern how people conducted their lives. This process had the greater purpose of "civilizing" them.[2]

Over time, politics moved beyond philosophizing about the common good to persuading and convincing others that the common good is defined by this or that specific understanding of the good. Taken to an extreme, some scholars, like Karl Popper, have even blamed the appearance of twentieth-century totalitarianism on Plato's notion of philosopher kings, taken to its worst imaginable extremes.[3] Some politicians have perfected the art of generating an idea of the common good and then universalizing it in such a way as to gain control over the personal lives of all those who live within the *polis*.

This is reflected in many ways through the proliferation of special-interest groups in American life today. There are not many places in our public life today where the sense of the whole competes well with the desires of the particular parts. Legislators seek special pork-barrel legislation for their own districts. If they don't, they won't be reelected. Lobbying groups, including Christian lobbyists, sway the public and Congress on behalf of their own special interests. Those in Congress, in their own self-interest, respond by pocketing the benefits offered by lobbyists to support special interests. Single-issue politics can rule the day anywhere and everywhere. It rules in government and in education. It often rules the day in denominations, in congregations, even in universities and theological schools. Belief in the principle that securing a victory for the whole is more important than achieving a victory for any one part suffers dramatically in American politics today.

Founders like Benjamin Franklin and Thomas Jefferson emphasized the Enlightenment presupposition that human beings were autonomous individuals bent on pursuing "their own self-interest." The liberalism found in the Enlightenment writings of Thomas Hobbes and John Locke emphasized the creation of a social contract, voluntarily entered into by these autonomous individuals, in order to "facilitate their personal security and private gain." The goal of public life was not to fulfill some particular vision of a common good; rather, public life served to increase the ability of all individuals to "secure their private ends." Public life in America, therefore, often serves individual gain more than the common good. When this philosophical liberalism emerging from the Enlightenment is connected to capitalism, the resulting political culture emphasizes individualism, wealth, and consumption. Public good, a notion of broader purposes with a strong sense of public virtue, is not high on the list of priorities.[4]

This was not always the case in American public life. In spite of their commitment to the Enlightenment value of individual autonomy, and despite their belief people were bent toward a tendency to pursue self-interests, founders, including people like Washington, Jefferson, Franklin, and Madison, all had a fairly clear sense of public virtue. They spoke unashamedly of improving the commonwealth, even if it meant significant self-sacrifice. Over the past two centuries, however, this sense of public virtue increasingly has been lost. These days, as Robert Bellah and others lamented in *Habits of the Heart,* and Alasdair MacIntyre explored at some length in his book *After Virtue,* the language of the public is controlled by the rhetoric of "personal rights" and of respect for the "rights" of others. "Our rights talk," argues Mary Ann Glendon, "in its absoluteness, promotes unrealistic expectations, heightens social conflict, and inhibits dialogue that might lead to consensus, accommodation, or at least the discovery of common ground." Public discourse today is devoid of language concerned with "virtues" and "the good" that might conflict with the individual. This does not mean, as Jeffrey Stout has pointed out, that language concerned with rights, and language concerned with virtues, cannot coexist. It just means that they don't coexist much in contemporary public discourse.

In one sense, politics moves people from the private realm into the public arena for the purpose of getting problems solved. It connects with people where they are, but ultimately moves them to someplace else. Politics is always an intimate concern, and it is spiritual. It becomes spiritual because it moves people to connect with forces beyond themselves. It connects them with others—whether through lifelong alliances based on shared views or through coalitions based on timely matters—rallies them, and motivates them to sign a petition, to protest, or to vote.

Yet politics also moves individuals from the public into their personal worldview. Like all human forces, politics can be manipulated to control the personal and ostensibly to rein it in. For example, just as people have used politics to define particular characteristics of civilization, they have also used it to define who was civilized and who was not. Women who transgressed against the traditional mores of the "cult of true womanhood" by working outside the home or by voicing their own opinion publicly were considered not civilized. People of color who sought freedom, justice, and equality because they neither understood nor accepted their station in life were considered uncivilized. Immigrants who left their homelands often at great risk and expense in the hopes of a better future in this country were not the least bit civilized in the eyes of native-born citizens fearful of what immigrants brought to their shores. To this end, politics often attempts to define the nature of truth for everyone within the *polis*, until there arises somewhere a force of the public powerful enough to change the narrative, break individually shared stereotypes and biases, and create a new political consensus about the meaning of truth.

The avatar for this chapter could be any of countless candidates in politics, but we have chosen Thomas Jefferson for somewhat obvious reasons. As the author of the Declaration of Independence, Thomas Jefferson started out with an abstract and metaphysical sense of what the new nation meant. The Declaration asserted that the colonists believed Great Britain's aim included the establishment of "absolute tyranny" over the colonies. In response to this perception, the Continental Congress proclaimed the colonies an independent nation. In effect, Jefferson and his fellow colonists negated the absolute sovereignty of monarchy and the military right of imperial might by invoking an even higher power's affirmation of their right to exist.

This dimension of Jeffersonian thought is made crystal clear in the opening lines of the Declaration's preamble: "When in the course of human events it becomes necessary for one people to dissolve the political bands which have connected them with another and to assume, among the powers of the earth, the separate and equal station to which the laws of nature and of nature's God entitle them, a decent respect to the opinions of mankind requires that they should declare the causes which impel them to the separation."

In addition, Jefferson used the Declaration of Independence to articulate the ideological shift from the objective rights of Englishmen advanced in the Magna Carta to the subjective rights of humanity ["mankind"] that would serve as the outright product of American independence. "We hold these truths to be self-evident, that all men are created equal," stated Jefferson in the

Declaration, "that they are endowed by their Creator with certain unalienable Rights, that among these are Life, Liberty and the pursuit of Happiness.— That to secure these rights, Governments are instituted among Men, deriving their just powers from the consent of the governed." The rights of humanity originate in a divine gift, which no government can take away.

Finally, the insertion of the oft-quoted phrase "pursuit of happiness" constituted a unique political thesis that remains one of the most provocative—if not perplexing—political ideas to this day. The origins of the concept can be traced to Jefferson's reworking of a key premise initially advanced in John Locke's *Second Treatise on Civil Government* (1690). In that text, Locke argued that governments exist to use their laws to enforce what is naturally and morally right. Locke asserted that the natural right to private property precedes the social compact that exists between the citizen and the nation-state. Therefore, the right to property arises because individuals extend their own personalities into the objects produced from the state of nature, so that, in Locke's words, the "life, liberty, and estate" (or property) of one person can be limited only to make effective the equally valid claims of another person to the same rights.[5]

Jefferson chose a different phrase to shift the emphasis and inserted "pursuit of happiness" in the place of "estate," consciously borrowing from Locke. By making "happiness," with all of its innate ambiguity and relativity, a political concern on equal footing with considerably more estimable political concepts such as life and liberty, Jefferson made a breathtakingly innovative move. Undeniably, the imaginative force and impassioned gravitas of Jefferson's preamble provided the Declaration's enduring impact within American life. Even though he was an unrepentant participant in the enslavement of others, his words provide a touchstone for any oppressed person or group who yearns for a better life.

By the time Jefferson became president of the new nation in 1800, this lofty rhetoric gradually had to be transformed into the mundane reality of governance. Scholars have described the election of 1800 that allowed Jefferson to ascend to the presidency as the "revolution of 1800," because the election included extensive verbal mudslinging and backstabbing within and between the political parties of the day. Having weathered the storm of the nation's first heavily contested election, Jefferson chose to be conciliatory toward his opponents in his first inaugural address. While he offered honorable statements toward all Americans in his first public statement as president, Jefferson acted to dismantle as much of the Federalist system as possible. In the hopes of quelling the grievances of his rivals and rallying the support of his allies, Jefferson shared these words in his first inaugural address:

Every difference of opinion is not a difference of principle. We have called by different names brethren of the same principle. We are all Republicans, we are all Federalists. If there be any among us who would wish to dissolve this Union or to change its republican form, let them stand undisturbed as monuments of the safety with which error of opinion may be tolerated where reason is left free to combat it. I know, indeed, that some honest men fear that a republican government can not be strong, that this Government is not strong enough; . . . I believe this, on the contrary, the strongest Government on earth. I believe it the only one where every man, at the call of the law, would fly to the standard of the law, and would meet invasions of the public order as his own personal concern.[6]

Jeffersonian idealism quickly collapsed into visions of life, liberty, and the pursuit of happiness that made very fine distinctions that privileged some people and disenfranchised many others. White men with property and education held all the rights and privileges of citizenship as their birthright. Women, African Americans (whether enslaved or free), and the poor could not vote because owning property quickly became connected to voting rights. The founders concluded that these people—women, African Americans, the poor—lacked the personal judgment and rational ability to exercise the vote in a democratic society. The "delicacy" of women, concluded John Adams, "renders them unfit for practice and experience in the great business of life." In the general order of things, "nature has made them fittest for domestic cares."[7]

Jefferson openly theorized that blacks did not possess the rational facilities to participate as equals with whites in the political process.[8] When thinking about the possibility of ending slavery in 1790 and the possibility of a future of free blacks in America, Jefferson stated,

It will probably be asked, Why not retain and incorporate the blacks into the state, and thus save the expence [sic] of supplying, by importation of white settlers, the vacancies they will leave? Deep rooted prejudices entertained by the whites; ten thousand recollections, by the blacks, of the injuries they have sustained; new provocations; the real distinctions which nature has made; and many other circumstances, will divide us into parties, and produce convulsions which will probably never end but in the extermination of the one or the other race.—To these objections, which are political, may be added others, which are physical and moral.[9]

And since the poor lacked experience in public affairs and did not own property, they could not be expected to exercise political power designed to ensure the protection of personal property.

Though many regard America as a Christian country, most are unaware that the first four presidents (Washington, Jefferson, Adams, and Madison) had virtually no connection to anything resembling orthodox Christianity. The Enlightenment influenced them far more than Christian doctrines. Though identified with Anglicanism, three of the four were influential deists and John Adams was a New England Unitarian. For them, belief in the supernatural convictions of Christianity stood counter to the dictates of reason and had to be abandoned. Yet each of them believed in the importance of religion and affirmed it should contribute to the establishment of peace and order within society.

Thomas Jefferson stands out as a key architect of religious freedom. As early as 1776, he worked in the Virginia House of Delegates to establish a new understanding of the freedom of religion, where all religions would be fully equal before the law. By 1779, as governor of Virginia, he proposed his "Statute for Establishing Religious Freedom." His bid in Virginia failed, and he headed to Paris as an ambassador for the new nation. After that, the main work of crafting the order of religious freedom in the new nation rested in James Madison's capable hands. For Madison and the other deists, the separation of church and state in America meant to separate religious institutions, especially the church, from government's institutions. They did not mean to separate religion from the public. On the contrary, the founders believed that religion would provide strong support for public virtue and morality. They hoped to distill the higher qualities possessed by all religions into a common morality that made sense for the new nation, stripped of the distinctive and peculiar religious beliefs (like the divinity of Christ or the sacrificial atonement theories associated with his death) that had little bearing on governing society.

According to some Christians, like Richard Neuhaus and others who argue for a greater accommodation, especially of Christianity, in American politics, the founders approved the First Amendment to the Constitution to protect the free exercise of religion rather than to prevent the establishment of religion.[10] In making this argument, Neuhaus states that governments should not be neutral about religion, but rather should side with those "who claim that religion has a 'privileged status' in the Constitution." This is, however, rather an outrageous claim.[11] When religion seeks access to government funding and power by claiming privilege, religion quickly crosses boundaries leading to some form of establishment.

Madison understood that religion could not be given constitutional privilege. This is why, in his view, the Constitution was properly a completely secular document, with no mention of a God or divinity in any form whatsoever. In his "Memorial and Remonstrance," Madison wrote,

> Whilst we assert for ourselves a freedom to embrace, to profess, and to observe the Religion which we believe to be of divine origin, we cannot deny an equal freedom to those whose minds have not yet yielded to the evidence which has convinced us. If this freedom be abused, it is an offence against God, not against man: To God, therefore, not to man, must an account of it be rendered.[12]

Madison wanted to keep institutional religious power from controlling government, so that politics could represent the art of compromise. However, throughout American history, politics has been known to take itself too seriously, forgetting compromise and, instead, assuming a kind of righteous certainty that is more often associated with religion. At times, especially in the twentieth century, politics in America has simultaneously shared the assumptions of a particular religion, those associated with popular and more conservative forms of Christianity. During these times, politics has looked a great deal like religion.

MYTHOLOGY

Americans have exercised a long-standing tendency to attach sacred meaning to their national history, both to the activities contained within it, and to the documents and monuments that emerge from it. Politics in America has always utilized strongly religious rhetoric in expressing its values and commitments. This rhetoric has conveyed the mythology associated with what it means to be an American. Beginning with the Declaration of Independence, Americans have emphasized rights and entitlements rooted in "laws of Nature and Nature's God." Not only are "all men created equal," but "they are endowed by their Creator with certain unalienable rights." To state things this way is not to make an argument supporting one side of at least two equally defensible positions, but rather to state the way things are, and ascribe to them a sacred significance that makes these conclusions necessary, unassailable, and beyond possible dispute.[13] Before anything else, this is a religious argument more than a political one. This historical document, defining the rationale for the development of a new nation, presents the gospel truth for all. The myth of liberty becomes the vein that runs through everything.

Even though this mythic origin story excluded Native Americans (whom Americans viewed as outside the social contract all together), women, blacks, and the poor, so compelling and complete was the message of the myth that each of these groups, and others later like gays, lesbians, and undocumented "illegal" immigrants, has utilized the message of this gospel to support both the full embodiment of their own civil rights and their struggle for liberation.

These civil rights movements succeeded in large measure because they tapped into the wide-ranging acceptance these themes already enjoyed among the American public. It's one thing to create this rhetoric; it's another thing to have faith in it.

When Martin Luther King Jr. marched nonviolently in Birmingham, with crowds of people singing Negro spirituals, a white grandmother and grandfather in Iowa, historically blinded by their own privilege, were able to sympathize more with them than those who wielded the fire hoses and controlled police dogs, because the actions of the blacks, rather than those of the white authorities, were appropriately expressing the American myth. The taproot of this anomaly can be traced to the fact that these common people living in America's heartland understood, even better than the founders did, that the political rhetoric designed to justify a revolution had, in fact, become real. Institutionalized systems of oppression and social control had actually become unjust precisely because the layers of meaning associated with the myth had transcended the rhetorical context of the myth's original expression. Due to the power of the myth, these groups worked to dismantle the master's house with the master's own tools. Yet, seemingly, the dismantling is never completely accomplished. In various contexts across the country, circles of power, whether represented in police uniforms (i.e., Ferguson, Missouri) or the offices of court clerks, and other civil servants (i.e., Kim Davis, in Rowan County, Kentucky), continue to assert and embody racism, homophobia, or gender bias in ways contrary to the myth they are sworn to uphold.

DOCTRINE

Among the doctrinal texts essential to the formation of our national character, the Declaration of Independence stands in stark contrast to the Constitution, which nowhere employs religious rhetoric. As the supreme order of law in a country that proclaims itself to be "a nation of laws," the Constitution is a thoroughly secular document.[14] While the Declaration of Independence is the motivating advertisement of the American dream, the Constitution is the owner's manual, marking how the society must be governed and how existing categories once taken for granted can be maintained and protected. Forms of resistance in American society are meant to be futile if they upset or overturn the social equilibrium established through constitutional means. This is why, despite the success of the women's liberation movement, the society has never passed an Equal Rights Amendment, and why, regardless of the realities of desegregation and the revocation of Jim Crow laws, America still understands the Voting Rights Act of 1965 as something that needs to be adjudicated in the U.S. Supreme Court.

In an ironic twist of American history, the Constitution, devoid of religious rhetoric or appeal, has assumed a sacred significance in its own right as the inerrant text to which all politicians, legislators, and judges must defer. A notable example occurred in January 2011 when newly elected Republican Tea Party members of Congress insisted on opening the new congressional term with a reading of the whole Constitution. The parallels of this event to Josiah's reading the newly rediscovered scroll of the Torah to the people of Jerusalem in 2 Kings 22 are telling.[15]

Jonathan Freedland, a British journalist, blamed the 2012 fatal Sandy Hook shooting spree in Newtown, Connecticut, on the sacrality attached to the U.S. Constitution. Other nations could easily revoke a law that provides easy accessibility to guns. In the United States, the Second Amendment is enshrined in a sacred text most Americans are loathe to change. As Freedland describes it, the right to bear arms has become a "rigid dogma" that has transformed a "document of liberation" into something that shackles Americans to "an outdated rule that makes easy the murder of schoolchildren."[16] Is the sacred nature of the Constitution related to the fact that mass shootings are an all-too-common occurrence in America? American dogmatism—strict recitations of doctrine, in this instance—overrides some measure of common sense when it comes to creating legitimate restrictions to the right of buying and bearing arms in America. With its depiction of a dystopian American society in the near future in which citizens annually participate in a 12-hour period in which all criminal activity—even murder—is legalized, one only need look at the surprising success of *The Purge* film series to bear witness to how deeply the right to bear arms and its related culture of violence pervades the American psyche.

Much as the Constitution is a secular document that has achieved a kind of sacred significance, American politics writ large is a secular endeavor that also assumes religious characteristics. Part of this sacred substance is due to the long-held American doctrine that the destiny of the nation stands for something beyond itself. Americans believe America is the kind of nation God intends all nations to be. Traditionally, the destiny of America has been described in two specific ways. One is best described as exemplary. American exceptionalism proposes that the country stands as a "light to the nations." In this case, the government consistently assures citizens that America is a clear representation of what God intends all places to be; America is the "city on a hill," a claim made at the heart of John Winthrop's classic 1630 sermon.[17] America, at its best, is the model for how to live authentically as a nation. Since the colonial era, politicians have evoked the enduring power of

Winthrop's vision of a "city on a hill" in order to define the nation as a beacon of freedom for the entire world.

The second way politicians have defined America's destiny is oriented more toward active mission. Many claim that America somehow bears a special responsibility to act on behalf of God in the world, to fulfill a doctrine of manifest destiny prescribed by God. This belief is based in a doctrinal claim that God has reserved a special place for America in the divine heart, and assigns America a special mission to perform in the world. America—proactively, independently, and some would say self-righteously—takes actions it understands to be in line with God's intention for the life of nations and humankind. American activities provide plenty of evidence for this orientation for well over one hundred years, particularly in the Spanish-American War, the Korean War, Vietnam War, and the wars in Iraq and Afghanistan, and even the contemporary and unconventional Global War on Terrorism. Whether viewed through the lens of role model or missionary, politicians and the American people have often understood both the history and destiny of the American republic in doctrinal terms as clearly standing "under God."[18]

Another key doctrine in American politics is found in the idea of the social contract. The social contract represents the cornerstone of political philosophy in Western civilization. The contract between individuals and the state is one predicated upon compromise. People within society have consented to surrender some of their natural freedoms to the state, in the belief that the state will provide necessary protections. Social-contract theory, with antecedents found throughout ancient times, biblical antiquity, and early developments in Western civilization, eventually influenced American government, particularly through the lenses provided by theorists like Jean-Jacques Rousseau and John Locke.

American politicians and later social activists have made the social contract popular and palpable for the public. They have done so by appealing to the ideas found within the Declaration of Independence. For Americans, the Declaration expresses the doctrinal commitment that government resides in the people and that government must recognize the equality of all people, as well as the belief that all people deserve both liberty and justice. These doctrines are theological because, as the Declaration insists, they reside in nature itself, placed there by "nature's God." For the most part, Americans, even those who have been judged by many to be outside the social contract, are swept up in the tide of religious fervor attached to this theological commitment. In 1972, for example, a U.S. Representative from Texas, Barbara Jordan, herself a descendant of enslaved Africans and sharecroppers, unashamedly and unapologetically affirmed, "My faith in the Constitution is whole, it is complete, it is total."[19]

Mark Hulliung has argued that the American revolutionary experiment truly established a "new order of the ages." Building specifically on John Locke's formulation of the social contract, Americans established a government that they believed nature itself mandated, a government bound to protect natural rights of its citizens (which did nothing for the natural rights of Native Americans to possess the land, since white Americans did not deem them citizens). While the notion of the social contract lost its power in Europe, replaced by utilitarianism and historicism, the idea maintained relevance in the new United States. Hulliung shows that when industrialization threatened the social contract in the late nineteenth century, and big business developed its own selfish theory of natural rights, land reformers and various progressive authors kept alive the ideas contained in the Declaration of Independence.[20] In this way, doctrine formed the basis for what Americans needed to live out through ethics, so that their profession could be carried out in practice.

ETHICS

While doctrine conveys the American creed, the ethics of American politics cultivates an ability to embody and empower beliefs, and to transform them into something concrete and cultural, in order to create an American way of life. American politics promotes an ethic of freedom and democracy and asserts these as universal norms for what it means to be fully human. Through this striving to be universal, America has consistently preserved its claim as the first world power, in spite of the challenges brought by both pluralism and globalization.

Well past the halfway point of the American Civil War, President Abraham Lincoln used his impressive oratorical prowess to recall the cadences of the Declaration of Independence to renew America's ethical commitment to the universal doctrines found in its social contract. "We here highly resolve," Lincoln promised the American people at Gettysburg, "that these dead shall not have died in vain, that this nation under God shall have a new birth of freedom, and that government of the people, by the people, for the people, shall not perish from the earth." Lincoln here expressed the soul of the social contract. Garry Wills explains the power of the Gettysburg Address by arguing that "a nation born of an idea finds that idea life-giving. And all attempts to re-enter that idea bring it and its adherents back to life. This is the 'new birth' always available to people begotten of a proposition in the first place. The 'new birth of freedom' in the last sentence of the Address takes us back to the miraculous birth of the opening sentence; and behind this image, too, there is the biblical concept of people 'born again' (John 3:3–7)."[21]

Roughly a month prior to his assassination, President Lincoln delivered his second inaugural address as the nation's bloodiest war neared its end, and in anticipation he sought to set the stage for the "new birth of freedom." At the very end of the address, Lincoln promoted an ethical social contract for the citizens of this "republic of suffering" by proclaiming, "With malice toward none, with charity for all, with firmness in the right, as God gives us to see the right, let us strive on to finish the work we are in, to bind up the nation's wounds, to care for him who shall have borne the battle and for his widow, and his orphan—to do all which may achieve and cherish a just and lasting peace among ourselves and with all nations." Resonating with the concerns of the people, Lincoln sought to reawaken Americans' belief that they had to strive to create liberty, equality, and justice for all.

When the social contract of the 1920s, represented in the Republican conservatism of Warren G. Harding, Calvin Coolidge, and Herbert Hoover, had failed, Franklin Delano Roosevelt and the Democrats sought a way to help Americans address fear itself by offering a more prophetic version of the social contract. As Roosevelt put it in his first inaugural address, "Throughout the nation men and women, forgotten in the political philosophy of the Government, look to us here for guidance and for more equitable opportunity to share in the distribution of national wealth. . . . I pledge myself to a new deal for the American people. This is more than a political campaign. It is a call to arms."[22] FDR's policies actually expanded an ethical understanding of the social contract to emphasize the responsibility of government to attend to the economic welfare of all those who lived within its domain.

At the onset of the 1960s, President John F. Kennedy's famous inaugural rhetoric emphasized how natural rights implied natural duties. He urged his fellow Americans, "Ask not what your country can do for you—ask what you can do for your country." Ethical duty rested clearly for Kennedy on the revolutionary-era "belief that the rights of man come not from the generosity of the state but from the hand of God. We dare not forget today that we are the heirs of that first revolution." As Americans, he vowed, we are ever "proud of our ancient heritage—and unwilling to witness or permit the slow undoing of those human rights to which this nation has always been committed."[23]

In his famous "I Have A Dream" speech, Dr. Martin Luther King Jr. also recalled the rhetoric of the Declaration of Independence to argue that the social contract had been left unfulfilled. King and all those within the sound of his voice during the March on Washington for Jobs and Freedom in August 1963 knew that the resounding promises of the Declaration of Independence were not equally experienced across the American landscape. King declared,

[We] have come to our nation's capital to cash a check. When the architects of our republic wrote the magnificent words of the Constitution and the Declaration of Independence, they were signing a promissory note to which every American was to fall heir, . . . a promise that all men, black men as well as white men, would be guaranteed the "unalienable rights" of "Life, Liberty, and the pursuit of Happiness." . . . Instead of honoring this sacred obligation, America has given the Negro people a bad check, a check which has come back marked "insufficient funds." But we refuse to believe that there are insufficient funds in the great vaults of opportunity of this nation. . . . Now is the time to make justice a reality for all God's children.[24]

King demanded that America bring its ethical practice into alignment with its doctrinal commitments.

In Ann Arbor, Michigan, on May 22, 1964, President Lyndon Baines Johnson announced his hopes for the creation of the Great Society. Riding the coattails of the faith in robust American liberalism expressed in FDR's New Deals for the poor, LBJ assumed America's prosperous economy made a Great Society possible, even in the anxious context marked by the Vietnam War overseas and rampant racism at home. Inspired by the deeply passionate critique of America in works like Michael Harrington's *The Other America* (1962), Johnson spoke of a new social contract that offered an expansion of the role of government to make good on promises to every American, regardless of race, gender, or class. Setting out to provide health care, affordable housing, a decent standard of living, early education, vocational training, housing, and urban development, while opening up immigration from Asia and Latin America, LBJ remained confident that the United States could live up to its beliefs.

Johnson urged Americans to join the battle to become the Great Society defined by the claims contained in the Declaration of Independence. "The Great Society," he declared, "rests on abundance and liberty for all. It demands an end to poverty and racial injustice, to which we are totally committed in our time."[25] However, as King observed just three years later, "the promises of the Great Society have been shot down on the battlefields of Vietnam, making the poor white and Negro bear the heaviest burden both at the front and at home."[26] LBJ's Great Society never got out of the starting gate.

President Barack Obama, on the occasion of his second inaugural address in 2013, reinvigorated this sacred rhetoric for a new generation with a power not often experienced in popular speech since the days of Martin Luther King:

What makes us exceptional—what makes us American—is our allegiance to an idea, articulated in a declaration made more than two centuries ago. Today we continue a never-ending journey, to bridge the meaning of those words with the realities of our time. For history tells us that while these truths may be self-evident, they have never been self-executing; that while freedom is a gift from God, it must be secured by His people here on Earth. . . . They gave to us a Republic, a government of, and by, and for the people, entrusting each generation to keep safe our founding creed.

Through a series of statements, alternating between repeated uses of "we've always understood," "we the people still believe," "we will defend," and "we must act," Obama highlighted both the doctrinal (the first two) and ethical (the last two) value of the social contract. Near the end of the speech, he summed up these themes again:

> We, the people, declare today that the most evident of truths—that all of us are created equal—is the star that guides us still; just as it guided our forebears through Seneca Falls, and Selma, and Stonewall; just as it guided all those men and women, sung and unsung, who left footprints along this great Mall, to hear a preacher say that we cannot walk alone; to hear a King proclaim that our individual freedom is inextricably bound to the freedom of every soul on Earth.

Obama's speech clearly connected the social contract to both the New Deal and the Great Society. But what makes Obama's 2013 inauguration speech most poignant is his inclusion of all those who had been so easily excluded by his predecessors in previous centuries and decades. The speech sounds the themes of women's rights, black civil rights, and LGBTQ rights by naming Seneca Falls, and Selma, and Stonewall. Each expanded the meaning of the social contract. Obama's confident belief in the power of the social contract seemed especially meaningful coming from a black man who was also leader of the free world. His understanding of the history, however, also enabled him to emphasize that the work of the social contract remains unfinished. Again, doctrinal belief in natural rights called forth an emphasis on ethical natural duties.

> It is now our generation's task to carry on what those pioneers began. For our journey is not complete until our wives, our mothers and daughters can earn a living equal to their efforts. Our journey is not complete until our gay brothers and sisters are treated like anyone else under the law for if we are truly created equal, then surely the love we commit to one another must be equal as well. Our journey is not complete until no citizen is forced to wait for hours to exercise the right to vote. Our journey is not complete until we find a better way to welcome the striving, hopeful immigrants who still see America as a land of opportunity. . . . That is our generation's task—to make these words, these rights, these values of life and liberty and the pursuit of happiness real for every American.[27]

For Americans, this American way of life is the ultimate life; this is far more than simple belief in "life, liberty and the pursuit of happiness." Without question, even though the idea of American exceptionalism appeared in much of the symbolism and rhetoric of the Revolutionary era, the Declaration frames the issue in such bold fashion as to make it an irrevocable facet of the American consciousness. Strict adherence to these moral principles, written during the eighteenth century, lives on as a nationalist ethos supporting American exceptionalism, civic duty, and the promises made to all adherents of the American Dream. Perhaps Will Herberg says it best: "The American Way of life . . . affirms the supreme value and dignity of the individual; . . . it defines an ethic of self-reliance, merit, and character, and judges by achievement: 'deeds, not creeds' are what count."[28]

National archivist John W. Carlin has argued that such moralism makes Americans exceptional to other nations and civilizations: "We are different because our government and our way of life are not based on the divine right of kings, the hereditary privileges of elites, or the enforcement of deference to dictators. They are based on pieces of paper, the Charters of Freedom—the Declaration that asserted our independence, the Constitution that created our government, and the Bill of Rights that established our liberties."[29]

This belief in American exceptionalism has been examined from a variety of perspectives. Ever since Robert Bellah's seminal essay, published in 1967, on "Civil Religion in America," Americans have struggled to understand how these doctrinal and ethical commitments have expressed themselves in a kind of national religion. This national religion has naturally co-opted many of the symbols of both Christianity and Judaism and provided them with new meaning. Civil religion is not a unilateral expression of religion. Sociological and theological study of it has revealed its complexity. Civil religion can be nationalistic, in which everything America represents is assumed to be representative of God's will. Nationalistic civil religion emerges particularly when American values are threatened, as they were with the September 11, 2001, terrorist attacks. In such cases, many confuse an attack on America with an attack on God.[30]

An inappropriate mixture of politics and organized religion always appears when politicians claim God's will is connected to any particular policy, whether liberal or conservative, but these days it seems much more of that practice is found among conservatives, most often those identified with the Tea Party movement. Sarah Palin's claim, made before young church leaders, that God's will required that a gas pipeline get built is only one such example. Actually, Palin offers many great examples, such as when she told Alaskans that her work as governor would be greatly impaired "if the people of Alaska's heart isn't right with God"[31] or her claim that it was "God's plan" for her to be chosen as John McCain's running mate.[32]

Some politicians believe the Bible should be used as the basis for every decision made by Congress—so long, that is, as Congress employs particular interpretations of the Bible and God's will (those that agree with the politicians in question). In August 2014, for example, just before a congressional recess, Rep. Steven Palazzo (R-Miss.) sent a Bible to every one of Congress's "535 members of Congress, calling on lawmakers to reflect on 'God's word' when deciding on 'policy decisions that impact America's future.' "[33] Former Congresswoman Michele Bachmann also has a tendency to be certain about God's will as applied to American politics, as when she declared that gay marriage is a "radical" experiment that, essentially, flies in the face of God.[34]

Another particular form of nationalistic civil religion also appears in politics when Christians and churches confuse political rhetoric intoning God with the divine being historically worshiped within Christian history. The former God is created from a very particular national and political history over the past two centuries, where God has been domesticated, and is basically predisposed to American values, desires, and purposes. The latter, historically at least, has been understood by Christianity as the Creator of all things, the One who equally loves and equally judges all peoples and nations. The two divinities are not the same.

As Sidney Mead once put it, all that mostly remains of the highly utilized and national political and rhetorical version of God is a disembodied sentimental smile reminiscent of Alice's Cheshire cat.[35] This confusion of the two very different expressions of "God" leads to misplaced efforts to equate Christianity and what it means to be American. Such unfortunately mistaken equations lead to misguided attempts to frame copies of Ten Commandments on courthouse walls, or ensconce them on marble monuments on state capital lawns, or perhaps to require all public school students to read the Bible and to pray in their classrooms.

But civil religion can also appear in more prophetic forms. Both Robert Bellah and Sidney Mead emphasized the founders' attitude of reverence for a transcendent reference, something or someone that judges all nations equally. Neither tried to make historic connections between the transcendent deity the founders emphasized and the God worshiped within Christianity. But both called for a prophetic civil politics, made possible when Americans resisted making an idol of national policies and recognized the existence of something beyond themselves. In such cases, civil religion calls Americans to represent global, rather than merely national, values. Advocates of prophetic civil religion in America always point to Abraham Lincoln as its supreme example. In that crucial second inaugural address, near the end of the Civil War, Lincoln warned Americans, both North and South, who each liked to think that God

had taken their side in the conflict, "The Almighty has his own purposes."
More to the point, Lincoln asserted,

> Fondly do we hope, fervently do we pray, that this mighty scourge
> of war may speedily pass away. Yet, if God wills that it continue until
> all the wealth piled by the bondsman's two hundred and fifty years
> of unrequited toil shall be sunk, and until every drop of blood drawn
> with the lash shall be paid by another drawn with the sword, as was
> said three thousand years ago, so still it must be said "the judgments
> of the Lord are true and righteous altogether."[36]

The fact that Lincoln is always the exemplary figure used to represent prophetic civil religion illustrates how rare is its actual expression in American
politics.

RITUAL

Rituals sustain the doctrines and ethics of American politics and call both
our beliefs and our practices to mind. Inauguration festivities, especially
surrounding the U.S. presidency, complete with the prominent role played
by the Bible, inaugural prayers, and the ritualistic ending to presidential
addresses with the solemn benediction "God bless America," enable Americans to express their religious hopes for the future. For example, Obama's
theme in 2013 for his inaugural ceremonies was "Faith in America's Future."

Sometimes inaugurations signal a future quite different from the past, as
was the case when Rep. Keith Ellison from Minnesota, the first Muslim member elected to Congress, insisted on using a copy of the Qur'an instead of the
Bible to be sworn into office. When challenged that his actions were fueling a
slide toward moral relativism in America, Ellison responded sensitively to the
symbolism at stake by choosing to use Thomas Jefferson's personal copy of
the Qur'an. His election and inauguration signaled a future where the American Way of Life, and the rituals that support it, must learn to accommodate in
tangible ways the meaning of both religious pluralism and cultural difference.

National holidays like Independence Day, Memorial Day, Martin Luther
King Day, and Thanksgiving remind Americans of the importance of both
the beliefs valued by America and the sacrifices necessary to keep them vital.
The daily recitation of the pledge of allegiance by school children across the
country ritualistically introduces and initiates a student into what it means
to be a citizen who lives in a nation "under God, indivisible, with liberty and
justice for all." When the national anthem marks the beginning of sporting
events across America, or "God Bless America" is sung during the seventh-
inning stretch, Americans ritualistically embody and express their hopes for

the country and its politics. But such rituals are not connected with Christianity. Rather, they are connected with some form of civil religion, quite distinct from traditional expressions of faith.

Confusion between civil religion and traditional faith is evident in arguments related to the legal battle about the pledge of allegiance, finally ending in 2010. Several court cases have been launched since 2000 protesting the words "under God" in the pledge of allegiance. The cases are instructive when it comes to understanding the ritual meaning of politics. Most of these cases have involved Michael Newdow, an emergency-room physician with a law degree, who acted as his own lawyer. In the first case, he argued that his daughter's First-Amendment rights were harmed because she was forced to "watch and listen as her state-employed teacher in her state-run school leads her classmates in a ritual proclaiming that there is a God and that ours is 'one nation under God.' "[37] Since this flap started, the girl's mother, Sandra Banning, has said she shares the public outrage about what Newdow has done. "She was up there proud as can be, reciting the pledge. . . . The child was not raised an atheist."[38]

On June 26, 2002, the U.S. Ninth Circuit Court of Appeals in San Francisco ruled that Congress violated the First Amendment when it passed a law in 1954 that added the words "under God" to the pledge of allegiance. Two of three justices (Goodwin who was seventy-nine and appointed by Nixon, and Reinhardt who was seventy-one and appointed by Carter) ruled that the words "under God" in the pledge of allegiance constituted a violation of the establishment clause of the constitution.

Response came quickly among the politicians. President Bush's immediate response was that the ruling was "ridiculous." Senator Tom Daschle (D., S.D.) called it "just nuts." Senators and representatives quickly passed resolutions condemning the ruling (99–0, and 416–3). Dozens of House members of both parties gathered on the steps of the Capitol to recite the pledge and to sing "God Bless America." Politicians knew how America would react, and they wanted quickly to be on the "right side." Americans, in a *Newsweek* poll, showed 87 percent support for the pledge containing "under God," compared to 9 percent opposing it. Of course, by a 54–36 percent margin, these Americans also said there was no reason for the government to avoid promoting religion.[39]

In his dissenting opinion, Justice Fernandez (sixty-three and appointed by the elder Bush) relied on the Seventh Circuit Court's previous consideration of the phrase "under God." That court determined that the phrase, in the context of the pledge, "is devoid of any significant religious content, and therefore constitutional." Another term historically used by the courts to describe this lack of serious religious content is "ceremonial deism." Phrases like "under God" and "in God we trust" serve a ceremonial purpose, rather than carry any deep or significant religious meaning. Fernandez, for his part, believed the words do convey "a vestige of the awe we all must feel at the immenseness of the universe and our own small place within it, as well as the wonder we must feel at the good fortune of our country."[40]

On March 24, 2004, the Supreme Court heard the case on appeal and decided that Newdow did not have standing to bring the case, since he was not the custodial parent of his daughter. In this way, the Supreme Court avoided making a ruling on the phrase itself. Newdow filed suit the next year on behalf of three unnamed families. The initial decision in the Eastern District Court of California favored Newdow, using the previous Ninth Circuit decision as a precedent. The case reached the Ninth Circuit on December 4, 2007, but the decision in the case was not published until March 11, 2010. This time, the Ninth Circuit ruled the pledge constitutional by a 2–1 margin. The two justices who argued that the pledge is constitutional had joined the Ninth Circuit Court after the original 2002 case. The only remaining judge of the three original judges, Justice Stephen Reinhardt, wrote the dissenting opinion.

The majority opinion of 2010 argued that the words "under God" are "(1) to underscore the political philosophy of the Founding Fathers that God granted certain inalienable rights to the people which the government cannot take away; and (2) to add the note of importance which a pledge to our nation ought to have and which ceremonial references to God invoke." The majority also emphasized that the Supreme Court has, historically, drawn distinctions "between patriotic [and ceremonial] mentions of God on the one hand, and prayer, an 'unquestioned religious exercise,' on the other."[41]

So, where the majority justices refer to this phrase as a "political philosophy" or a "patriotic mention," the dissenting Justice Reinhardt, writing the minority opinion, stressed the religious nature of the phrase. He argued, quoting from the 1954 congressional record, that the amended pledge, with the addition of "under God," was intended by Congress, to teach "the schoolchildren of America" to "reassert their belief . . . in the all-present, all-knowing, all-seeing, all-powerful Creator."[42]

When the Supreme Court heard the original pledge case in 2004, eventually declaring that Newdow did not have standing to bring the case, a significant number of religious leaders submitted a "friend of the court" brief that offered the following argument. If the language of "under God" is taken seriously, it should be removed from the pledge in a nation as pluralistic and diverse as America. If the language of "under God" is viewed as primarily ceremonial in nature, then having children speak it in public schools is, from a Christian point of view, to force children to take God's name in vain on a daily basis.[43]

Thus, there is an interesting irony in the pledge-of-allegiance controversy. Inside the Court, lawyers who take the words seriously as important religious words argue they should be taken out of the pledge. Those who view them as merely ceremonial argue they should remain. Thus the words remain because they are merely ceremonial. The pledge of allegiance is a ritual in American politics. The Court's rulings have termed it "political philosophy," a "patriotic" or "ceremonial" mention of God, rather than a religious one, even though the word "God" makes the pledge appear at least nominally religious. In short, to recite the pledge is not to describe the United States as a nation living under the domain or judgment of a divine being (as in Christian or Jewish or Muslim beliefs); instead, the pledge represents a ritual reinforcing for those who recite it of a sworn allegiance to the values for which the flag stands. On the nation's best days, those values are the ones historically identified as unity, indivisibility, liberty, and justice. On occasion, however, other values, those associated with power, colonialism, self-righteousness, and consumerism, have been connected to the flag as well.

Appropriate rituals relating to the American Way of Life have been grafted onto the life cycle of Americans, following them throughout their lives. Whether these rituals involve getting a Social Security number at the same time one's parents received their child's birth certificate, pledging allegiance to the American flag, filling out voter registration cards and casting ballots, celebrating national holidays, paying income taxes, attending ball games or political conventions, singing the national anthem, or receiving one's first Social Security check, they enable our society to create social investment in the political process. If citizens have no investment in the future prospects of society, they can easily become indifferent toward it. An important integration occurs as one is ritualistically initiated into American society. At least occasionally, these rituals seem to carry a rather clearly defined religiosity connected to American politics.

EXPERIENCE

Political rituals enable individuals to experience politics, to gain a firsthand understanding of beliefs and practices that can help cultivate both adherence and patriotism. Each generation can reference some cultural or political event that for them becomes a central marker by which they experience in their bones what it means to be an American. For older Americans today, the salient moment might be the assassinations of John F. Kennedy, Martin Luther King, and Robert F. Kennedy during the 1960s or the official end of the Vietnam War in 1975. Younger Americans might mark the explosion of the Challenger on January 28, 1986, or the Columbia on February 1, 2003. For members of the millennial generation, those who had at least reached school age by 2001, the tragic events of September 11 created a community of experience out of disconnected individuals as if they were one.

As a therapist has put it, "The experience, the visceral, psychic mind-heart continuum experience, was a collective experience. . . . That level of communal experience outweighed the personal story. . . . It didn't matter who you were talking to—relief worker, direct victim, other therapist—you were all the same body."[44]

In the midst of terrorism perpetrated on American soil, spiritual and personal transcendence emerged through an awakened and experiential sense of personal and corporate patriotism. David L. Atheide has commented:

> The collective response to the terror attacks was framed as a communal patriotic experience that provided opportunities to "come together" and be "united" in a "coalition of war and humanitarianism." Numerous messages also appealed through nostalgia to a U.S. past of moral and military dominance, authentic life styles, and traditional values (e.g., family, respect), as well as institutions of social control (e.g., police, fire departments, and military). National symbols were renewed through the mournful language of victims and vengeful promises of future action by the military on our behalf. Leaders, with the aid of the mass media, repeatedly bolstered the assertion that the moment of attack and tragedy was an opportunity for Americans to renew their commitments to freedom and the American way of life.[45]

Written in 1984 and originally sung at Reagan's political convention, Lee Greenwood's song "I'm Proud to Be an American" returned to prominence following September 11, because it captured well the way many Americans experience their faith in American politics. "And I'm proud to be an American where at least I know I'm free. . . . 'Cause there ain't no doubt I love this land, God bless the U.S.A."[46]

In America's recent history, large numbers of Americans have taken their level of experience to that of the ultimate sacrifice. Since early 1973, America has relied entirely on a volunteer armed force. In spite of restrictions naturally imposed by a dependence upon volunteers, America has had little difficulty in fielding a global military presence. This remains true even though the level of recruitment has not always met the military's expectations. Recruiters often have come up short of recruitment goals despite persistent efforts to reach out to high schools, college campuses, and local Walmarts, informing young women and men what the military could do for them. September 11, 2001, changed all of that. Recruiters in every line of service watched in amazement as people, many of whom would never have thought before of enlisting, lined

up to defend America and the nation's honor. Army sergeant Cheri Depen-
brock concluded, "It was all about patriotism. . . . I think half those kids would
have joined if we hadn't paid them."[47] Such is the power of a singularly significant experience of American patriotism.

While events can evoke a sense of patriotism that, especially in the face
of terror, is rather homogenous, the reality is that what is experienced as
patriotism for some creates dissonance in the experience of others. Patriotism sometimes defines a narrow path, where status quo politics upholds
a normative experience of what it means to be American. In these cases,
counterexperience becomes a significant aspect of political activity and
appears in the form of political protests. Sometimes these are born of experiences of one's uniqueness, usually embodied in one way or another when
compared to the "standards," and emerge through racial politics, gender
politics, and sexual politics, to name a few. These persons are no less patriotic than those who hew the line of traditional American politics. The
grassroots organizing found in civil rights protests, freedom rides, pro-
choice and pro-life rallies, the women's liberation movement, gay-pride
marches, and the Occupy Wall Street demonstrations are all representative
of a brand of patriotic protest.

These outliers hearken back to America's founding principles, and understand America to be a land that supports protests against all tyrannies, no
matter when or how they arise. They organize themselves for a more perfect
union, grafting their cause onto the Declaration itself. As historian Simon
Hall has noted,

> As well as being deployed in the service of a range of very different,
> at times even opposing, causes . . . patriotic protests have also been
> construed in a number of different ways. While the Black Panthers
> emphasized the Declaration of Independence's justification of the
> right to overthrow despotic government, anti-busing and tax pro-
> testers preferred instead to highlight the Founders's fears of a strong
> centralized government; and whereas gay rights activists' focus on
> the right to the "pursuit of happiness," those opposed to abortion
> stressed the Declaration of Independence's guarantee of the "right to
> life." Generally, progressives have sought to narrow the gap between
> America's lofty promise of liberty and justice for all and the actual
> experience of oppressed and marginalized groups. Conservatives, in
> contrast, have tended to emphasize the nation's traditional values
> (rooted in Judeo-Christian morality), recall the early history of small
> town America and celebrate the Republic's historic achievements.[48]

In America, alternative experiences of patriotism leading to protests have
accomplished significant political change.

INSTITUTIONS

Institutions lend to myth, doctrine, ethics, rituals, and experience an illusion of truth and immortality that individuals and communities alone can neither foster nor sustain. Political institutions, especially those associated with the three-pronged nature of checks and balances found in American politics, are intended to create laws and produce policy (legislative), evaluate law and protect rights (judiciary), and enforce laws (executive). Yet institutions also represent the variety of political ideas within America. Political parties, lobbyists, and unions function as political institutions of considerable influence in the country.

Even the public school system is a political institution, at least in the way it socializes the nation's children to the ethos of American culture, especially the venerable tradition associated with its history, and such concepts as the right to vote, civic duty, the role of government, and social responsibility. Historically, public schools have exposed children to some level of familiarity with America's mission in the world and the multitude of symbols that convey its special meaning. Public schools convey the importance of patriotism, the history of American accomplishment, and the details of myths associated with them. They engage children in rituals and practices that help them understand their relationship to the country. Children in most states first learn to sing patriotic hymns in public-school music classes. In addition, public schools teach children the meaning of the holidays associated with American culture and inculcate within them the early habit of observing them.[49] As Sidney Mead put it, when Americans separated church and state, public schools developed and assumed the role traditionally filled by churches, the role of educating citizens, "to make possible and to guarantee the dissemination and inculcation among the embryo citizens of the beliefs essential to the existence and well-being of the democratic society."[50] Indeed, public schools can serve as vehicles through which politics moves, operates, and connects to the people it affects.

Political parties, of course, also connect directly to the people. As much as people imagine that political parties have been the be-all and end-all of American society, they are actually a fabrication coming after the fact. In the *Federalist Papers*, James Madison argued passionately against forming partisan organizations in the burgeoning American republic. He believed political parties would lead to constant bickering among elite leaders of the nation and would ultimately result in both an inefficient and ineffective mode of government. Simply put, while political parties are entities within the government, they should never represent the entirety of governance itself.

As one of the framers of the Constitution, Madison stated that partisanship invariably has its own "noxious" qualities and often leads to divisive risks, including "dangerous schisms" and "violence, especially in the ascendant party." So long as Americans adhered to a strict interpretation of the Constitution, Madison argued, they could keep the nation together in the face of various self-interests. Interestingly, he remained thoroughly unconvinced by Richard Henry Lee's contention that the existence of the press itself could serve as a "remedial power . . . over the spirit of party." Even if political parties might be an inevitable and necessary evil of government, Madison did not place much confidence in the press to curb the thirst for power found in politics.[51]

More than likely the current state of affairs in politics in America is actually, in some ways, the fulfillment of James Madison's worst nightmare. The arbitrariness of contemporary political parties and their leaders, and their great fondness for a deadlocked political system between them, has shown all too well just how "noxious" political parties can become. When a political party creates an institutional altar demanding worship at all costs, the results can be devastating for the country. Party politics overcomes national interest and the common good in every instance.

The Democrats and the Republicans, with their primaries, caucuses, conventions, and blue state vs. red state demographic rivalries, are political institutions designed to initiate, guide, and educate citizens-turned-constituents to assume a particular perspective on the nation. They provide a specialized political space in the public square. For those political junkies who pay attention to such matters, the media frenzy, public debates, and campaign fever during election season help people to match faces with names of the various players. Through the politicians basking in these spotlights, people see grand-sized images of themselves.

As Richard Hofstadter has noted, "As popular democracy grew strength and confidence, it reinforced the widespread belief in inborn, intuitive, folkish wisdom over the cultivated, oversophisticated and self-interested knowledge of the literati and well to do."[52] In many cases, this means politicians are elected more by how they popularly connect with constituencies as charismatic leaders than because of the extent of their knowledge or experience. Candidates might also connect with constituencies based on celebrity earned elsewhere, or by appealing to existing discontent with current party leadership, or both, as seems to have been the case for Donald Trump, a real estate developer and reality television star, during the 2015–2016 presidential nomination and election cycle.

In essence, political parties and their associated institutions, like denominations and churches, also narrow the focus of those things with which people can identify, thereby creating a false sense of security and understanding. Because of the insularity of party politics in our society, citizens who are deeply evangelical don't need to question how one can be pro-life in abortion and hawkish about capital punishment or matters of war at the same time. If scientists can program computers with artificial intelligence and implant the minds of mice, as Marty Kaplan recently put it, with false memories, so too can institutions introduce, invest, and inspire constituencies to believe in false truths and empty promises, calling for blind faith in political platforms or party ideals.

Marty Kaplan, referring to the work of Robert Bellah and others on the emergence of radical individualism, pointed out that President Ronald Reagan masked the dramatic rise of consumer capitalism by constant reference to the rhetoric of traditional values. "The genius of Reagan's rhetoric," writes Kaplan, "was to assert that we can have it both ways—that the private quest for money and power is compatible with the yearning for public connectedness. Reaganism encouraged Americans to believe that there is no trade-off between unleashing the cowboy and empowering the community."[53] The power of the Reagan public-relations juggernaut convinced millions of Americans that, despite the record of massive historical experience to the contrary, no tension properly exists between these two goals. Americans found the rhetoric compelling.

Charismatic political leaders can convince those they lead to surrender to blind faith in politics. In such cases, Americans who follow a leader or party faithfully may end up accepting propositions they otherwise might have questioned. They become convinced, for example, that there are weapons of mass destruction where there are none. As Donald H. Rumsfeld, secretary of defense during George W. Bush's first presidential term, told one American reporter inquiring whether he still believed in the existence of WMDs in post-invasion Iraq, "The absence of evidence is not evidence of absence."[54] Occasionally, the double-speak of politicians is more obvious than it is at other times.

Today, the two major political parties are more interested in self-preservation and maintaining the vitality of their brand than they are about purposefully imagining new ways of governing, addressing serious cultural issues, and involving more citizens in the body politic. For example, liberal moderate Republicans, in say the ilk of Mark Hatfield, Nelson Rockefeller, Olympia Snowe, and Lincoln Chafee, have all but disappeared. Meanwhile, the Blue Dog (read conservative) Democrats, prevalent during Bill Clinton's presidency, are finding it difficult to gain any foothold in their own party. Some argue, given the calcified stances of both Republican and Democratic parties, that it is high time to shake up the two-party system.

There is certainly plenty of room for a few third parties to sound themes silenced in the face of a cacophony defining the mainstream of both parties. As Sean Wilentz points out, "no third party has knocked off one of the reigning two, and none has taken power." Third parties succeed to the extent that they "take a cry from the margins of American life—an issue, or an interest, or a prejudice—and force it onto the agenda of the political elite." Once they are successful in reaching the elite, they usually then disappear into irrelevance. Given the context of today's political culture, however, perhaps only a robust multiparty system could accurately represent the interests of the full range of diversity within American politics.

Insurgent movements in American politics during the early twenty-first century seem to be fueled by anxiety and a spirit of frustration or failure transformed into self-righteous discontent. On the right, candidates find support from high-powered political PACs, well-heeled organizations, and influential figures like Karl Rove's American Crossroads, Ralph Reed's Faith and Freedom Coalition, FreedomWorks, and conservative benefactors like the Koch brothers (David and Max) and Sheldon Adelson. This fact enables a candidate like Donald Trump, who largely funded his own primary campaign, to claim he was his own man. However, as primaries turn to national elections where a party's candidate seeks the presidency, even candidates like Trump generally must become connected to the troughs connected to political fundraising.

On the left, the democratic socialist Bernie Sanders ironically like Trump also bragged that he avoided PACs, to the consternation of both Hillary Clinton and the vast majority of the Democratic Party establishment. But whether one talks about the PACs, the wealthy Trump, or the financing of Sanders by a mass collection of the small donations of the middle and lower classes, money still seems to control the electoral process in America. Now with the *Citizens United v. Federal Election Commission* decision, big-money professionals are buying access and using their skill in high-level influence peddling to purchase politicians and U.S. elections even more blatantly.

On both political extremes, the process is the problem. For the broad base of financial and political supporters of the Tea Party, backing a well-articulated and systematic endgame related to their grievances has led to disenchantment, as successful candidates make inevitable political compromises for the sake of governing. For example, Rick Scott rode into the governor's office in Florida on Tea Party grievances, but once he arrived, given the sizable deficit of the budget, he found that he needed to accept funding associated with Obamacare in order to have the money to govern.

Where the Tea Party is considerably homogeneous and centralized, the Occupy Wall Street movement is dramatically heterogeneous and decentralized. The movement has prided itself on not having a single voice or easily listed set of grievances, and now finds itself in suspended animation. It speaks powerfully to some core American principles but has been unwilling to organize or create leadership because, ironically, such efforts would result in structures similar to those they critique. In an interesting way, both the Tea Party and the Occupy Wall Street Movement emerged during a shared historical moment, from opposite poles of the political system, find themselves unable to accomplish goals, because implementing successful means to reach them tends to violate their own commitments.

Contemporary American politics seems to breed cynicism. People are sent off to change Washington, but ultimately Washington changes them. The ideal of trusting a political figure to accomplish the people's business has long been tainted by two necessities. On the one hand, all successful politicians need to stay on the proverbial hamster wheel of political fundraising if they hope to stay in politics. On the other hand, if they hope to achieve anything approaching effectiveness in governing, they have to be able to compromise, to make sacrifices on ideals they were sent into office to uphold. In both respects, the more closely one is identified with either left or right, the harder it is to operate with any degree of success. The machinery of politics nearly always frustrates the truly committed voter, whether left or right. The power of political institutions in American life often means that politicians, not unlike ministers or missionaries, find that the faith they begin with is not always the faith they find themselves practicing.

Certainly the tolerance of the American public for violations of the public trust has increased in recent decades. Yet Americans are still capable of being scandalized by the actions of their politicians. The last few decades have possessed no shortage of such scandals, including Watergate, Abscam, the Iran-Contra affair, the Keating Five, and sexual shenanigans (such as the Clinton-Lewinsky sex scandal and actions of other politicians). One need only look at the damage suffered by the presidency during both Watergate and the Clinton impeachment hearings to conclude that institutions nearly always suffer due to the sins of those intimately connected to them. As the Benghazi debacle clearly demonstrates, one does not even necessarily have to be guilty of anything for a supposed scandal to gain traction in ways that affects a politician's reputation or gums up Congress in such a way that it is distracted from tending appropriately to the peoples' business.

Whistle-blowing is easier today than during the era of Daniel Ellsberg and his publication of the Pentagon Papers in 1971. But all whistle-blowers must still take a leap of faith, usually involving personal risk, that something matters and that there is somebody out there who cares. They believe doing the right thing is its own reward. Even contemporary self-styled whistle-blowers like Julian Assange, Chelsea Elizabeth Manning (born Bradley Edward Manning), and Edward Snowden are taking grave risks in following their beliefs that something wrong needs to be righted. Like the transgressions of individuals, the sins of institutions are likely to emerge one day or another. Yet today, given the realities defined by both the USA Patriot Act and the USA Freedom Act, certain political institutions like the National Security Agency, vested as they are in concentrated and often hidden special interests, have become so powerful in American politics that they now threaten to undo the ability of Americans to govern themselves effectively.

In American culture, an oversaturated media landscape, now including social media, has made fairness and objectivity a much harder commodity to find. Some of us are old enough to remember the days when the public insisted on "objective" news accounts, meaning a fair representation of all sides of an issue and an attempt to understand the stakes. The days of widely trusted and politically unaligned journalistic voices like those of Edward R. Murrow, Walter Cronkite, Chet Huntley, and David Brinkley are over. There is serious question whether or not today's media is actually equipped to pull off a Bob Woodward and Carl Bernstein style of investigation. Ultimate value is placed in personal opinions, which fly nonstop. Today's pundits find themselves becoming the news rather than simply reporting it.

People define their politics more by the offerings of Glenn Beck, Rush Limbaugh, Stephen Colbert, John Oliver, Bill O'Reilly, Trevor Noah, Rachel Maddow, Ann Coulter, Jon Stewart, or Bill Maher than by understanding what is actually happening in the political arena. The clearly aligned views on the news offered by Fox News and MSNBC mirror the kinds of religious propaganda found at the heart of media televangelism. Each of these networks has faithful followers devoted to the sermonizing of news pundits on a nightly basis. To this often-ideological media mix, add the convoluted and highly eclectic institutional universe created by social media, and one discovers a ready-made outlet for daily devotionals and active sharing of personal testimonies.

Other institutions deserving brief mention here are nongovernmental organizations or NGOs. Even though the formalization of NGOs is a relatively recent development, these grassroots movements enjoy a significant history. In the late nineteenth and early twentieth centuries, the nation witnessed the rise of the Populist and Progressive movements. These forces helped to reestablish for many Americans the conjoint principles of popular democracy and popular sovereignty. The notion that everyone should have access to the levers of power within government led to the rise of organizations like the National Association for the Advancement of Colored People, the National American Women's Suffrage Association, the American Socialist Party, the International Workers of the World (the Wobblies), the Populist Party, and the Progressive Party. The idea that people should have a say in the most urgent and pressing issues of the day, so they might govern their own lives in the ways they deem best, gave rise to groups like the Women's Christian Temperance Movement, the American Civil Liberties Union, the National Urban League, the Sierra Club, the Hull House Movement, and the social gospelers, to name a few.

While NGOs are independent of both government and politics, they are social institutions wielding political interests, usually in ways different from institutions associated with party politics. They work to provide equitable and sustainable development where the government has failed. In many ways, and for many people, NGOs represent voices not always heard or respected in traditional political organizations. They represent the political interests of these voices far better than more recognized political institutions. By operating through charitable service, community organizing, advocacy, and empowerment, these organizations do not necessarily wave the American flag, but do exercise some influence in determining how it waves. Contemporary examples might include the efforts of organizations concentrating on the environment, human rights, disaster relief, and economic development.[55]

The power of politics often draws in institutions that are supposedly by nature nonpolitical. When the Progressive National Baptist Convention becomes closely identified with the Democratic Party or when the Republican Party seems mostly affiliated with the religious right, the church as institution is drawn into the political fray in a way that contradicts its standing as a nonpolitical organization. Churches and the Christians who weekly occupy them, in spite of the clear separation of church and state in America, often willingly worship at the altar of politics.

MATERIALITY

American political life possesses many material items that generate a notion of reverence often attached to America's self-understanding as a nation. Most of these items are not Christian in their religiosity, but carry a strong sense of sacred meaning nonetheless. Americans revere the eternal flame at John F. Kennedy's grave, the Washington Monument, the Lincoln and Jefferson Memorials, the shrine of our major documents at the National Archives, and the Vietnam War Memorial. All of these sites in the nation's capital generate reverence, and perhaps even a sense of awe among those who visit them.[56]

Political power is also able to baptize the material associated with Judaism and Christianity with alternative meanings, such as placing "In God We Trust" on all American money. Another material example, of course, is the use of the Bible in courtrooms and political inaugurations. The use of the Bible on these occasions has nothing to do with its content portraying a biblical God who is concerned with the redemption of human beings, or its message describing the faithfulness of either Jews or Christians. Rather, the Bible in these contexts is used as an object to ensure truthfulness and convey solemnity; the Bible helps to communicate the fact that this truth-swearing ritual matters, but its meaning in these cases has nothing to do with either the Jewish religion or with Christianity.

The iconic approach to the Bible always subordinates biblical values to whatever American political thought might need at the moment. It takes phrases from the Bible that Christianity has applied to the church and applies them to the American nation, phrases like "a city upon a hill," "the new Israel," "a light to the nations," the "servant of the Lord," and "the chosen people." A particularly disturbing example of applying new meaning to the phrases of the Bible occurred on September 11, 2002. Speaking on the first anniversary of 9/11, President Bush closed his address to the nation from Ellis Island with the following words:

> Tomorrow is September the 12th. A milestone is passed, and a mission goes on. Be confident. Our country is strong. And our cause is even larger than our country. Ours is the cause of human dignity; freedom guided by conscience and guarded by peace. This ideal of America is the hope of all mankind. That hope drew millions to this harbor. That hope still lights our way. And the light shines in the darkness. And the darkness will not overcome it. May God bless America.

The last two sentences, prior to the traditional benediction, are a direct quote, without any quotation marks or note or reference from John 1:5: "And the light shines in the darkness. And the darkness will not overcome it." That passage in the Bible describes the Word of God, in whom "was life, and the life was the light of all people" (John 1:4)." But here Bush lifts the words of John 1:5 out of context and uses them to refer to "the ideal of America" as "the hope of all mankind," and its role in the world. These biblical words have been filled with new, and very different, content. When politicians quote the Bible in the public arena, most are not primarily interested in espousing Christian themes. Rather, passages from the Bible serve as convenient proof texts for expressing what one already believes to be true. The Bible is transformed into a supporting text for a political agenda.[57]

Perhaps the most important symbol carrying the nation's meaning in its material fabric is the American flag. The flag carries the history of the national struggles on behalf of "liberty and justice for all." It symbolizes the meaning of the nation itself and binds people together in the American experiment.

The United States flag code stipulates all manner of conduct in relation to the flag. The code governs all matters related to the display and handling of the flag, and protects the reverence associated with it. The flag must never be dipped or crumpled. Flags cannot be displayed upside down except as a signal of dire distress, used as apparel or drapery, or used in any form for advertising. The flag must never be stepped on or allowed to have any part of it touch the ground. Even the question of how to wear a flag lapel pin is addressed in the ode (it must be worn close to the heart). The code requires the motion of the right hand being placed over the heart. In short, the code ensures the American flag is the most revered material object in political culture.

Of all the altars examined here, politics is the one most likely to rival the traditional faiths in terms of ultimate allegiances. Perhaps this is due to the fact that politics tugs on so many of the same strings as the traditional faiths, hopes for a better world, calls for justice, freedom, and community. Especially in America, politics expresses a publicly religious rhetoric, as in the American motto, changed in 1954 from "E Pluribus Unum" to "In God We Trust"; in phrases like "under God" or "God bless America"; and in borrowing otherwise religious symbols like the Bible in order to redefine their meanings or to use them for political purposes. Christians, particularly, seem prone to connect Christianity to the civil religion that is so pervasive in the United States. In such cases, their Christianity is often conflated with or confused by the meanings connected to civil religion.

On the same day the Eighth Circuit Court released its 2010 decision about the pledge of allegiance, it also rejected Michael Newdow's other case attempting to remove "In God We Trust" from money and from its standing as the national motto. The same two justices representing the majority argued that the national motto is merely of a "patriotic or ceremonial character" and "has no theological or ritualistic impact." The Supreme Court refused to hear the appeal. Though the courts have tried to make a distinction between the ceremonial deism, expressed in political phrases like "under God" and "in God we trust," and religion, the rest of the country is not so adept at distinguishing such subtleties.

5

Sports

Religion and sports seem, at first glance, to be seriously at odds with one another. In sports, in contradiction to the words of Jesus, "the last won't be first; the last will be cut."[1] The moral ethos of most organized religions emphasizes restraint in satisfying one's own appetites, in order to meet the needs of others. Above all, religion is about a willingness to surrender oneself to something transcendent to the self, or something that provides greater meaning for life. Sports, on the other hand, is all about winning, achieving victory over against the other. While lip service is often given to emphasize how sports teach and exemplify teamwork to young people, it is usually more about competition with a "killer instinct" that reaches the ability to crush an opponent.

If there is any sacrificing going on, it might involve sacrificing time with family, or occasionally sacrificing one's health in order to win. In sports, the competitor plays through pain to help the team gain victory and sacrifices the body to achieve personal glory. If Muhammad Ali was arguably the greatest athlete in the twentieth century, his life story can certainly be used to represent the claim that the true sportsman lives and even dies by his commitment to the sport. Professional sports, in whatever league, is about ambition and achievement, whatever the sacrifice. Rather than restraining the self, sports put the self on a grand stage, one usually connected with glory and fame. All professional athletes are concerned with accolades, with garnering an appearance on the highlight reels on ESPN's SportsCenter or a spot on the Wheaties box. These days, sports is also about the money and the marketing, the collection of material resources, for the athlete and the franchise. Perhaps these characteristics explain why active athletes and professional sports at large have had difficulty finding ways to safeguard athletes from life-threatening or fatal injuries. However, Ali's life also demonstrated that sports leaders, if they choose, can utilize their popularity and fame in positive ways to play major roles in demanding that society change for the better.

Perhaps there is no better example of the incongruity between religion and sports than what happened on the football field in 1990 as the University of Colorado Buffaloes found themselves pursuing a national college football championship. Bill McCartney, who had founded the Christian movement Promise Keepers during that same year, coached the team. Promise Keepers seeks to help Christian men revitalize their homes and communities by living with integrity. Connected to a muscular and masculine brand of devout and conservative evangelical faith, McCartney has influenced the lives of tens of thousands of men through the work of Promise Keepers. Yet in that first year of his organization's existence, he found himself coaching a game between his Colorado team and Missouri when a rare event occurred. With his team trailing 31–27, the officials made a crucial mistake. They failed to flip the down marker on a second-down attempt by Colorado to score close to the goal line. When they got to what should have been the fourth down, the quarterback spiked the ball to stop the clock, and, on what was actually the fifth down, the Buffaloes scored a touchdown.[2]

The year 1990 just happened to mark the fiftieth anniversary of an accidental fifth down that enabled Cornell to beat Dartmouth in 1940 to continue an eighteen-game winning streak. The Cornell coach and president, in the aftermath, looked at the facts and forfeited the victory. Would McCartney's Christian concern for integrity yield the same result?[3] No. McCartney quoted 1 Corinthians 4:4 and said, "My conscience is clear, but that does not make me innocent. It is the Lord who judges me." The victory came within the rules of the game as administered by the officials. That year, Colorado won the national title. Eight years would pass, well after McCartney's retirement, before he would express any public remorse about the episode.[4] Winning is all-important in sports. Triumph is what matters, and often other values dwindle by comparison.

Standing as a counterpoint to the conflict of values between sports and religion, there are the glowing and spiritually inclined superlatives launched by lovers of baseball. John Sexton, president of New York University, described, for example, *Baseball As a Road to God*. In a review of Sexton's book, Richard Lischer of Duke Divinity School wrote,

> Not many authors write about professional football and basketball in poetic, moral or religious terms because these sports do not tell us who we are in quite the way baseball does. The human being is not by nature a bone-crushing hunter or a swaggering show-off. We

have our allotted innings and play them out as best we can, but always within the friendly confines of eternity. We are the only creatures who hew to the immutable laws of birth and death even as we dream of their transformation.[5]

While Lischer critiqued those who go overboard with their religious associations, there exists no shortage of authors these days who celebrate the positively religious nature of the game of baseball, and others who have done so in days past. They find grace in its structure, and faith and hope generated through the experience of the game itself. Some even talk about conversion, transformed lives, and ways the game has led to an authentic experience of what it means to be human in the presence of God. But surely Lischer is right when he asks and answers the question whether baseball is a road to God. "Well, no, not exactly. At least no more than hiking in the Appalachians, volunteering in a hospice, reading Emily Dickinson, listening to John Coltrane, making a friend or raising a child."[6]

To recognize that both sports and religion represent a distinct moral ethos, or to refuse to recognize baseball as a "road to God," is not in either case to deny that baseball or other sports possess inherently religious characteristics, or inspire rituals and behaviors that can legitimately be described as religious in nature. These days, scholars who examine phenomena in religion, sports, sociology, and anthropology are all analyzing the connections between sports and religion using their own methodologies and reaching their own, usually differing, conclusions about this relationship.[7] Yet all agree that religion and sports share certain similarities and interact in interesting ways.

One of the greatest stories in American sports is found in the triumph represented in the Jackie Robinson story. Robinson's legacy is celebrated by Major League Baseball every year on April 15, the anniversary of the date (1947) when he broke the color barrier in the major leagues. On Jackie Robinson Day, both players and umpires across the country wear the number 42 in his honor. The road to that official recognition was never easy, and never seemed complete during his years of playing at Brooklyn, even though he batted .311 lifetime and averaged twenty-four stolen bases a season during his prime. Finally, on July 23, 1962, the day the Baseball Hall of Fame in Cooperstown inducted Jackie Robinson, he felt the full measure of the triumph when he confessed at the beginning of his speech, "Today, it seems that everything is complete."

Jerry and Mallie Robinson, in an on-again, off-again marriage, gave birth to Jack Roosevelt Robinson in Grady County, in southern Georgia, on January 31, 1919. Biographer Arnold Rampersad notes that between 1909, when Jerry and Mallie were married, and Jackie's birth, Georgians witnessed more than 125 lynchings across the state. Into the context of continuing white hostility and active persecution and repression toward black residents that yielded only "widespread poverty, disease, and crime, as well as cynicism and despair," Jackie arrived as the fourth son and fifth child of the couple. His maternal grandparents had been born enslaved, but had been able to raise all fourteen of their children on land they owned and farmed. An active church life figured prominently in Mallie's side of the family, and she grew to affirm the importance of family and God in facing successfully the challenges posed by the racism prominent all around her.[8]

Taken by Jerry Robinson's charm, as were many other women following their marriage, Mallie married Jackie's father on November 21, 1909. Living in abject poverty, Jerry and Mallie eked out an existence as farmers working on Jim Sasser's plantation. An incredibly resourceful woman, Mallie worked out a sharecropping arrangement with a reluctant and racist Sasser, who at one time had told her she was "about the sassiest nigger woman ever on this place," and their life improved considerably. That did not last long, however, as Jerry was in and out of the marriage and eventually left with another woman. Without Jerry around to work the farm, Sasser evicted Mallie and the children from their home, placing them in barely habitable locations. In May 1920, Mallie packed up her five children and joined seven other relatives on a train headed to California, where her half-brother had successfully set down roots.[9]

Fortunes turned for the young Robinson clan that year. Mallie found work as a maid in Pasadena for eight dollars a week. Then, when the family employing her moved, she was hired by another family and ended up working for them for more than twenty years. She and her sister's family lived with her half-brother for two years. Her sister Cora cared for the kids while Mallie and Cora's husband, Sam, worked. Mallie, along with Cora and Sam's family, bought a house together in 1922, the same year Pasadena leadership constructed the Rose Bowl, which housed one of the most prestigious college football games every year. The more prosperous the city became, the more problematic the city's increasing black presence became for white leadership.

While the Robinsons' life improved in most ways, the city passed increasingly severe restrictions to keep blacks out of certain areas of the city and in the most menial of jobs. In 1924, Mallie's sister's family bought their own home close by, and the Robinson family took sole possession of the first house. Jackie knew this as home until he left the house in 1941. The house provided a measure of security, even though somebody at one time had "burned a cross on the front lawn." But the family could not eat security, and Mallie often found it difficult to provide enough food for the growing kids and all the visiting relatives Mallie tried to help through the years. They made do with whatever they had on hand. Mallie's faith in God provided the strength to persevere, even thrive as a family.[10]

Very early in his life, Jack experienced athletics as a path to acceptance. As Rampersad puts it, "whites as well as blacks bowed to his gifts. . . . He and other gifted young athletes in Pasadena, black or white or Asian-American, competed against one another without allowing race to drive a permanent wedge of hatred or resentment between them." Mallie had chosen their location well, as Jack grew up in the shadow of the Rose Bowl, where he worked selling hot dogs, and not too far from Brookside Park, "with its fine array of sporting facilities for baseball, basketball, tennis, and swimming." He found his identity in sports, and tended to neglect his studies, skating by on his athletic abilities, with a passion for winning in every competition. Yet he also had a fragile self-esteem, uneasy with the fact that he did not have a father, and uncertain about how to handle his own nagging self-doubt about his worth as a human being.[11]

Jack's brother Mack, four and a half years older, introduced him "to the glory and the glamour of sports." A sprinter and broad jumper, Mack overcame heart trouble to win a spot on the 1936 U.S. Olympic squad. During the Olympics in Berlin, Mack finished second place behind the better-known African American, Jesse Owens, in the 200-meter dash. When he returned stateside after the Olympics, he set a world's record. Mack, like Jesus, never received any recognition from his hometown. When he arrived in Pasadena following the Olympics and the "triumphant post-Olympics tour on the Continent," he did so without receiving any fanfare (of course, Jesse Owens received little fanfare either). Racism allowed him a job as a street sweeper, which he often did while wearing his U.S. Olympic jacket. Mack's experiences, according to later reflections from Jack, had "soured him on life completely." Looking at the life of his brother, a black man who reached the pinnacle of athletic excellence, symbolized by a silver medal in the most significant Olympics in history, but ended up sweeping streets in bitterness, Robinson said in 1949 that he intended to "resolve to make the best of things."[12]

Jackie Robinson played all the sports in high school and excelled in most of them. The common elements he brought to his participation included unbelievable athleticism and a fiercely competitive nature. Robinson hated to lose. He carried his sports abilities to the Pasadena Junior College, where for two years he excelled in baseball, football, basketball, and track. Blacks made up less than 2 percent of the school's student body, but all activities and facilities were liberally available to them. During Jack's junior-college years, and in the midst of one or two small dustups with police, Robinson met the new young minister, Karl Everette Downs, who had arrived to minister at his mother's Methodist church.

Through his developing relationship with Karl, Jackie made new connections with the faith of his mother. "Faith in God then began to register in him as both a mysterious force, beyond his comprehension, and a pragmatic way to negotiate the world." Robinson began to mature and recognized he was not alone in the world. The importance of his mother's tenacity, and the role her faith played in it, became increasingly clear to him. As that happened, he began to nurture his own faith in God.

He also refined his baseball prowess in those years. During his second year in junior college, he had a phenomenal year, leading the school to the divisional title. He "batted .417 and scored forty-three runs; scoring in all but three of the games, he struck out only three times and stole twenty-five bases." When Pasadena youth put nine of their finest against the Chicago White Sox in March during spring training, Robinson hit well, stole second against the White Sox catcher, Mike Tresh, and made an impressive stop off the bat of Luke Appling, the American League batting champion the previous year, which he turned into a double play. Jimmy Dykes, the manager of the Sox, declared, "Geez, if that kid was white, I'd sign him right now." Other California players his age, like Ted Williams and Bob Lemon, were signed in 1938, but Jackie's brilliant early years were lost to the major leagues forever. Yet, on occasion that summer, more than five thousand fans gathered to watch him play a game of competitive softball in Pasadena's Brookside Park for a team sponsored by Pepsi-Cola.

The next year, his last in junior college, Robinson played football in front of crowds of 35,000–40,000 in the Rose Bowl, most of whom came simply to see Robinson quarterback. In that undefeated season, he scored seventeen touchdowns and 131 points. He then led his basketball team to the conference crown. Even though the junior college located in Pasadena provided a bit of an oasis for Robinson, the city itself did not. He resented the treatment of blacks by the police and the vast majority of the citizens of the city. He and other members of his family experienced personally the racism of both the city's establishment and its residents on a number of unfortunate occasions.[13]

He became the first athlete ever to letter in all four sports his first full year (1939–40) at UCLA.[14] When Robinson arrived at UCLA, a black track star named Tom Bradley (future mayor of Los Angeles) had been actively working to raise awareness regarding racial barriers in the university. Numbering only about 50 among the 9,600 or so students, blacks could not live in the village of Westwood and experienced other restrictions. However, white students and administrators tended to appreciate black athletes, as UCLA sought to increase its standing among schools like USC, Stanford, and Oregon. That first year, Jack, as a running back, joined two experienced black football stars, Kenny Washington and Woody Strode.[15] They met the heralded national champions from the previous year, Texas Christian University, in their first game. Expected to lose, UCLA won, 6–2.

Just over 103,000 people watched the last game of the season against USC, which ended in a scoreless tie. Though he missed two games of the season due to injury, Robinson's team finished the year undefeated, but with three ties. This tied them with USC for first place, but USC got the Rose Bowl bid, because UCLA had more ties. "Had Robinson not missed two games, UCLA almost certainly would have gone to the Rose Bowl." Despite having unbelievably successful seasons, neither Washington, a senior, nor Robinson, a junior, was named to any postseason honors. Jack ended the year having better seasons in football, basketball, and track than in baseball. Though he had a great year fielding, his hitting slumped rather dramatically.[16]

Robinson's last year at UCLA (1940–41) had its ups and downs. He met and began dating Rachel Isum, a seventeen-year-old first-year student, whom some five years later he would marry. Robinson had a good year on the football field, finishing second in the conference in offensive statistics, but the team won only one game. In basketball, Robinson won the league's individual scoring title for the second year in a row, but again received no league honors. The UCLA paper, the *Bruin*, lamented, "Prejudice 'Rumored' to Have Played Major Role in Selection" to the all-conference team. After the basketball season, on March 3, Jack decided to leave UCLA, despite being close to finishing and despite protests from all the coaches and, most especially, from Rachel. As Rachel thought about those days, she simply said, "He had had enough." Professional sports (NFL, NBA, MLB) allowed no black athletes in those days, so Jack took a job about six hours north of Los Angeles as an assistant athletic director with the National Youth Administration, an agency established by presidential order to respond to the Great Depression.

After a few months, with the increase of America's preparation for war, the army moved in and took over the facilities in September. The month before, Jack had the opportunity to play in a charity football game that pitted college all-stars against the reigning champions of the NFL, the Chicago Bears. In Chicago, before more than 98,000 fans, Robinson scored a touchdown in a losing effort. Over the course of the next few months, Robinson played some semiprofessional football in Honolulu, Hawaii, but struggled with an injury and some poor play. He left Hawaii on December 5, two days before Pearl Harbor. When he returned to Los Angeles, he found work as a truck driver for Lockheed Aircraft in Burbank, returned to his old house, and contributed financially to maintaining the family residence, which housed extended family as well.

At nearly the same time that Jimmy Dykes, manager of the Chicago White Sox, invited Jackie to work out with the team at Brookside Park, the army ordered Jackie to report for induction. He reported on April 3 and ended up in Kansas for basic training, where he excelled. Many expected he would be admitted to Officer Candidate School (OCS) when he finished in July. However, the army refused his application, along with those of any other black soldiers who had the audacity to apply, and assigned him to take care of horses at Fort Riley. Secretary of War Stimson had concluded that "leadership is not imbedded in the negro race yet" and attempts to make them commissioned officers were doomed to failure.[17] Eventually, Jackie proved him wrong and graduated from OCS. He served well as a second lieutenant, but after experiencing several other instances of blatant racism, Jackie eventually received an honorable discharge due to medical disability (bone chips in the ankle) in the fall of 1944.

Free now from the service, Robinson sent a letter to the owner of the Kansas City Monarchs. The team offered him a contract and ordered him to report to Texas for spring training in April 1945. He spent the months between discharge and spring training directing the athletic program at a struggling black college in Austin, Texas, led by his old friend Reverend Karl Downs. Even though he had not played organized baseball for years, and had a bum ankle, Robinson tore up the Negro League with his bat and his baserunning. Largely through the efforts of Wendell Smith, a black reporter, Robinson caught the attention of Branch Rickey, president of the Brooklyn Dodgers since 1943. Robinson suddenly figured into Rickey's emerging effort to break the color line in baseball.

Ironically, Jackie planned to leave baseball in 1945 to seek a coaching job in high school and marry Rachel on February 10, 1946. On August 24, 1945, while Robinson stood on the field in Comiskey Park before a game, Clyde Sukeforth, acting on behalf of Branch Rickey, made contact with him. On the morning of August 28, Robinson met with Rickey in his office in Brooklyn. Kept secret until his formal signing at a news conference on October 23 in Montreal, the city hosting the minor league club where Jackie would begin his professional career, the news took Major League Baseball, and the nation, by storm.

Why was Jackie's signing so significant? According to David Chidester, baseball "is a religious institution that maintains the continuity, uniformity, sacred time, and sacred space of American life."[18] In this way, Chidester emphasized that baseball acts as a container for American tradition, the continuity of what it means to be American. He quotes Donald Hall to say that baseball "is a place where memory gathers." Cultural memory, at least as curated through nostalgia, is highly influential in creating the present in

America. If American cultural memory makes blacks invisible, then blacks are external to the core American experience of what it means to be an American. Chidester also stresses that baseball provides a place of uniformity and community, providing a sense of belonging for those who inhabit the space. Baseball represents the "sacred space of home," that feeling of comfort you get when you know that things are just as they seem. Major League Baseball, in its policies and its command of this particular sacred space, made sure blacks knew they did not belong in sacred spaces in America.

Though he likely never thought of it specifically in religious terms, Jackie Robinson knew in the depth of his experience that baseball served as the "functional religion of America."[19] Throughout his youth into adulthood, he used his athletic prowess and competitive edge to gain a measure of acceptance in the white worlds he negotiated. Sports, and especially baseball, touched a nerve in the American psyche. When you could contribute to a team's ability to string together victories, you could win your way to acceptance, even acclaim, among the fans supporting the team, no matter how racist they might otherwise be. When the opportunity to play professional baseball appeared, Jackie knew from experience it meant not only the possibility of a paycheck, but the serious possibility of creating acceptance for blacks within American culture. Branch Rickey knew that as well. Sports provided blacks an opportunity to move from the margins to the center of American life, to show they were as human, and as American, as anybody else.

William Baker has described how many outsiders in the American experience have used sports to demonstrate their "American-ness." Over the years, Mormons and Jews and urban Catholics have utilized sports to show just how American they could be. They quickly learned that "prizefights and ball games were godsends, tickets to the American mainstream."[20] Joseph Dorinson has described how Jackie Robinson, Hank Greenberg, and Joe DiMaggio, each in his own way, "by their talents, strength of character, and dignity transformed the public stereotypical notions held of their heritages."[21] Blacks, Jews, and Italian Catholics all benefited from their baseball prowess.

Jackie's fortunate break in the major leagues, given the religious and cultural power of sports in America, sped up the racial integration of American culture. Reverend Wyatt Tee Walker, a close associate of Martin Luther King Jr., said that King once told him, "Jackie Robinson made it possible for me in the first place. Without him, I would never have been able to do what I did."[22] Even though King's alleged statement smacks of more than a bit of hyperbole, it is true that the integration of baseball, and particularly the example of Jackie Robinson on the playing field, helped to accomplish cultural acceptance of increasing participation of blacks in American life. During his years playing the game, Jackie consistently used his fame to criticize racism in the country and to speak out about civil rights for all African Americans.

When Robinson retired, he became a vocal advocate of civil-rights causes, working on behalf of the NAACP. He also served as chair of the board for a bank in Harlem that rapidly became the biggest black-owned bank in the nation. The years following 1957 were among the most difficult for blacks to negotiate in the modern period. As a visible leader, Robinson tended to anger everybody at some point or another:

> when he denounced anti-Semitism among blacks; when he attacked Adam Clayton Powell for urging blacks to abandon the NAACP and support the Black Muslims; when he resigned from the NAACP in 1967 because it opposed his connection with Nelson Rockefeller and because he resented the fact that it hadn't given more voice to younger, more aggressive black leaders; when he denounced police brutality in the treatment of the arrested Black Panthers in New York City in 1968; and in 1971 when he publicly criticized his friend Nelson Rockefeller for authorizing the assault on rioting prisoners in the Attica penitentiary, most of whom were black. Jackie was uninterested in adhering to any inflexible political perspective; his sole commitment was to integration and improved social conditions for black Americans.[23]

Only the Boston Red Sox, the Detroit Tigers, and the Philadelphia Phillies had failed to integrate their teams by the time Jackie retired. Over the course of the next three years, each brought black players to the big leagues—though grudgingly in all three cases. For Jackie Robinson, sports operated as a source of value and meaning. Sports spoke to his need to find acceptance as a human being and a provided a transcendent purpose for his life. Through his experience, and through his embodiment of ultimate concern for racial and social justice, he provided opportunities for others to discover meaning for their lives at the altar of baseball and other sports.

In addition to releasing a flood of black talent, Jackie's decade in baseball also opened the gates to American baseball for players born in the Caribbean and in Latin America. The international ramifications of the integration of baseball are themselves significant. Minnie Minoso, the first black Cuban player, and Roberto Clemente, the first Puerto Rican, both owe their entrance into the professional game to the groundbreaking career of Jackie Robinson, as do the slew of international players who followed them.[24]

Until 1953, Major League Baseball had sixteen teams, all located in ten cities spread across the midwestern and northeastern United States. Jackie affected both the international market of baseball and the market at home. The influx of potential professional talent led to an expansion of teams. This transition also included breaking trust between teams and their communities. Teams began moving to new locations in the country to increase market shares. After the Brooklyn Dodgers and the New York Giants moved west in 1958, teams began to fill in across the country. Today, there are thirty major-league teams.

Though the Dodgers were not the first team to move, Walter O'Malley's move of the Dodgers to Los Angeles symbolized a shift in baseball, from an era when baseball represented "a faithful expression of its communities" to a time when baseball became "an impersonal business competing not for people's hearts but for their entertainment dollars."[25] This shift, combined with attitudes about money in both American culture and the sports that reflect it, now threatens to undo much that Jackie Robinson helped to accomplish. At the time of integration, nobody could have foreseen the implications of the evolution of sports after the influx of money provided by the modern economy of sports. Integration in sports, like the accomplishments of desegregation and civil rights in American culture more generally, did not finally resolve the underlying issues. Sports is not a miraculous panacea for all forms of social injustice in this country. A critical examination of the mythology associated with sports helps to make sense of these things.

MYTHOLOGY

Some people use mythology to obscure the truth, to create narratives designed to misrepresent truth, or to create alternative realities that serve some prior purpose. We could talk about the mythology that Abner Doubleday invented baseball in Cooperstown, New York, a myth that has little basis in fact but secured for the game an "All American" reputation.[26] Or we could describe the many myths that surround certain of its stars, like the way Babe Ruth during the 1932 World Series could call the spot in Wrigley Field where he was about to place the home run he hit on the next pitch. Myths like these are similar to those told about George Washington associated with American civil religion.

We could talk about the myth that sport is a "manly" thing, and that women who can compete with men in various sports are actually freaks of nature. Mildred "Babe" Didriksen, perhaps the greatest female athlete of the twentieth century and the woman most responsible for the development of women's professional golf, actually developed a reputation as a "freak" for her athletic prowess across the sports of tennis, basketball, baseball, swimming, and golf. Allen Barra wondered "how many great female athletes we might have had" in that century, had it not been for the long-unchallenged assumptions associated with the myth that female athletes were unequal to their male counterparts.[27] Any religious expression that takes itself seriously ultimately must work to expose false myths, in order to serve whatever truths we can imagine through human narratives (as, for example, represented in the career of Jackie Robinson).

In 1928, John Tunis wrote about "The Great Sports Myth" that had developed, in his view, due to sportswriters in major newspapers, for they "regard the whole sporting panorama with an almost religious seriousness." Americans, he wrote, "do not seem to find religious prophets to exalt," so "we turn hopefully to the world of sports." The first aspect of the myth of sports in America, he said, was that "competitive sport—any kind of competitive sport from prize fighting to squash tennis—makes for nobility of character." Tunis argued that precisely the opposite was true, so far as he had experienced it. In the quest "for victory, victory, victory, unpleasant traits of all sort are brought out." He rehearsed the practice of creating hate for the opposing team, found in the motivational work of some college and professional coaches. Tunis's words call to mind the scandal associated with the New Orleans Saints, when coaches paid bounties to those who could knock opposing players out of the game due to injuries. Tunis concluded more than eighty-five years ago that the myth that sports teaches self-control and how to accept victory with humility and defeat with grace is simply not true.

Further, Tunis challenged the myth that international sports events create warm bonds of friendship between both nations and individuals.[28] Even though it helps to make his case, Tunis would have been shocked, writing as he was in 1928, to learn that more than 25,000 security police and soldiers had to be in place around the stadium in Rio de Janiero for the final game of the World Cup between Argentina and Germany played on Sunday, July 13, 2014. Fights broke out between Argentinian fans and Brazilian fans on the beach and in the area outside the Maracanã Stadium, where the game was played, likely because Argentinians chided Brazilians a bit too much about their team's poor showings against both Germany and the Netherlands.

The notion of myth we'd most like to discuss is, in the words of Joseph Price, where myth "as narrative construct . . . is able to stimulate dreams and cultivate hope." Price particularly used A. Bartlett Giamatti's belief that baseball and myth "became part of the same American story" to illustrate his point. "Baseball," Giamatti writes, "is part of America's plot, part of America's mysterious, underlying design . . . the plot of the story of our national life." Giamatti defines that plot as the ability "to be free enough to consent to an order that will enhance and compound—as it constrains—our freedom." In essence, both America and baseball, for Giamatti, embody the virtues of a freedom to become whatever one can or will be, in a context that is limited enough to keep it from succumbing to chaos.[29]

The mythical understanding that baseball and other American sports generally mirror the best in American culture has led to the expression of one of the most important myths associated with sports. The myth of the level playing field is one that possesses extraordinary power to stimulate dreams and cultivate hope, particularly among the youth in America. The belief that anybody can make it, if they just work hard enough, if they just hone their skills and train with the necessary discipline. Professional sports, so it goes, are open to everybody. Even the chief justice most responsible for furthering the cause of civil rights, Chief Justice of the Supreme Court Earl Warren, assumed the legitimacy of the level playing field: "I always turn to the sports page first, which records people's accomplishments. The front page has nothing but man's failures." Here he alludes to the purity of sports, itself a mythical concept, and the belief that merit is always properly rewarded. But this myth is difficult to sustain in today's climate.

At one time in baseball, there were so-called industrial leagues, often sponsored by local steel mills or mining companies, where serious baseball talent could be developed. There were other leagues, like the All-American Girls Professional League and the Negro leagues, which nurtured budding talent in the sport and offered a more democratic approach to playing the game, one open to all genders, races, and classes. Mickey Mantle and Willie Mays, one white and one black, yet both well-experienced in the art of living in the midst of poverty, were among the last players to come from these leagues. The industrial leagues, as well as the other leagues, all died out in the wake of integration and the emerging connections between baseball and television.[30] Today American sports has become more oriented toward the elite—not exclusively, but increasingly so—especially at the highest levels of competition.

Jimmie Lee Solomon points out that black participation in Major League Baseball has drastically declined in recent years. In the mid-1970s, black baseball players made up about 27 percent of all major leaguers; in 1986, 19 percent were black. In 2015, the number stood at about 7.8 percent. Solomon tags the cost of baseball as chief among a variety of reasons. In urban settings it is difficult to find the green spaces required for baseball. Without a solid support system and financial sponsorship the purchase and maintenance of baseball equipment can be an unwelcome or even burdensome expense. Blacktop surfaces and a basketball hoop are easier to maintain. All one needs is one basketball and a pair of sneakers in order to play. Solomon points out that the athleticism associated with basketball and football make them easier to learn later in life, while baseball requires the development of technical skills earlier in life. Mentors, usually fathers, who Solomon notes are often absent in African American homes, are needed to teach those skills. The phenomenon of fatherlessness (the dearth of black fathers and male mentors within the African American community), Solomon opines, might be a contributing factor to why so many promising athletes never acquire either the technical prowess or nostalgic connections to this particular sport. It is amazing to think how something like missed chances to play catch in one's youth might yield countless unintended consequences.

Major league teams have also developed academies in Latin America, preferring to develop international talent over finding ways to nurture African American talent at home. As of 2015, more than 28 percent of major league players were born in other countries, the vast majority (24.2 percent) from Latin American countries, most from the Dominican Republic and Venezuela.[31] Only about 4 percent of Latino players were born in the United States, in spite of the fact that the nation's largest minority population (over 17 percent) is Hispanic American. The interesting fact here is that Major League Baseball teams do not have to draft international players or pay them the going draft wages. Instead, they can develop the talent in Latin America through their camps as individual teams, outside the draft system, and pay players the major-league minimums when they start. This may be one reason team owners prefer Latin American–born players over both homegrown Hispanic and African American players.

In addition, baseball's marketing lacks qualities that attract black youth, especially when compared with the marketing of basketball and football. There are racist assumptions present in marketing that conclude baseball is too slow compared to more intense, fast-paced sports, and therefore it lacks allure for young black athletes. Further, colleges and the NCAA emphasize the revenue sports of football and basketball over baseball. Solomon noted that eighty-five football scholarships are offered at every Division I university, compared with an average of only 11.7 provided for collegiate baseball, so that most baseball scholarships are divided between several players.[32] As a result of these and other factors, baseball is no longer the go-to sport for American youth. This fact poses a challenge to its status as the American pastime.

The National Football League integrated in 1946. Player rosters across the NFL, as of the 2014 season, are around 66.3 percent black. Less than 1 percent of NFL players are Latino, and only 1.1 percent are Asian. In 2015, African Americans represented about 14.3 percent of population in the United States, Hispanic Americans about 17.4 percent, and Asians about 6.3 percent. NFL office management (29.3 percent women) and office support staff (31.4 percent women) each stand at about 9.2 percent African American. There are no black majority owners in the NFL (97 percent white and 3 percent Asian, and 9 percent women). Among head coaches, 15.6 percent are black (5 out of 32 as of January 2015), down from a high of 25 percent in 2011. Black assistant coaches have remained relatively stable at 31 percent for several seasons. At least up through 2013, the last comprehensive look at these statistics, there have been no African American CEOs or presidents in NFL franchises (again, 97 percent white males). Only 6 percent of vice presidents are black (17 percent of vice presidents are women). Among general managers, 19 percent are black (81 percent white, no women). Some 12 percent of all senior administrators are black (20 percent of senior administrators are women). Of all members of NFL administration, 11 percent are black (29 percent are women). Only 4 percent of NFL team physicians are black (2 percent are women). Some 17 percent of head trainers are black (83 percent white). The power structure in the NFL, in spite of the dominant percentage of black players, is still largely white.[33]

Today African American players make up more than 80 percent of NBA rosters. Professional basketball integrated in 1950, three years later than professional baseball. Since then, blacks have overtaken the sport as players. Even with those numbers, a black athlete in high school has a better chance of being struck "by a meteorite in the next 10 years, than getting work as an athlete."[34] A recent sociological study suggests there may be even more to the picture than meets the eye initially. The study examined whether it is generally true that players rise from the ghettos to play in the NBA. The conclusions are somewhat surprising: "we demonstrate that the majority of NBA players come from relatively advantaged social origins and that African American players from disadvantaged social origins have lower odds of being in the NBA than African American and white players from relatively well-off families."[35]

Among blacks, a child from a lower-income family has a 37 percent less chance to play in the NBA than a child from a middle- or higher-income family. Among impoverished whites, the percentage is 75 percent less likely. And a black child with only one parent at home is 18 percent less likely than a black child in a two-parent household to play in the NBA. Blacks from poor backgrounds are underrepresented in the NBA compared to the general population. As Peter Keating indicated when he reported on this story for ESPN, "it now takes more resources—a lot more—to compete at the highest level." He continues: "We believe that skills always trump circumstances. But that's a myth. . . . Yes, your talent is important. But your very first teams—your family and your earliest support structures—matter an awful lot too."[36] It remains true that middle-to-upper-class youth with two-parent families, black or white, have a big leg up over those who might have much better talent but are being raised in lower-economic social settings by a single-parent household.

This dynamic is spreading across all sports in America. Select leagues for soccer, tennis, baseball, football, and basketball exist for those as young as eight to ten. They require considerable financial commitments to hire qualified coaches, enter the most competitive of leagues, and travel to the best tournaments. These select teams require first-rate training facilities and high-quality equipment. Parents have to get their kids to practice sessions, usually at least twice per week, and may have to travel some distance to get them there. Not only is it difficult for single-parent households to afford this kind of training; it is nearly impossible for one parent to do the hauling necessary to get kids where they have to be. The best talent among young children is siphoned off early from public sports leagues and diverted into private select leagues. Though some of these leagues provide scholarships to disadvantaged youth, the vast majority of players come from advantaged middle-to-upper-class households with two parents. The playing field of sports is more than a bit lopsided these days, matching the power dynamics associated with other cultural and economic aspects of American life.

For African Americans, it is even harder to find and keep work as a coach in the NBA. In 2005, ten of thirty coaches were black, but one analysis demonstrated that white coaches kept their jobs 50 percent longer than black coaches, meaning that white coaches always have a longer period of time to prove their abilities. Black coaches lasted an average of only 1.6 seasons.[37] An incident involving an NBA owner in April 2014 raised the question whether it might be time to examine the extent of structural racism found within the NBA. The NBA banned Donald Sterling, owner of the Los Angeles Clippers, from the NBA for life due to racist comments he made to a girlfriend that she recorded and released to the media. The NBA acted quickly. But did its actions address the deeper issue? Is there equal opportunity in professional basketball?

In the wake of the Sterling event, Tom Ziller examined the hiring practices for first-time head coaches of NBA teams over the past five years. Of the nine rookie coaches hired in the summer of 2013, seven of them were white. In the past five years, the NBA hired eleven coaches who had never played the game; the last ten of them have been white, and the eleventh is an Asian American. In the last decade, no NBA team has hired a black as a first-time head coach who has not played the game professionally. In twenty years only four blacks have been hired, compared to twenty-six white first-time coaches, who have never played a game in the NBA. Ziller points out this may be due to the fact that only one NBA owner is black (Michael Jordan) and one is Indian-American (Vivek Ranadive). The twenty-eight other teams have white ownership. Ziller also notes that "only five NBA general managers are black." He concludes, "We talk about Donald Sterling's plantation mentality, but that's fish in the barrel. What about the NBA itself? This is a primarily black player pool, reporting to a primarily white coaching pool, hired by primarily white executives and getting paychecks from almost exclusively white team owners.

Now the players are paid extremely well, and this is nothing—nothing, nothing, *nothing*—like slavery. But the power structure is pretty familiar."[38]

Hockey broke the color line during the 1957–58 season. Yet today there is only a handful of African American or African Canadian hockey players. As of the 2014 season, there were approximately nineteen black players across the entire NHL, some of those originating from locations other than America or Canada. That is about 2.6 percent of NHL players. There are thirty teams, each with a roster of twenty-three players. The number-one-rated player in the 2013 NHL draft was Seth Jones, son of former NBA player Popeye Jones and an African American kid. The Nashville Predators drafted him 4th overall. The Edmonton Oilers drafted his younger brother, Caleb, 117th overall in the 2015 draft.

Professional soccer has a larger number of black players, but is nearly all white at the top. As of 2014, among major league soccer players, 10.6 percent were African American and 24.1 percent Latino (from across the world). There are no black majority owners (three Latino), coaches (two Latino), CEOs/presidents (one Latino), general managers (one Latino), or athletic trainers (two Latino). There are three vice presidents (two Latino), three senior team administrators (twenty-three Latino, representing 10.6 percent), one black team physician (one Latino), and one black assistant coach (nine Latino, representing 14.3 percent).[39]

The playing field across professional sports is not quite as level as one might think at first glance. As of 1961, blacks and other ethnic groups were allowed to play on tour with the PGA. In 2014, there were only eighty-five African American PGA club professionals, statistically insignificant when considering there are 28,000 pros.[40] In spite of the fact that Venus and Serena Williams have dominated the women's tennis tour for more than a decade, there is just a handful of black professional tennis players on tour. The economic aspects of the inequalities for aspiring players of any ethnic heritage are as significant as the racial discrimination that still seems evident in the power circles dominating professional athletics.

Regardless of how we are prone to congratulate ourselves for breaking down color and class lines, or creating a context in America where merit and hard work always pay off, the idea of sports as a level playing field is far from a reality. Sports, in fact, remain the microcosm of the American myth writ large. We can point to the Jackie Robinsons, the Michael Jordans, and the Williams sisters to gauge social progress. We perpetuate the myth that anybody can make it if they "just do it," as Nike claims, or if they can only "be like Mike," as the Gatorade commercial so eloquently puts it. Yet a closer examination shows that sports continue to mirror the power dynamics present in every other aspect of American culture. Sports become the most visible of public arenas where people's private passions, prejudices, and privileges have full sway. At some point, these racial limitations within sports will likely be broken down, but future generations should mark progress by measuring it against a significant and systemic racism fully evident in the long history of professional sports.

DOCTRINE

Belief in sport can take any number of forms. Sometimes they are more "folk beliefs" than genuine beliefs. This happens in cases where fans act as if they believe they can influence the outcome of a game by doing particular things: growing a beard during the hockey playoffs, wearing their lucky jersey, or turning their cap inside out and placing it on backwards in a rally-cap position. Perhaps one of the most popular cultural examples is the Pat Salitano Sr. (played by Robert DeNiro) character in the Oscar-nominated film adaptation of *Silver Linings Playbook*. Salitano lived out the depth of his commitment to the Philadelphia Eagles by orchestrating his family's entire life to enhance the Eagles "mojo" on any given Sunday. Salitano's behavior comes closer to an expression of rituals than an expression of belief. But Salitano's rituals are based on his supernatural belief that his behavior somehow makes a difference.

There are other folk beliefs or superstitions connected with sports. For example, athletes seem to believe bad luck is associated with an appearance on a *Sports Illustrated* cover. A good many Chicago Cubs fans believe in the "Billy Goat curse" originating in 1945. When the Cubs banned Billy Goat Tavern–owner Billy Sianis from being able to bring his billy goat to games, due to the goat's smell, Sianis cursed the club and said there would never again be a World Series at Wrigley. More than seventy years later, there has not been another World Series at Wrigley Field even though fans have expended a variety of efforts to break the curse. Large numbers of fans continue to express hope that the new year will be the year.[41]

The Boston Red Sox fans have dealt with a similar curse. In the six years before the Boston Red Sox traded Babe Ruth to the Yankees, they won a World Series about every other year. After that trade in 1919, the Red Sox had to wait eighty-six years before winning their next championship (2004), while the Yankees won twenty-six championships during the same period. Some blamed the long drought on the "curse of the Bambino." The power of such curses is not, of course, empirical, but rather derives from the spiritual sensibility that believes in them. Occasionally, sincerity of belief leads to a self-fulfillment of things that otherwise certainly stretch credulity.[42]

There are beliefs in sports that are clearly based in empirical data and verifiable through statistics. In baseball it is nearly always better not to swing when you face a 3–0 count. There is wisdom in orchestrating a sacrifice bunt with a man on second base with one out or no outs. Do not attempt a two-point conversion early in a football game. In a close basketball game with less than a minute left, the team trailing should foul the team that is ahead and, if possible, put its worst foul shooter on the line. Other beliefs in sports are less verifiable, falling nearly into the category of mythology. In this latter category are beliefs like colleges and athletes are always better off when they play in Division I intercollegiate athletics, or that the higher level the competition, the better the sport builds character.

Other doctrines seem to possess more merit, due either to their practical ability to inculcate the hope that indeed salvation (a victorious season) is possible, or because they connect so well with common sense. An enduring doctrine of the first type is the belief that "there is always next year." Optimism and hope derive from this belief, for athlete and sports fan alike. In expressing it, one is clinging to the eschatological hope that, no matter how bleak the current season or experience has been, victory still remains out in front somewhere. At least two beliefs, commonly belonging to all sports, connect with the second type.

First, athletes generally believe in the importance of self-confidence for athletic success. Interviewed just before his last professional All-Star Game in July 2014, Derek Jeter stressed the role his self-confidence had played in his career. Joe Girardi indicated a few years ago that self-confidence was "one of the things that has made [Jeter] such a great player, the belief in himself that he can always right it if something's going wrong."[43]

A second belief that dominates the world of sports is that hard work must always accompany natural ability in order to succeed. Vince Lombardi used to say, "It's not whether you get knocked down; it's whether you get up."[44] The only way you can get back up is to work hard enough before you get knocked down. Anson Dorrance, the woman's soccer coach at the University of North Carolina, whose teams have dominated the sport for decades, winning twenty NCAA championships, put it this way: "The vision of a champion is someone who is bent over, drenched in sweat, at the point of exhaustion when no one else is watching."[45]

Sometimes sports leaders—particularly great coaches like Amos Alonzo Stagg, Vince Lombardi, Red Auerbach, Pat Summitt, John Wooden, and Phil Jackson—achieve a status of revered spiritual teacher, a dispenser and delineator of wisdom, not only about the game, but about life. They gain their status as spiritual teachers through the victories they have racked up.

Their wisdom would seem hollow without the victories to back them up. These coaches mediate the belief system of sports; they hand down the acceptable doctrines, some with more profundity than others. These beliefs provide players with a code of conduct by which to live. For many, the beliefs they have adopted through participation in a variety of sports provide the only belief system that functionally operates for them in life. They live their lives by adherence to various sports clichés. Don't lose hope when things don't go your way today; there's always tomorrow. Victory is somewhere in your future, if only you believe in yourself and your abilities. If you work hard to develop those abilities to your fullest potential, you can become successful in your everyday living.

RITUAL

Like fans, players engage in ritualistic behavior, often as a matter of routine, to keep order in their minds and to feel prepared for the moment of competition. Michael Jordan always wore his college shorts under his professional uniform. Wade Boggs became an expert on how to cook chicken, because he observed a dedicated ritual where he had to have chicken before every game. Neymar (Brazil's premier soccer player) must always receive a pregame pep talk from his dad before taking the pitch for an important game. Rafael Nadal, with fourteen Grand Slam singles titles, takes a cold shower before every match and then sets two water bottles, one cold and one at room temperature in front and left of his chair on the court, making sure that the labels face the same direction, and drinks from them in a precise order during the match. Tennis players bounce the ball a specific number of times before serving; batters run through rituals before facing the next pitch; and Tiger Woods always wears red on the final round of tournaments.

Though it is doubtful any of these rituals, in and of themselves, has a dramatic impact on the outcomes of competitions (after all, Neymar fractured a vertebra in the 2014 World Cup), without them, the athletes would likely compete differently; and *that fact* could impact the outcomes. These rituals prepare the athletes, provide them with a sense that all is right with their world, that there is order in the universe, enabling them now to do what they need to do.

These rituals are largely individual in nature. The important connection between symbols and rituals tends to indicate that the meaning of rituals needs to be, in some sense, social or communal. These kinds of rituals relate to virtually every aspect of sports. In a traditional ritual that goes back to

1880, an international rugby union of New Zealand, the All Blacks, performs a traditional Māori *haka* dance just before playing every international match.[46] Fields of play must be prepared in particular ways, as sacred space must be tended and placed in the proper order before every service. Umpires spend an hour or two to rub all baseballs with mud to prepare them for the game. Players and coaches work out the signs they will use for that day's game, rituals that will make sense only to those who wear the same uniform and profess the same loyalties. Fans wear face paint, distinctive clothes, and participate as a community in sacramental beers, hot dogs, and, these days, warm pretzels and nachos. Organs play at the right moments, and fans clap their hands in unison. Chants begin, waves roll across all kinds of stadiums. Winners of championships celebrate with champagne in clubhouses, after, in some sports, coaches have been doused with Gatorade. And every NHL champion drinks from the Stanley Cup and gets a chance to take it home with him.

By all these actions, players and fans are connected to a wider sense of meaning and to a broad tradition that in some sense shapes them so that they are different from what they would be without the experience. Carl Diem, who organized the 1936 Olympics in Germany, created the ritual of the Olympic torch relay. The suggestion likely originated in the propaganda ministry in Berlin, but that possibility is not often raised in connection with Olympic history. On June 30, 1936, the torch was lit in Olympia, Greece, in the ruins of a temple, and then carried, one kilometer at a time, by runners who fit the Aryan profile, all the way to Berlin (3,422 kilometers). Describing the Olympics in general, Carl Diem wrote, "Over the modern event of the Olympiad lies the magic circle of the historical-old and the divine-pious. . . . The things that open the celebration: Bell sound—fanfares—festive procession—choir singing—speech—oath—flags—pigeons—light symbol, all this means solemnity, equal-ranking to a church celebration without copying it, and a deep emotion is everywhere, quite comparable to a religious celebration hour."[47]

In the late 1930s, the Dutch philosopher Johan Huizinga wrote a book he titled *Homo Ludens*, translated "Man the Player." The book, now a classic, has been translated into various languages across the world. In examining flourishing societies, Huizinga finds one central aspect in common: the element of play. For Huizinga, play and ritual have much in common: "The ritual act has all the formal and essential characteristics of play . . . particularly in so far as it transports the participants to another world."[48]

One way that rituals and play transport participants is the way they seem to deal with time. "In each case," observes Thomas Carter, the ritual or gaming activity takes place in a temporal frame that is considered removed from everyday time." Time in rituals and in sports seems especially separated from ordinary time. Time is marked by innings, or holes, or sets and matches, or quarters and halves. As players and fans are separated by ritual and play from ordinary time, some scholars of religion and sport argue they have entered a liminal state, a sacral state within which they experience something akin to spirituality, or certainly a lifting of their own spirits. Carter believes the better term might be liminoid, a distinction made by sociologist Victor Turner, who pointed out that "liminoid phenomena are spectacular performances in the process of being commoditized, whereas liminal phenomena are not—and possibly cannot be—transformed by capitalist forces." According to Turner, "one works at the liminal, one plays with the liminoid."[49]

Besides the ritualistic connection to the capitalist system in American sports, many rituals in sports are also connected to the civil religion the nation solemnly observes. Players remove helmets or hats, set hockey sticks and basketballs aside, and place hands over hearts, as the "Star Spangled Banner" is played or sung before every game. The ritual has its roots in the first game of the 1918 World Series, when a relatively small and quiet crowd showed up to see the Boston Red Sox play the Chicago Cubs. More than 100,000 Americans had already died in the war, and the mood was somber. During the seventh-inning stretch, the crowd roared to life when a military band struck up the song. The Cubs repeated it in game two. When the series moved to Boston for game three, the Red Sox moved the song to the start of the game and introduced wounded soldiers who had received free tickets. From then on, the song was played during the Series and for holiday games.[50] After Pearl Harbor, the ritual became an every-game event, as it took strong root in the fertile soil of baseball.

This ritual prepares the teams for the moment of battle and places them psychically and emotionally on the same plane. It also serves to adjust the emotion of spectators appropriately. In the big business of sports, where each tries to define itself as the American game, it never hurts to connect the flag with the sport. Especially was this evident on September 17, 2001, when baseball resumed after the attack on the Twin Towers. In Los Angeles, while a female police officer sang the anthem, Dodgers and Padres worked with firemen and police officers to unfurl a huge flag that covered nearly the entire infield. After 9/11, Major League Baseball adopted the ritualistic practice of singing "God Bless America" during the seventh-inning stretch, in addition to the fan favorite "Take Me Out to the Ball Game," sung together as a congregation and played by many of the teams. In this way, baseball has linked the core values of American culture with the game in yet one other way, while also indicating solemn concern for the American way of life during an era of terrorism.

ETHICS

All sports are clearly governed by guidelines, rules, and handbooks of policies and procedures. Those who officiate each sport become professionals in their own right by knowing all these details. Like the ethics associated with many other aspects of culture, sports ethics can be understood as deontological, in many respects. Deontological ethics judges the morality of actions by whether the activity falls within the confines defined by a rule or set of rules. Was the ball passed while the forward was in an onside position? Did the base runner run outside the base path? Did the tackle get a head start before the ball was snapped? There are countless rules, and countless judgments are made by officials concerning the actions of the athletes.

In deontological ethics, whether or not one acted within the rule is more important than the consequence. So long as the hit on the quarterback or the wide receiver or the catcher at home plate was a legal one, the fact the opposing player had to be hospitalized as a result does not figure into any judgment concerning the play itself. Teleological (consequential) ethics would be more concerned with the outcome of the act, and virtue ethics more interested in the virtue of one's character and how that was embodied in one's activities. Since these hits are allowed by the rules, they do not violate the ethics of the game itself. It isn't cheating if the activity can be construed as being within the rules of the game.

Cal Ripken once pointed out that there is nothing in the rules of baseball that prohibits deceiving umpires.[51] Others succeed in cheating, regardless of the rules, even when the NFL rules otherwise, because they use the court system to overturn decisions of the head office, and only "underlings" end up taking the fall when footballs are illegally deflated. Those who administrate the sports are not immune from outright ethical abuses either, as the bribery scandal involving FIFA and Sepp Blatter in 2015 illustrated all too clearly. Ethics in sports are more deontological than consequential, with little interest in virtue, no matter how much it claims that the best "man" wins. Many fans and players carry this ethical approach into their daily living; they claim to live within the rules, and they don't worry about the consequences or whether it was the most virtuous thing to do.

When players do what has never been done before, there is no way to assess that activity ethically, so it requires a new round of rule-making, either to affirm or disallow the new state of affairs. For example, Bob Gibson so dominated the National League as a pitcher in 1968 that MLB lowered the height of the mound the next year. Roy Williams broke the ankle of Terrell Owens when he tackled him by the back of his jersey in a December 2004 game, so the NFL banned "horse collar" tackles. When Lew Alcindor (later known as Kareem Abdul-Jabbar) dominated college basketball, the NCAA banned the dunk after the 1967 season, but had to reinstate it in 1976 because the dunk was good for basketball. In 1981, Lenny Randle got on hands and knees to try to blow a slow rolling fair ball into foul territory without touching it. That possibility was banned by MLB the next year. Kevin Garnett (1995) and Kobe Bryant (1996) went straight from high school to the NBA ("prep to pro"), where previous expectations favored college experience or at least a year separating high school from the professional leagues. In 2005, the NBA sought to set a minimum age of twenty; the union opposed age limits. The compromise reached between them established the rule that a player has to be nineteen and a year removed from high school. Sportsmanship is about abiding by the rules, but players have often altered the game, forcing rules to adjust to them, through their creativity or superior skill.

The meaning of ethical behavior in sports can extend to situations off the field. In most cases, these situations continue to include a violation of rules. Knowing that the league prohibited use of performance-enhancing drugs (PEDs) caught by existing drug tests, players took a "deceive the umpire" kind of approach to the rule. They hoped they could stay ahead of the science of drug testing, or time their use so as to avoid detection. Their moral persuasion in this regard rested in their ability to play better, to move their game to the next level. Justification in deontological ethics is often a highly individual phenomenon. Rules can be bent for a higher end. PEDs enabled them to be better than they otherwise could be. The PEDs did not give them the talent or make the sport easier; they simply provided the fuel and made sports more dynamic. Players needed no other rationale.

Yet the Bay Area Laboratory Co-Operative (BALCO) scandal started the tumbling of the house of cards built by the players using PEDs. A 2002 government investigation of the laboratory revealed proof that a good number of professional athletes had been using banned substances to enhance their performances. These included people like Jason Giambi, Barry Bonds, Marion Jones, and Bill Romanowski. The BALCO scandal has been followed by the 2013 scandal associated with the rejuvenation clinic of Biogenesis of America. A number of players, among them Alex Rodriguez, Ryan Braun, and Nelson Cruz, were suspended from baseball for a noteworthy number of games due to their use of PEDs. Then there is the long history of allegations concerning Lance Armstrong, seven-time Tour de France champion, finally confirmed by Armstrong in 2013 after nearly a decade of denials. Armstrong forfeited all seven of his titles.

Pete Rose, one of the hardest-working ball players ever to play professionally, is permanently banned from baseball due to his proclivities toward gambling. He played twenty-three seasons, managed the last two while he played, and then managed an additional three years. He made seventeen All-Star appearances. He remains the all-time leader in base hits (4,256) and games played (3,562). Yet he is banned from ever being recognized by the Hall of Fame, due to the fact he gambled on games in which he either played or coached. Rose admits he gambled on the Reds, but claims never to have bet against them.

Players also damage the integrity of their games through their personal behavior. Many players have ended their careers by getting caught up in drugs or alcohol. Like any other segment of the population, some percentage of athletes get wrapped up in criminal activity of one kind or another. Young players often have too much money and too much time on their hands, leading to wrong choices that eventually lead to the wrong kinds of publicity or exposure. Some athletes reach the point of thinking they are so much larger than life that they can get away with murder. Former New England Patriot tight end Aaron Hernandez, twenty-four years old, found himself indicted and convicted for murder in 2014, and sentenced to life in prison.

Football suffered a serious black eye throughout the 2014–15 season due to the behavior of its players. After the news became public that Ray Rice, running back with the Baltimore Ravens, had assaulted his fiancé, the NFL, under the direction of Commissioner Roger Goodell, suspended Rice for two games. The news of the slap on the hand brought protests from women's groups and organizations supporting victims of domestic abuse. Eventually, the commissioner had to issue an apology. "My disciplinary decision led the public to question our sincerity, our commitment and whether we understood the toll that domestic violence inflicts on so many families," Goodell said in a letter to team owners. "I take responsibility both for the decision and for ensuring that our actions in the future properly reflect our values. I didn't get it right. Simply put, we have to do better. And we will."[52] Goodell's office issued new guidelines regarding discipline in cases of domestic abuse. In the midst of all this NFL drama, the elevator video, capturing some of the full force of Rice's assault of his fiancé, became public. In the wake of its release, the NFL suspended Rice indefinitely, and the Baltimore Ravens released him.

Other cases plagued the NFL throughout the year; one of the more visible of these involved Adrian Peterson, running back for the Minnesota Vikings. Peterson faced charges when he beat his four-year-old son with a switch. Peterson, while allowed to play in the wake of the initial charges, also finally faced indefinite suspension. In the wake of the 2014–15 NFL season, the sports world faced increased public scrutiny. The public now expects accountability. To this point, most major sports leagues, but especially the NFL, NBA, NHL, and MLB, have done little to deal appropriately with the domestic violence so often associated with their sports. As the hoopla surrounding defensive end Greg Hardy and the release of pictures of his battered girlfriend the next football season indicates, the NFL still lacks a substantial ability to respond until pressed to do so.

Joseph Price points out that ethics in sports is also connected to the "values embedded in its rituals and underlying its social relationships." Here he points especially to the values of "equality, freedom, and a rugged sense of individualism."[53] Of course, one could mention others as well: the values of hard work, discipline, and especially the benefits associated with winning and achieving success. These are all values that are represented in significant ways throughout American sports; they are also one other way that sports reflects culture, as these particular values have long permeated and defined the American way of life. As Carlyle Marney, an old Southern Baptist preacher, once put it so well, Americans are addicted to an ethical approach to life that might be described as "salvation by successing."[54] In this kind of culture, particularly in American male sports culture, success, always accompanied by things like wealth, strength, and power, often becomes the measure of a man.

EXPERIENCE

In the long history of sports in America, religious experience has been closely associated with athletics. Amos Alonzo Stagg transformed football when he joined the University of Chicago in 1890. Greatly affected by his participation in the YMCA, Stagg originally planned on becoming a minister. When his former professor of biblical literature at Yale became president of the University of Chicago and offered him an appointment as coach and director of physical culture, Stagg made his ministry college football. Stagg's friend James Naismith, the man credited with inventing basketball, and a Presbyterian minister, also brought his religious inclinations to his experience as an athlete. Both Naismith and Stagg gave us the pregame prayer.[55] The examples are legion, right down to contemporary football and baseball players who pray openly on the field during or following a game, and Tim Tebow, who etched Bible verses into his eye-black.

Yet experiencing sports religiously is meant differently here. Joseph Price quotes David Chidester's essay, "The Church of Baseball," to talk about how many fans enjoy "extraordinary moments of ecstasy and enthusiasm, of revelation and inspiration" when they watch sporting events.[56] In 2006, David Foster Wallace wrote for the *New York Times* an article entitled "Federer as Religious Experience," which captures this sentiment:

Federer is of this type—a type that one could call genius, or mutant, or avatar. He is never hurried or off-balance. The approaching ball hangs, for him, a split-second longer than it ought to. His movements are lithe rather than athletic. Like Ali, Jordan, Maradona, and Gretzky, he seems both less and more substantial than the men he faces. Particularly in the all-white that Wimbledon enjoys getting away with still requiring, he looks like what he may well (I think) be: a creature whose body is both flesh and, somehow, light. Genius is not replicable. Inspiration, though, is contagious, and multiform—and even just to see, close up, power and aggression made vulnerable to beauty is to feel inspired and (in a fleeting, mortal way) reconciled.[57]

Fans, just by watching sports, getting caught up in it when the perfect double play is completed or an impossible golf shot is pulled off beautifully, can be transported for a moment to some other realm. Psychologists are reaching generally the same conclusion, as evidenced in Nigel Barber's conclusion that "sports spectatorship is a transformative experience through which fans escape their humdrum lives, just as religious experiences help the faithful to transcend their everyday existence."[58]

Jordi Xifra once described how the soccer club Barcelona FC "bestows social energy" on its fan base that helps the fans meet "the need for community belonging" and provides for them a measure of "emotional unity."[59] An article appearing in June 2014 described how, for Latino/a fans, soccer was "virtually a religious experience."[60] The experience of millions watching the delayed transmission of the Olympics on American televisions in 2012 and 2014, when nearly all fans in the United States already knew the outcome, illustrates the power attached to the need to see things for themselves, to experience it personally. Sport certainly can provide a powerful, religious-like experience for its fans.

For the players, the experience is embodied religious experience. It has to do with the physicality of performance, of feeling mind and body work together in some action that reaches excellence or near perfection. When it does happen, the experience can produce a high, a sense of radical transcendence, of feeling as if one has reached another plane of existence, a moment of incredible clarity and self-awareness. This might be described, in the terms William James used to describe religious experience, as ineffability (an indescribable experience) or as *noesis* (an experience of having one's outlook changed or transformed by an event).[61] Scholars from both scientific and religious perspectives are beginning to explore the meaning of embodiment for sport (and for religion).[62] In doing so, they are also siding with Merleau-Ponty concerning the significance of "embodied consciousness," and challenging the old Cartesian assumptions discussed in chapter 1.

Klaus V. Meier has analyzed the significance of this shift in understanding for sports. For Meier, it is important to understand that "the imposition of meaning is not caused by a universal constituting consciousness, but rather by bodily experience." The body is "a self-transcending subject." By engaging "with the world it appropriates centres of meaning which go beyond and transform it."[63] The world is a lived rather than objective experience. This shifts the purpose of human endeavor from, in Cartesian terms, the need to live as a spiritual thinking essence to, in phenomenological terms, an intention to live as a fully embodied being-in-the-world. If it is true that meaning itself arises "through the body's power of expression," then sport provides "opportunities for the creation of new worlds and the structuring of previous perceptions."

> Totally immersed in sport, man formulates and extends his powers, sense of self, and personal expression. The unfolding of meaningful activities unfolds man; through instances of dynamic individuation and self-discovery, man creates and affirms himself in sport. . . . New awareness, self-perceptions, and meanings are elicited during participation in sport situations. . . . The participant knows and experiences his body, and therefore himself, as he is, immediately and directly through concrete intermingling with the world in projects which express his unique being.[64]

This shift in human understanding of mind and body makes it possible to understand what athletes actually experience at the highest level of competition. They interact with the world around them, in the environment of the court, the rink, the baseball field, or the football field, and the body becomes a work of art perfectly blended with its surroundings, at one with the world in ways that teach heightened self-awareness. Sport becomes a "celebration" of women and men as "open and expressive embodied" beings and it enables an experience of that reality that most can describe only in religious terms, as spiritually empowering.[65]

In the nineteenth century, a movement now titled "Muscular Christianity" developed in Great Britain and spread across the pond. The movement stressed both health and "manliness." The heritage of the movement connected the physicality of sports specifically to the male experience. Church leaders underlined physical exercise for men, the creation of healthy bodies competing in a variety of sporting contests to develop appropriate character building among men. These emphases spawned the development of national parks and playgrounds, and organizations like the YMCA and the Boy Scouts. The movement sought to counter the "overfeminization" of culture in both Britain and the United States.

Theodore Roosevelt became a staunch advocate of the movement. With the influence of Roosevelt and many church leaders, Muscular Christianity connected Christianity with an evangelical promotion of sports, mostly for men. These evangelicals argued the bodies of women were made to produce children and to take care of the home.[66] Twentieth-century versions of Muscular Christianity flourished in a variety of ways. In 1976, Frank DeFord of *Sports Illustrated* referred to the movement as "Sportianity" and called the movement to account for its uncritical love of sports, overlooking steroids, cheating, recruitment violations, and the like. Sportianity, he concluded is "more devoted to exploiting sport than serving it."[67]

Today an awareness of the importance of embodiment in both sports and religion has led to feminist critiques of gender constructions as related to sport.[68] Professional sports remains a field dominated by men. Some inroads are finally appearing, such as when in August 2014 the NBA San Antonio Spurs hired Becky Hammon, a sixteen-year veteran of the WNBA, as an active, heavily involved assistant coach. In July 2015, the NFL Arizona Cardinals announced they had hired a woman assistant coach, Jennifer Welter, who played ten seasons with the Dallas Diamonds of the Women's Football Alliance, to coach inside linebackers during training camp and preseason on an "internship" basis. Welter also became the first woman to play in a men's professional game with the Texas Revolution of the Indoor Football League. Coaching as an assistant, even if only a term appointment, with an NFL franchise represents another groundbreaking move for women in professional sports. The NFL made another important move in June 2015 when it announced the hiring of Sarah Thomas, previously a Conference USA official for football games, as the first woman among the 122 NFL officials. She is a full-time member of Pete Morelli's NFL crew and began officiating games during the 2015 season.

Yet women's sports remain undervalued and too easily dismissed. Though a professional women's basketball league has survived, women's soccer and baseball leagues have both failed. Attempts to create viable women's football have met with insuperable challenges as well, including an attempt at a Lingerie Football League, rebranded today as the Legends Football League.[69] Where women do play sports, North American culture is more consumed with focusing on the heterosexual appeal of female athletes, or lack thereof, than on their athletic abilities or accomplishments. There are online lists with such titles as "100 Hottest Female Athletes of All Times."[70] Helen Lenskyj points out that the Women's National Basketball Association "was reported to have held 'beauty sessions' during its 2008 rookie orientation."[71] Media evaluate men by their performance, and women by their appearance. Women's athleticism, their experience in their bodies *as athletes*, is rarely adequately covered.

Media emphasis on heteronormativity, and appropriate roles for the genders, has also contributed to lesbian and gay invisibility in the world of sports.[72] Penn State University officials protected two different forms of abusive power operating in their sports programs. Lenskyj stressed that even though the full details of the Jerry Sandusky mess at Penn State were duly reported, media remained silent about the fact that Rene Portland, head women's basketball coach, had a "no drinking, no drugs, no lesbians" policy her entire career at Penn State (1980–2007). Even though her policy had been well known, both by the university community and the media, silence reigned until she was finally dismissed in 2007, due to a discrimination lawsuit.[73]

Coverage of NBA player Jason Collins's public coming out and the drafting of gay football player Michael Sam by the St. Louis Rams held some promise in counteracting heteronormativity in the media, at least for gay males. Yet Michael Sam failed to hang on in the NFL when both the Rams and Cowboys released him. Sam signed a two-year deal with the Montreal Alouettes of the Canadian Football League in May 2015. He left camp the day before the first preseason game for personal reasons that have never been clearly articulated. He returned briefly, played in one game on August 7, 2015, and then left the team, citing concerns for his mental health following a "difficult" twelve-month period in professional football.

The underlying stereotype of sports, due to traditional understandings of masculinity in sport, is that all female athletes are lesbians. Because of this, advocacy efforts on the part of lesbian athletes, like Billie Jean King and Martina Navratilova (tennis), Sheryl Swoops and Brittany Griner (Women's National Basketball Association), and Megan Rapinoe (US Women's Soccer National Team), are rendered nearly invisible. Inappropriate and discriminatory gender perceptions common to the gendered hierarchical assumptions found among the media abound, related to both heterosexual females and lesbians, not to mention transgendered persons. Feminist studies, which consistently analyze media constructions of women's participation in sports, call for a deeper understanding of the meanings associated with an active feminine embodiment in sport.

Sexism pervades even when we talk about homosexuality and the transgendered. The media attention accompanying Bruce Jenner's transition to Caitlin Jenner itself illustrates the point (for example, few are paying much attention to the transition of Chastity Bono to Chaz Bono). Further, the increasing interest and tolerance in transgendered rights and experience among the older generations of Americans, known for homophobia and heterosexism, can legitimately be connected to the spokesperson and model Caitlin Jenner, in that she is revered first as the all-American athlete Bruce Jenner, a genuine "man's man"—which does not disappear even after transition.

INSTITUTIONS

The various professional leagues define the societal presence of sports in America. As indicated in a number of ways in this chapter, these leagues both represent and promote society's values and, on rare occasions, prophetically push society to new understandings. Each league creates its own image and exerts considerable control in marketing and maintaining that image. Each seeks to secure the trust and confidence of the American people. Most leagues find some way in championship games or series, in addition to the traditional singing of the national anthem, to make an appeal to patriotism or the importance of honoring military sacrifice for the nation (using F-16 flyovers, for example).

The stadiums and fields across the nation feature effective use of architecture and landscape to fit their surroundings, yet also to provide testimony to the grand nature of the events they host. There is a particular reverence accorded the national heritage represented in the older ballparks like Fenway Park (1912) and Wrigley Field (1914) for baseball and even Soldier Field (1924) for football. These stadiums are institutions in sport, but they also constitute for many fans an important aspect of the materiality contained within religious experience. When fans gather in any of the stadiums or arenas for professional or college games, the atmosphere is electric, and the crowd, even when rooting for different teams, is seemingly transformed and brought into full communion with one another, often through a variety of rituals. For home team fans, additional connections with one another are assured as the organist strikes up "We Will Rock You," by Queen or "Na Hey (Kiss Him Goodbye)" by Steam. The stadiums bind the social fabric of fandom together and enable them to identify, not only with their teams, but also with each other and with the values associated with the major sports in America.

Finally, fans often make their ritualistic pilgrimages to their favorite Hall of Fame, whether in Toronto (NHL), Cooperstown, New York (MLB), Springfield, Massachusetts (NBA), or Canton, Ohio (NFL). The Halls provide a complete and complex history, usually interwoven with the major events and social issues associated with the American past, whether connected to the Great Depression and poverty, war, politics, or race relations. They help the fan fully integrate sports with American culture, usually without being accompanied by any form of acute critical sensibility. The history simply is. The Hall connects them to it, complete with the greatness of the game and its players, and a feeling that it is all possible only in America. For most visitors, the various Halls evoke a sense of awe and wonder as fans find themselves somehow spiritually at home in the midst of the holy material found in those chapels.

Players have their own experiences of sports arenas. They are the cathedrals within which players are the focus of attention. However, for the athletes, perhaps the most consecrated social location in these cathedrals is the locker room. It is the sacred space of refuge, a sanctuary away from fans and reporters (except for specified time periods). Since locker rooms are only for the initiated, they become a haven where players can be themselves fully and freely, a place where they come clean with one another. It is the only real space available to them. The genuine communion of the saints takes place there. In the locker room, players become bound to one another for life through shared tears in the wake of defeat, moments of inspiration provided by words uttered by coaches and captains, and of times of exuberance while celebrating victories and dousing one another with champagne. In locker rooms players gain a complete sense of being part of something larger than themselves.

Locker rooms come with their own cultures. In the arena, games are being played; people put on their best game faces, and the game is on. In the locker room, there are no games; all is known for exactly what it is. Naked butts abound. Nothing remains hidden. When a player does not meet the expectations associated with this culture, the player has to make an adjustment to the "real" world of the whole.

The well-publicized harassment of Jonathan Martin by Richie Incognito on the Miami Dolphins football team raises new questions about locker rooms. Martin did not fit the culture of the Dolphins locker room. He seemed "soft." The coaches asked Incognito to work on him, to get him to "man-up." Incognito's onslaught of harassment and insults did not work; Martin left the team and went home. When media uncovered what happened, and the NFL launched an investigation, the responses were telling. Media and the public, like the players, had difficulty making sense of a football player who wouldn't fight back.

Players believe what happens in the locker room stays in the locker room. This is why the response of some athletes to the imbroglio was that it should have stayed private. It was a team matter. The fact that such harassment in the workplace is illegal is irrelevant in the testosterone world of the NFL. The NFL demands toughness of all its players. Either get with the program or leave. Even teammates who might have sympathized with Martin and had their own reasons for criticizing Incognito were prone to feel that Martin's actions violated not only the inner sanctum of the locker room but the culture of football itself.

MATERIALITY

The sports world is filled with items that excite the five senses and create a visceral connection that ignites the experience of the fan. This is especially true when one visits the Halls, but it is palpable when one catches a foul ball at the ballpark, or slaps the hand of an NBA player as he makes his way in or out of the tunnel, or makes contact with the professional golfer as she or he walks to the scoring tent after a round. The Halls specialize in the relics, the personal belongings of the saints and the tangible memorials of both players and teams venerated by all who know anything about the circumstances of their significance.

The world of sports memorabilia has become a big business in the United States. Family-owned stores specialize in baseball cards, autographs, and actual pieces of uniforms players wore or equipment they used in games. Fans also buy official apparel new off the shelves and wear it faithfully to games or even to work. Sporting authorities and those who play at their game's highest levels somehow seem to possess the ability to endow material goods with transcendent meaning. Occasionally, that meaning is measurable for a time in exorbitant economic fashion, as when Mark McGwire's seventieth home-run ball sold for $3,005,000 or Honus Wagner's baseball card delivered $2.3 million. The value does not always hold up. McGwire's ball, since the steroid scandal, is worth considerably less today, while Wagner's card continues to escalate in value.

Captured in the ability of material objects to transport those who encounter them to a different place, to claim some toehold of power over their psyche or alter somehow their perception of the world around them, is a snapshot of the religious power contained in sports. Whether sport is truly a religion or not will continue to be debated by scholars of religion, sports, sociology, and anthropology for decades to come. However, few of those analyzing the question will deny that many people, fans and athletes alike, are affected, even formed, by sports, resulting in passion, practice, commitment, and community that mightily resemble or surpass the effectiveness of traditional religions.

6

Science and Technology

All the topics covered in this book are complex, but perhaps none more so than science and technology. Where does one begin? Where do we end? We can't cover it all. We could start with the discovery of fire and move on from there. But that would make for a rather long story. Certainly the turn from magic to science in the history of human understanding is relevant for a discussion like this one. The work of Copernicus and Galileo was far ahead of their time. For the religious during those days, the unknown or mysterious nearly always connected with the Divine. When those contributing to the development of science began to uncover natural secrets, the religious authorities could get rather defensive.

The origin of the word "science," or *scientia*, is connected with the concept of knowledge. Science is the world of ideas, of theoretical knowledge. Technology is its application, where science is made purposeful. Both have a long history, well before the scientific revolution or the Enlightenment.[1] As long as science is mostly or purely theoretical, its truths can be ignored by any who have other understandings. But when science is applied and clearly demonstrates its truths through its applications, those truths can no longer be denied without being accompanied by profound experiences of cognitive dissonance. One could deny that people can fly until the Wright brothers broke through human denial at Kitty Hawk. No one at the time could have accurately imagined the future that resulted from that one act, including the capability to control drones, some armed with all manner of new-weapon technologies.

Science and technology are both inevitably connected to progress. The principle of progress is such that in order to keep up with our own conditions in the present, we are compelled to move forward. We have to work harder and move faster. There is no standing still. To stand still is to die. As Woodrow Wilson put it in a 1912 campaign speech, "We shall have to run, not until we are out of breath, but until we have caught up with our own conditions, before we shall be where we were when we started. . . . And we should have to run twice as fast as any rational program I have seen in order to get anywhere else. I am, therefore, forced to be a progressive, if for no other reason, because we have not kept up with our changes of conditions."[2]

It is not just knowing something or inventing something that is the point. These two serve some other thing, which is generally progress. To continue to be human is to progress—or so most of us believe. To maintain one's humanity necessitates progress. Science and technology provide the means to that end. Yet not all progress is equal.

What happens when human beings develop the means to do things, but the means are far ahead of the ability of a human moral compass to determine whether such things *ought* to be done? Of course that is a religious question, the legitimacy of which some would deny. Is there a realm of knowledge that should be off-limits for human beings? The perception of sin or the "fall of humanity" found in the Western religious traditions is often tied to understanding what happens when human beings try to acquire knowledge about, or gain control over, things that go beyond the knowledge or dominion the Divine has intentionally given to us. What happens when human beings bite the apple or build the tower?

In one sense, technology addresses human limitations posed by human conditions. When one loses an arm or a leg, technology can through prosthetics restore at least a semblance of what was lost. Much of what we seek through both science and technology has to do with our desire to restore a sense of normalcy, or at least what we perceive to be normal. Perhaps that is why Prozac and Viagra are two of the world's most popular drugs today. Of course, unintended consequences often accompany the creation of semblances. Medicine calls such things "side effects."

Why does technology go beyond what is necessary to restore the lost? For example, why must human beings go to the moon, when we are creatures of the earth? John F. Kennedy considered that question on September 12, 1962:

We set sail on this new sea because there is new knowledge to be gained, and new rights to be won, and they must be won and used for the progress of all people. For space science, like nuclear science and all technology, has no conscience of its own. Whether it will become a force for good or ill depends on man, and only if the United States occupies a position of pre-eminence. . . . Why choose this as our goal? And they may well ask why climb the highest mountain? . . . We choose to go to the moon in this decade and do the other things, not because they are easy, but because they are hard, because that goal will serve to organize and measure the best of our energies and skills, because that challenge is one that we are willing to accept, one we are unwilling to postpone, and one which we intend to win.[3]

Kennedy assumes human beings are meant to do seemingly impossible things. Technology, fully developed, will serve both progress and the human condition. Kennedy does not have much doubt about that. In the middle of the Cold War, for him, Americans and not the Russians will be the ones to do it right, and the ones who will win. Therefore, Americans must do it. While his perspective in these matters might properly be disputed, one of his conclusions cannot. Technology definitely has no conscience of its own.

There are some people, of course, often branded as Luddites, who have doubted much good can come from further technological innovation. The main concern for Luddites originated not necessarily from a disdain for technology (many were machine operators) but, rather, from a fear that the development of new and better machines would displace them. Richard Conniff points out that Luddites feared not technology but the implications new technologies brought for the human condition. Luddites asked, "What does technology do to our humanity?" For them, technology was not automatically bad; human beings could always live with technology—so long as they were able to understand its relationship with the values associated with what it means to be human.[4]

Many think the Amish oppose technology. Actually, they are more like the original Luddites. Where most Americans assume any new technology is inherently a good thing, the Amish question whether that is indeed the case. As historian Donald Kraybill has put it, "They're more cautious—more suspicious—wondering is this going to be helpful or is it going to be detrimental. Is it going to bolster our life together, as a community, or is it going to somehow tear it down?"[5]

Such questions are not readily on the moral radar of most Americans today as we tweet, e-mail, or use our smart phones to navigate our worlds. We like our technology. Some joke that even the Luddites, some of whom appear to use the latest in viruses to defend their spaces, are radically dependent upon it. As one Internet site put it, "Luddite invents machine to destroy technology quicker."[6] In fact, the tendrils of technology are so far-reaching in our personal and public lives that their force seems omnipotent, omnipresent, and omniscient. Due to our cultural dependency on technologies, we often worship at this altar and surrender to its salvific ability to play the role of God for our lives.

Historian David Noble has shown how religious convictions have driven cultural developments in science and technology for more than a thousand years. In the ninth century, theologian and Neoplatonic philosopher John Scotus Erigena argued that human cultivation of the mechanical arts served both to create human "links with the Divine" and to provide a "means of salvation." His argument led to efforts to extend humanity's sovereignty over the rest of creation. Science and technology promised a return to the garden of Eden, when Adam possessed knowledge concerning everything. Nature contained the divine secrets. If human beings could understand nature, they could understand divinity itself. The goal, however, has always surpassed a desire simply to understand God; it rests also in the development of human perfection. Noble's book *The Religion of Technology* explored four examples of what he called "technologies of transcendence," looking closely at contemporary work in nuclear technology, space exploration, genetics, and artificial intelligence.[7]

Each of these explorations has hoped to develop new horizons, to free human beings to transcend the historical and contemporary limitations imposed upon them. This is why President Richard Nixon declared, in the wake of Apollo 11's return from the moon, "This is the greatest week since the beginning of the world, the Creation."[8] Many people working in artificial intelligence today believe the day is not too distant when the content of the human brain can actually be downloaded; a literal "eternal life" seems just around the corner.[9] The implications of successfully mapping human DNA (the Human Genome Project was completed in 2003) promise even more. Scientific developments building on these maps now aspire to the ability to erase any defects associated with the human condition itself—in essence an attempt to master characteristics historically attributed, according to more traditional expressions of religion, only to "God the Creator."[10]

Few have understood this contemporary cultural or contemporary human tendency more than tech guru Steve Jobs, who, with the force of a divine call, dedicated his life to matching technology with a hope to empower human ability. As Jeff Goodell puts it, "more than anyone else on the planet, [Steve Jobs was] responsible for fusing the human realm with the digital, for giving us the ability to encode our deepest desires and most intimate thoughts with the touch of a finger."[11] If one imagines Michelangelo's vision of the outstretched human finger coming into contact with the finger of God, one gets the general idea. The power of having all one's songs at hand, or a computer being available in a handheld smartphone, exceed all expectations of what might be possible even just a few years ago.

Steven Paul Jobs was born on February 24, 1955, into a seemingly untenable situation.[12] His mother, Joanne Schieble, a graduate student at the University of Wisconsin, developed a relationship with a Syrian student named Abdul Fattah Jandali. Her father's strong disapproval of the resulting pregnancy led

Schieble to place the baby for adoption with a couple in San Francisco, Paul and Clara Jobs.[13] Steve Jobs had a troubled, moody, and rather self-absorbed childhood. Through a couple of moves, Jobs ended up in the emerging Silicon Valley.

At age fourteen he met Steve Wozniak ("Woz"). Though Woz was five years older, he and Jobs combined computing and a geeky sense of humor to enable a lasting collaboration. At seventeen Jobs also connected with Chrisann Brennan, began a relationship, and attempted to educate her about the value of LSD and primal-scream therapy. When he graduated from high school, he spent a wild summer in a mountain cabin with Chrisann. Jobs assumed a feast-or-famine approach to life. He pushed all kinds of limits to satisfy his insatiable desire to know and experience all things. Leaving Chrisann behind, Jobs enrolled in Reed College. "After six months, I couldn't see the value in it," he recalled. "I had no idea what I wanted to do with my life and no idea how college was going to help me figure it out. And here I was spending all of the money my parents had saved their entire life. So I decided to drop out and trust that it would all work out OK."[1]

The birth of Apple came after Jobs took a brief sojourn to India. The company began as the Homebrew Computer Club, where Jobs and Woz built their first computer in his parents' garage. Jobs came up with the name "apple" because, on his return from India, he had stopped to visit an Oregon apple farm. He provided the vision for the company and saw a future for personal computing that few imagined at the time. Ironically, Apple's success brought out the worst in Jobs. He had reconnected with Chrisann Brennan. When she became pregnant, "Jobs refused to provide her with any financial help, yet he was violently opposed to her giving the baby up for adoption and had his friends pressure her not to have an abortion."[15] After Lisa's birth, a DNA test confirmed his paternity. Jobs ignored both Chrisann and Lisa.

He demonstrated the same lack of sensitivity and responsibility at the office. Managers at the company feared his tendency to follow his impulses. Jobs just wanted to build an "insanely great" machine.[16] He never thought much about the cost that might be involved to produce it. With Jobs, passion meant everything. Debi Coleman, a member of his development team in the early 1980s, described him as a kind of Rasputin: "You did the impossible because you didn't realize it was impossible."[17] When management at Apple drug its feet, Jobs simply put together his own team, stole ideas existing elsewhere in the valley, added his unlimited imagination, and assembled the Macintosh.

Previous personal computers, like the one released by Adam Osbourne in 1981, seemed adequate. But adequate was not enough. Jobs wanted beauty, perfection, and transcendence. As Hertzfield put it, he wanted to do "the greatest thing possible, or even a little greater." Jobs cared little about the money, or the competition. He wanted perfection.[18] The Macintosh provided the world's first example of WYSIWYG ("What you see is what you get") in personal computing especially as it applied to both a graphical user interface and to word processing. The result was revolutionary.

After the Mac's debut, Jobs pushed Woz out. Riding a rocket, Jobs knew enough to realize he needed some expert help. He sought out John Sculley, the CEO of Pepsi and recruited him to run Apple. In the end, Jobs simply couldn't yield to expertise. The board chose to side with Sculley. That quickly, Apple cut Jobs out. The ordeal forced a bit of soul searching, dealing both with his original familial abandonment and now the betrayal perpetrated by his personally created Apple family. During this period, Steve Jobs embarked on his own vision quest of sorts. He traveled in Italy and the Soviet Union. He contacted his biological mother and met a sister, Mona Simpson, whom he did not know he had. He used the time to get to know his daughter Lisa.

Within two years, Jobs developed a new corporate venture with every intention of rising from the ashes like the mythical phoenix. He created NeXT. He hoped to build the perfect computer that would represent "his revenge on the bozos at Apple who had tossed him out."[19] Typical of Jobs, his drive for perfection led him to believe he could design a computer that would play music even more beautifully than any human could—a proposition Joan Baez found repugnant when Jobs pitched it to her in her home. While she did not say it aloud, she found herself thinking, "How could you defile music like that?"[20] For Jobs, however, it only made sense—technology had to make everything better. To think otherwise would be nothing short of sacrilegious. NeXT became an epic failure.

Biographers mark two events as the reasons Jobs overcame his tendencies to wallow in bitterness. First, he met and fell in love with Laurene Powell. The relationship and resulting family life brought new stability and maturity to his life. The second shift in Jobs's demeanor accompanied his connection to Pixar. He bought the company in 1986 from George Lucas for a mere five million dollars. After developing an animation studio, he turned to Disney Studios and made a deal for distribution. Eventually, *Toy Story* emerged, Pixar went public, and Jobs had turned his five-million-dollar investment into a billion-dollar addition to his personal fortune. Jobs accomplished with Pixar what he had failed to do with NeXT; he epitomized the classic example of the "comeback kid." Both corporate and creative communities touted his virtuosity all over again.

Around 1996, Jobs convinced Apple's leadership to buy NeXT's software for $400 million and use it to build a new operating system, which eventually became OS X. In the process, Apple named Jobs an "informal adviser."

Soon the board hired him to reassume leadership of the company. As Jeff Goodell tells the story, Jobs "halted Apple's disastrous decision to allow other computers to clone Macintosh's operating system, . . . went humbly to Bill Gates and struck a deal to keep Microsoft software running on the Mac . . . and unleashed a talented designer named Jonathan Ive, giving him free rein to build great computers."[21] Jobs's visionary interest in creating other electronic gadgets added the icing. Apple was back.

In 2003, Jobs learned he had pancreatic cancer. Following the pattern of a lifetime, Jobs worked as a mode of catharsis, ever reaching toward perfection. The iPhone and the iPad both followed his cancer diagnosis. Although Jobs died at the young age of fifty-six, he lived longer than he thought he might. Living on a borrowed clock, he used the unexpected time "to complete the spiritual journey he had begun as a kid in the apricot orchards of Silicon Valley." While he will long "be remembered as the man who brought the human touch to our digital devices," perhaps more importantly, in the end, he lived long enough to bring "the human touch to Steve Jobs."[22] Jobs biographer Walter Isaacson opines, "The saga of Steve Jobs is the Silicon Valley creation myth writ large: launching a startup in his parents' garage and building it into the world's most valuable company. He didn't invent many things outright, but he was a master at putting together ideas, art, and technology in ways that invented the future."[23]

Consumer behaviorists and marketing experts Russell Belk and Gülnur Tumbat argue that the community of Mac users has a sacred devotion to the company's products and the aesthetic they exude. After a series of interviews with Mac users, Belk and Tumbat dubbed this phenomenon "the Cult of Macintosh." Belk writes, "This religion is based on an origin myth for Apple Computer, heroic and savior legends surrounding . . . Steve Jobs, the devout faith of its follower congregation, their belief in the righteousness of the Macintosh, the existence of one or more Satanic opponents, Mac believers proselytizing and converting nonbelievers, and the hope among cult members that salvation can be achieved by transcending corporate capitalism."[24]

The "cult of Mac" operates religiously by advancing beliefs about Apple, the Mac operating system, and subsequent devices that have helped millions of consumers understand themselves and the world around them through the use of technology. Throngs of loyal followers have also nearly deified Steve Jobs. Taken to an extreme within Apple's "corporate mythology," Jobs has been portrayed not only as a "savior" of the corporate brand, but also as a creative deity who embodied the power (literally and figuratively) both to create and to destroy.[25]

Jobs produced the complete experience for the consumer because, as he put it, "customers don't know what they want until we've shown them."[26] He understood himself as building upon everything that had gone before, but making an undeniable contribution in the process. "It's a wonderful, ecstatic feeling to create something that puts it back in the pool of human experience and knowledge."[27] For Jobs, like the Edisons and Fords before him, satisfaction lay in the inevitable act of progress, moving technology and the human race forward. He built "for the masses" in a way that left no room for error. He wanted to provide for consumers "a controlled experience" they could completely rely upon.[28]

Jobs believed a properly designed computer emerged only when hardware and software were inextricably bound to and created for one another ("closed source"). Only this kind of computer could multiply the efficiency of the human mind.[29] Any other approach was heretical, because it sacrificed functionality to work across platforms. Jobs could not brook such sacrifices. The open-source approach of either IBM or Microsoft, according to Jobs, placed profits above creating the perfect human experience and thereby represented evil incarnate. The battle Apple set up with both enterprises, driven by a dogmatic devotion to perfection through a closed source approach, represented religious wars at their worst. The orthodoxy of Apple must fight all heretical and heterodox competitors; the company has been very successful in using the "ecclesiastical courts" in defending the faith. If anyone doubts that, just ask Samsung.[30]

The "apple" Jobs offered was no forbidden fruit, or alien intrusion, but rather represented the true source of knowledge, where there would be a complete compatibility, a mutuality and reciprocity, between the demand of human need and the supply of the machine's provision. The human and machine could become one, with the iPod , iPhone, iPad, Apple Watch, and other devices providing intuitive experiences anyone—even a young child—could enjoy and share. Jobs and his Apple could provide all the answers because, in his view, nobody understood the questions better than he did. A writer for *The Guardian* declared:

> Someone once said that one of the advantages of religion is that it offers security in return for obedience. This point was not lost on the late Steve Jobs, the co-founder, savior and high priest of Apple. And it led Umberto Eco, in an essay published in the 1980s, to describe the Apple Mac as a Catholic machine, in contrast to the IBM PC, which Eco characterised as a Protestant device. His reasoning was that the Mac freed its users/believers from the need to make decisions. All they had to do to find salvation was to obey the Apple way. All the important choices, including whether a mouse should have one button or two, had been made for them, whereas the poor wretches who had to use a PC had, like the Calvinists of yore, to make their own salvation: installing expansion cards, anti-virus software, wrestling with incompatible peripherals and so on.[31]

While Steve Jobs's life has ended, his legacy has changed the landscape. He made technology serviceable as an effortless and efficient extension of human needs and desires. In the pantheon of science and technology, Jobs is one of the most revered of saints, because he made the spirituality of technology accessible to all. In a Martin Buber kind of way, Jobs shifted technology from the "self and the other" to the "I and Thou" modality. In the I-Thou relationship, human beings are aware of each other as being interconnected and unified in their existence, not perceiving each other as separate and isolated, but rather being engaged and involved in each other's whole being.[32]

We are connected to our technology in a way that makes us nearly one with it as well. We are now evolved to the point where we are not just I-Thou, but are also iMac, iPod, iTunes, iMovie, iPhone, or iPad. Many see technology as a path to a more perfect self, or a self that matters more with it or through it than without it. We believe in our technology and everything connected with it. We become doctrinally committed, even when it doesn't make sense to do so. Above all, we believe that technology helps us evolve.

MYTHOLOGY

Those captivated by the doctrine of progress seek human perfectibility in every aspect of their lives. They believe in a mythology that life is what you make of it (we become what we imagine ourselves to be), based on both discernment and will—the choices each of us makes. This progress can also be expressed on its flip side with the degradation of the quality of human life, a situation where we reap what we sow (as in Margaret Atwood's *MaddAddam* trilogy). Such themes are amply evident in contemporary science fiction films and books.

Today's scientists often cite science fiction, particularly the *Star Trek* phenomenon, as inspiration for their careers. Mae Jemison, the first African American female astronaut in space, found inspiration in the show's diverse crew, making it seem possible for her to do things she had never imagined. "I think the other thing that 'Star Trek' did was it basically said that humanity would make it through all of the conflicts and catastrophes that we were facing." Jemison is among many who see their lives through the lens of creating science fact from the world of science fiction.[33] As Stephen Hawking put it, "Science fiction . . . is not only good fun but it also serves a serious purpose, that of expanding the human imagination. We may not yet be able to boldly go where no man (or woman) has gone before, but at least we can do it in the mind."[34]

Moving beyond science fiction, the creators of speculative fiction typically envision a world or civilization arising after disasters such as nuclear warfare, pandemic, extraterrestrial attack, extinction level event, cybernetic revolt, technological singularity, dysgenics (biological degeneration), supernatural phenomena, divine judgment, climate change, or absolute resource depletion. The time frame may be immediately after a catastrophe, focusing on the travails or psychology of survivors, or considerably later, often including the theme that the existence of precatastrophe civilization has been forgotten (or romanticized/mythologized). For instance, postapocalyptic stories often take place in an agrarian, nontechnological future world, or a world where only scattered elements of technology remain. There is a considerable degree of blurring between this form of science fiction and that dealing with dystopian social orders or disastrous visions of human nature.

A prime example of a speculative fiction film is *Prometheus* (2012). Envisioned by director Ridley Scott as a prequel to his classic film *Alien* (1979), the film raises provocative concerns about the rise and fall of the human race in quintessentially cosmic terms. Set in the year 2093, after identical ancient inscriptions are discovered at various archeological sites scattered across Earth, suggesting that extraterrestrials contacted—and possibly even created—humanity, the story follows the crew of the spacecraft *USCSS Prometheus* as they venture out in space to find these alien predecessors. The ship's inventor, tech tycoon Sir Peter Weyland, launched the state-of-the-art starship in 2091. Once the team of explorers realizes that these would-be "makers" actually intend to destroy humankind, they must fight a terrifying battle to save the Earth from alien extermination. Throughout the film, many of the characters are plagued by questions about the intentions that lay behind humanity's creation. Only one character, Dr. Elizabeth Shaw, demonstrates anything resembling traditional religious faith.

As author Margaret Atwood suggests, where science fiction seeks mostly to entertain, speculative fiction attempts to make the reader rethink her own world and worldview.[35] Speculative fiction, especially in the world of films, contains many mythical themes. What does it mean to be human and/or humane? What is our relationship to the sacred in times of crisis? How much have we taken for granted the splendor of the natural world or divine grace in our midst? In what ways has our dependence upon technology simply remade the world in our own flawed images? If the world were to end, could humans start over again, and how would we begin? What would we keep about human nature, and what would we leave behind? What if speculative fiction is really simply the effect of people's desire to work out frustrated (or frustrating) eschatology?

Consider, for example, the *Matrix* trilogy. The films describe a world controlled by sentient machines where humans live in a perceived reality called the Matrix, a virtual world created by the machine overlords to keep the human population docile and under their control. Neo, and friends in revolution

Morpheus and Trinity, rebel against the machines. They increase the size of the rebellion by recruiting others who have woken from the "dream world" of the Matrix to the real world. As one blogger puts it, "the film contains many references to the cyberpunk and hacker subcultures; philosophical and religious ideas such as Rene Descartes's evil genius, the Platonic *Allegory of the Cave*, the brain in a vat thought experiment, and homages to *Alice's Adventures in Wonderland*, Hong Kong action cinema, spaghetti westerns, dystopian fiction, and Japanese animation."[36] The runaway success of the *Matrix* franchise extended itself through the production of comic books, video games, and animated short films.

In the end, the self-realization of the main characters led to Neo's self-sacrifice, a deus-ex-machina moment. The machines had created an imaginary world with a clear and certain destiny. The world contained only an illusionary semblance of free will, just enough to satisfy the expectations of the human minds inhabiting the world, but not a reality strong enough to frustrate the design, or destiny, set out by the machines. Neo, like fictional protagonists such as Dorothy (*Wizard of Oz*), Frodo (*Lord of the Rings*), and Jake (*Avatar*), becomes the Christ figure by enacting genuine free will. He confronts "the god of the machines," the thing that represents the greatest obstacle to self-realization (equivalent to Dorothy traveling "behind the curtain," or Frodo heading for "the seat of evil," or Jake making his way to Pandora). As the ultimate embodiment of free will and self-realization, Neo confounds the nearly certain destiny defined by the power of the machines. He surrenders himself to both destiny and machine as an act of free will in order to save the essence of human existence, which is defined in all such stories by the notion of free will itself.

In this kind of mythical world, there is no need to wish for what you don't have. If you think it, you can do it. Life is basically a matter of self-realization. Self-realization provides the key to salvation. Technology often exceeds humanity's intent and takes on a life of its own, challenging humanity's dominion over the world. The spark of life, the powerful sense of self-awareness animating technology, creates the eventuality that humans themselves are now a threat. While *The Terminator* films imagine a genocidal machine culture that wants to purge humanity from the face of the earth, the *Matrix* presents a sophisticated technology that finds a way to sublimate humanity to serve its own purposes. It is left to Neo and his crew to rein in the power of technology so the latter may once again aid the human quest for self-fulfillment.

Thus we have yet another take on the happy ending, the belief that self-realization naturally leads to human fulfillment. Everything that you need to succeed, you already have in your possession. Get in touch with yourself, and you will see the world as it is. All the god you need is within you already.

If you call upon all the resources at hand, you can play a role in the ultimate triumph of good over evil. Life is what you make it. True salvation does not come in being rescued from some power outside of the self. Rather, it results from the actions of the self, either alone or collectively with those who choose to make a difference, to use fully the resources they have at hand. The only heaven you will know is the one you make for yourself. You can create your own happy ending. In Neo's case, to provide a happy ending for the world, he realized he had to sacrifice himself to save others, a common theme in religious mythologies. The importance of the happy ending, where science and technology are concerned, often translates into an ethic that emphasizes you should use everything you have at hand to produce the possibility of a better life.

DOCTRINE

Most of the time when people think about the evolution debate, whether consciously or not, it is framed around *Inherit the Wind* and the so-called Scopes Monkey Trial of 1925. Part of this fascination is wrapped up with where good people of faith are trying to prevent the forces of modernism from stealing their faith and Bible from them or, alternatively, where the scientists are trying to protect reason from the backward arguments posed against it. Hollywood has framed the lingering passions. Many on the left romanticize the victory, as if Scopes settled the matter once and for all. Meanwhile, those on the right, portrayed as country bumpkins, have demonstrated cultural staying power, evolving into astute politicians wielding considerable power in America's pulpits, polling places, and public forums. Ironically, while opposing evolutionary theory, the right has evolved in rather sophisticated ways.

While those on the left celebrate the victory of science's ability to liberate human beings from the prison of religious dogma, they adhere to this scientific triumphalism with a kind of inerrant literalism reminiscent of religious fundamentalism. Meanwhile, there are those on the right who tend to believe most human beings are heading straight to hell. Despite such a steadfast notion of human sin and imperfection, most of them keep up their property values, work to increase their efficiency and profitability, market their conservative values through slick advertising, massive digital screens, mobile devices, and online streaming, and seek to take advantage of whatever human advances prove useful to their otherworldly causes. Those on the right are quick to use whatever innovative means they can to produce the most regressive of ends.

In short, and again ironically, few dispute the premise at the heart of natural selection: that human tendencies propel human beings to cultivate progress and perfection, even if their cultivation is vested in the bet against human perfectibility. Therein lies the central doctrine undergirding both science and technology. Faith in progress marches on, whether lodged in the inevitability of human progress itself or lodged in the human ability to make progress in demonstrating the futility of belief in human progress. The latest in science and technology is employed in every way possible. We believe in its effectiveness, either to make us better versions of ourselves or to convince others of the absolute rightness of *our* ideas.

ETHICS

Martin Luther King Jr. once concluded that Americans "have unconsciously applied Einstein's theory of relativity, which properly described the physical universe, to the moral and ethical realm."[37] But King, like many others, was inappropriately confusing the theory of relativity with relativism. The theory of relativity creates anything but moral relativism; actually, it tends to create its opposite—moral certainty. In his theory of relativity, Albert Einstein advances Newton's laws of physics by showing us that, though the laws of physics are the same for everyone, how we encounter certain events may differ, based on our particular contexts and circumstances. As he was working out his theory, Einstein realized that mass distorts the space-time continuum. Our very being, or anything that has mass, possesses a gravitational pull on earth and on those within it. Without the knowledge of science, we as humans would neither know the impact our presence has on the earth nor the impact that the earth has upon us. To possess this knowledge should create due diligence, requiring us to be reflective about the impact our very lives and presence have upon the earth. To refuse to acknowledge this understanding is to do damage to the surroundings that to some extent depend upon our responsibly managing the fact of our existence in the world.

Ethics is about why people do what they do, in order to discern what they ought to do. It is a reflection on action, in order better to inform action. Why ought we do one thing instead of another? The ought is driven by law, desire, or consequences. When we examine the pros and cons, we know better what we ought to do. But there is nothing unpredictable or equivocating about the theory of relativity. There are no pros and cons. The theory of relativity, in a sense, is sovereign and tells us how things remain in order. It accounts for randomness in the reasonableness of a theory that has forced all scientists to account for the force of gravity in their understandings of reality.

If one assumes that the sovereign (theory of relativity) demands that everything in the universe happens for a reason, one also assumes one can unlock the relation of all things to one another. The theory of relativity preempts ethical thinking with the belief that when one understands the relation of all things to one another, one will know with certainty what one must do. The ethical mandate is nothing less than to explore fully the absolute extent of our knowledge, and to continue expanding knowledge, no matter the cost. Then human beings will know perfectly well what they must do in any circumstance, or at least those who place complete faith in science and technology believe this ultimately can be the case. The question always remains, however, whether the vast majority of people will want to do it, whatever it is, or whether some, perhaps the knowledgeable few, will believe, for the good of all, that they are ethically compelled to make sure all people will do it.

EXPERIENCE

The evangelical appeal of technology proves this point. Everybody must participate in it in order to be human. The Internet began as a government tool to bypass traditional modes of communication but has graduated to the mass market. Today, one can hardly communicate without it. The mass appeal makes it seem that one is not civilized if not connected. In much the same way that one has a faith community, a neighborhood, or a social organization to lend to themselves an identity defined by their connections to others, increasingly individuals are finding their identities shaped by virtual communities, populated by people whose hands they have never touched, living in houses they have never visited. The more intimate people are with technology, the more remote their human relationships can become. A whole new world can be found in the dark Internet, estimated to have more than five hundred times more information than is found on the surface web. Much scarier is the Dark-Net, a smaller portion of the underground Internet, where drug, sex, and weapons trafficking and other illegal activities proliferate.

The technological push for progress has depersonalized the way people relate to one another. The artificiality of technological advancement has not rendered human contact irrelevant. It has added a degree of superficiality to human relationships, while contributing to an illusion of more intimacy than people have ever experienced. One can have eight hundred friends on Facebook but have nobody to call in a time of need. The online community is detached but hypersensitized; people who have trouble expressing their feelings to trusted and personal friends provide full disclosure to random strangers in the context of a contrived online intimacy.

With today's "catfishing" trend, setting up false identities to find online romance, people these days become personas more than persons. Some are reeled in and can develop deeply complex emotional connections with a personality that's created solely for the purposes of manipulation or exploitation, or for the thrill or experience of just doing it. National news followed the saga of Manti Te'o, who led Notre Dame to a bowl championship series game in 2012 and had fallen in love with a girl who existed only in the virtual imagination of somebody who knew Te'o. Contemporary sites specialize in providing opportunities for full and graphic sexual activities (computer love, Internet sex, net sex, mud sex, cybering or conversex, C2C or C4C) with another person by using your body, your computer's camera, microphone, and keyboard.[38]

As the professional and self-righteous hack of the Ashley Madison website revealed, people use their computers to find convenient access to extramarital affairs. The complaints of Madison's users indicate that most of them valued the sanctity of their relationship with a cyber company more highly than the sanctity of the actual relationship they had with a marital partner. Further, the red-light district has moved online, where college kids (both men and women) and people next door are performing sex acts via livecams for tips. As Brian McKnight's song "The Front, the Back, the Side" (2013), sung with his son, graphically illustrates, many live experientially much more successfully in two dimensions than in three. In contrast, rather than celebrating the possibilities, Kate Bush's song "A Deeper Understanding" (1989) offered an early and prophetic exploration of the dysfunctional result whenever computers replace interpersonal contact.

Nothing represents this World Wide Web of virtual reality like Facebook. Surpassing the progenitors of social media pages Friendster and MySpace, what was meant for college students to keep in touch with one another has developed into a platform where millions of people can reconnect with family and old friends. Or, as many seem to prefer, can make "friends" of people they have never actually met. Facebook is what one makes of it. The positive aspects of the connections it enables are well known and experienced by many who use it on a daily basis. Yet Facebook can present a religious experience for many users. Within a decade of its appearance, Facebook has become the place where people go to emote, confess, congregate, post virtual memorials, write electronic journals, pray to God, venerate ancestors, and receive absolution.

While the privacy settings on Facebook are becoming more muddled and misleading, the public displays of faith in an artificial connection and its associated salvific power blur the lines between private domain and public information. On Facebook, the personal is always public. People are warned on every front about the dangers to privacy posed by this kind of participation. While there's every reason to retreat, people nonetheless are pushing forward. There seems an inevitable lure to bare the soul through social networking that causes otherwise conscientious people to throw all caution to the wind. As the old hymn opines, today's Facebook faithful "cannot have rest or be perfectly blest until all on the altar is laid."[39]

As a "touch screen generation," the young are now growing into a world we can only imagine. Hanna Rosin, in an *Atlantic* article, asked what it means for their development without offering a specific answer.[40] Teenagers have especially embraced all aspects of social media. But the immaturity of teen years often accompanies this embrace. They exercise few filters and their anonymity, mostly more perceived than actual, allows for the full exercise (rather than exorcism) of the worst demons of human nature. For this generation of teenagers, the threat posed by cyberstalking or cyberbullying actually leads to elevated suicides. Then there are the adults who prey on youth online to satisfy personal impulses. Chris Hanson of NBC's show *To Catch a Predator* has offered a television reality show to draw out some of these characters.

The blogging world began in earnest during the 1990s. For people who did not want to put a great deal of effort into blogging, microblogging emerged. And today the combination of microblogging and social networking surfaced with Tumblr. Tumblr, now owned by Yahoo, delivers more than 20 billion page views per month. Users are able to "effortlessly share anything," including "text, photos, quotes, links, music and videos." And people do share everything, from cute pictures of family to hardcore porn, and everything in between.[41] Whether you post with Tumblr, tweet in mini form with Twitter, blog with Blogger, stream with Skype, chat with Google or by other means, snap "selfies" with Instagram, share photos with Flickr or with "private photo sharing" apps like Snapchat, upload with YouTube, or pin with Pinterest, you can now let the whole world know what you are thinking or doing instantaneously. There are multitudes of personal worlds "to follow" the intimate expressions played out for eyes and ears everywhere.

RITUAL

All who are connected online have their daily rituals with technology. From the time we awake, whether or not awakening is aided by clocks or music or alarms, we brush our teeth with electric toothbrushes, check our e-mail, make our first connection with Facebook for the day, or pick up our remotes to watch our televisions at whatever our ritual time might be for doing so. Throughout our day, we perform the rituals that keep us wired and connected with all we deem important.

To take on religious significance, however, rituals are about transformation. In some way or another, they change us, our communities, and the environments around us. Scientists have to do the research to produce the medicine that will be effective. Doctors must provide a careful and ritualistically performed examination of a patient that enables the diagnosis behind a pharmaceutical or surgical prescription. Patients must faithfully take the pill at the appropriate hour. These kinds of rituals are essential to connect the healer and the healed. According to Abraham Verghese, professor at Stanford University School of Medicine, "being skilled at examining the body has a salutary effect beyond finding important clues that lead to an early diagnosis. It is a ritual that remains important to the patient. . . . Rituals are . . . a way of saying: 'I will see you through this illness. I will be with you through thick and thin.' It is paramount that doctors not forget the importance of this ritual."[42]

Other studies are beginning to show that, alongside the power of medicine, the mere performance of certain rituals—for example, taking placebo medications with a faithful hope in their effectiveness—scan lead to improvement for patients without the actual aid of either technology or science.[43]

According to physician and CNN medical journalist Sanjay Gupta, hospitals—and particularly surgeons—engage the ritual of the "morbidity and mortality conferences (M&M)" every Monday morning. They review bad outcomes of the previous week's surgeries, to facilitate introspection and critical reflection concerning their role as surgeons and to ferret out any possibilities of human culpability in the week's fatalities. Of special importance is the fact that the M&Ms are undertaken in the presence of one's peers. These are secretive gatherings—not at all accessible by any who are not professionally initiated within the inner circle. They provide a candid way to deal with failures and contribute to new knowledge that ultimately might lead to increased preservation of human life. The ritual allows vulnerability with one another and a chance to confront fears, doubts, and limitations. Their innate abilities, years of training, acquired expertise, and accumulated experience provide confidence they are well prepared for the task at hand. Yet, when all those things fail, the M&Ms provide a ritualistic path, "if you're lucky," to "a chance at redemption."[44]

INSTITUTIONS

All religions take as a given the importance of their social organizations, the places that enable them to survive and preserve their teachings and values. In one sense, perhaps the premier institution associated with science and technology is the Internet itself. The Internet is well named because it has created a powerful *net*work for community, and everything it communicates has been *inter*nalized. As one blogger has posted, "almost nothing goes in and out of our minds except what we get from social media."[45] It is almost impossible for most of us to go off-line.

We live in a time when the Internet actually seems infinite. The Internet is bottomless, an endless frontier, and no longer time-limited. If it happens, it is usually reported within seconds. News sites once trailed behind print versions. Now news appears instantaneously, if not officially, through tweets, Instagrams, or other instant "reporters" using whatever connected devices are at hand. We live in a world where Tom Matzie, an everyday citizen, tweets "off the record" comments of Michael Hayden (former director of the NSA) that are overheard on a train and cause an instant stir. As Hayden put it afterward, "Everybody's a reporter."[46]

In 2011, statistics suggested that one in eight people considered themselves addicted to the Internet.[47] According to ITU's more contemporary statistics, there are 7 billion, 85 million active mobile cellular connections in the world (that is 96.8 per every 100 inhabitants worldwide). That compares with 3 billion, 459 million active broadband subscriptions in 2015 across the world (47.2 percent of the global population). In the world, 46.4 percent of people have Internet access at home (81.3 percent in the developed world).[48] The membership to this "church" is growing across the world on a daily basis. And in contrast to most religions, those of us connected are likely to experience some form of worship at its altar on a daily basis.

How does one access the Internet as an institution? Search engines serve as the Internet's narthex. Through them, we enter the sanctuary that preserves knowledge, the history of human experience, the data of our tradition. Google accounts for more than 68 percent of all searches in America, and more than 88 percent market share of all worldwide searches (including mobile devices).[49] Pamela Jones Harbour, in a *New York Times* op-ed piece, wrote,

> In that role, Google is not just an eponymous verb but perhaps the most central conduit of information in the nation—and, indeed, on the planet. No other search engine comes close. Google is not just a "search engine company," or an "online services company," or a publisher, or an advertising platform. At its core, it's a data collection company. Its "market" is data by, from and about consumers—you, that is. And in that realm, its role is so dominant as to be overwhelming, and scary. Data is the engine of online markets and has become, indeed, a new asset class.[50]

We depend on Google to be the vehicle providing us access to the ever-flowing stream of knowledge that meets us where we are, no matter who we are. When an ivy-league PhD in Hebrew Bible, an ordained minister friend of ours, encounters anyone who expresses confusion about what to do or how to do something, she simply says, "Google is my mama."

The Internet is now the institution that stores all our stuff. With the emergence of "cloud computing," where we can now store infinite amounts of the most meaningful and heartfelt corners of our lives, the Internet has completed its move to the realm of the ephemeral; but this move does not make it any less real. This is an institution without bricks and mortars. Much like heaven or hell, we can't locate its physical space or map its geography. Yet, for those who believe in it, even place their trust in it, we become desperately dependent on its existence. It provides the relevant information when we most need it. We depend on it for the sights and sounds of the most precious moments in our lives. As a matter of faith, we are told "cloud computing" will never fail and will never need rebooting. We know there is a physical footprint somewhere, in server farms located somewhere in time and space. Yet none of us can touch the part of it that is ours, find it with our GPS, or physically walk through its halls to check on our contents personally. That's one powerful institution.

We could talk about other institutions, like the scientific labs and businesses that investigate the science or create the technologies that emerge from it, and the universities that enable research and development. Universities also offer both continuing education and degree courses in the virtual world for certificates or actual transcript credits. Online for-profit colleges, like the massive University of Phoenix, are garnering large numbers of students by turning education into a mass-market phenomenon found largely online.[51]

We could certainly include the marketplace of cumulative companies and their stores that deliver the devices into the hands of the enthusiasts, or the grant-funded labs and hospitals that provide the research and utilize the best technologies to treat the illnesses afflicting the human condition. We could also devote some space to the museums, like the Smithsonian, the Henry Ford or local science museums, places that house the vast accumulation of historical materials and introduce our children to the story of technology through the ages and its impact on our lives.

MATERIALITY

In twenty-first-century America, it is nearly impossible not to encounter the materiality associated with technology during most moments of any given day. From the food we eat to the clothes we wear to the transportation we use, there is no avoiding it. No matter how complex your life, technology has created appropriate materials to help resolve the complexity. In some cases, technology also makes our complex lives more daunting. While we can understand the role that social networking plays for people who are lonely, we also have to recognize technology must assume some responsibility for having caused the loneliness in the first place.[52]

In extreme cases, not only have people allowed technology to replace relationships in their lives; the material of technology now accessorizes their lives. For some, handheld personalized devices have become virtual appendages—leaving many feeling naked without them. Not only is it difficult for many to disconnect from the entangling web; it is equally disconcerting for many to think about separating from their handheld devices.

The need to be branded by a certain device or pacified by its presence is equally important. Even when one is disconnected, the material nature of technological devices as an accessory to one's persona allows us to feel more properly dressed. The device both comforts and communicates. It becomes a cultural signifier communicating our identification with the modern technological world with an appropriate style or flair that also says something about us. Much like religious symbols (the cross, the bindi, the yarmulke, or the hijab), something like wearing the Google Glass or strapping on a Fitbit or brandishing an iPhone communicates who you are, what is most important for you, and indeed provides a measure of material comfort to soothe a troubled soul.

These things increasingly serve to identify us with a particular "denominational" community as well. We readily identify with those we spot wearing or holding our devices. Today some are experimenting with actually incorporating technology in cyborg fashion. For example, Steve Mann, a professor at the University of Toronto, has worked to develop wearable computing.[53] Other technological developments, in the areas of implantable silicon silk electronics and Quick Response Codes, seek to build bridges between the body and technology.[54] The goal is to develop the possibility of a transhumanist future, where human beings may move into posthuman territory.

This chapter has emphasized the connected side of technology. Certainly, there are many other lenses we could use as well. The material culture connected with medical technology certainly belongs here. Consider the story of Henrietta Lacks, the black woman living in poverty and dying with cancer; her cells contributed to the development of such things as gene mapping, in vitro fertilization, and the polio vaccine. All this was done without her knowledge and with no benefit to her family. She died in 1951, but her cells, harvested at Johns Hopkins Hospital, lived on and were sold and resold. They call it the "HeLa immortal cell line," and it has been continuously used for medical research since the days before her death. Her cells were the first human cells to live longer than a few days after being divided and grown. Though the Supreme Court ruled in 1990 that this kind of material cultivation can no longer be commercialized, the HeLa cells have provided basic material for medical research for more than half a century.

Like Henrietta Lacks, all of us have cells. Her case makes us realize how valuable is the material we have within us. Today private and government labs are pursuing possible production of human stem-cell chimeras or hybrids in order to harvest human organs. Given the early controversies that accompanied in vitro fertilization and later stem-cell research, we can expect even a much greater hue and cry to come. Honestly, however, it likely won't stop anything. Technology is helping us understand how to unlock the potential contained in human DNA. When these secrets are more fully understood, human beings can increase both the quality and quantity of the years we live on the planet. Medical technology is making incredible progress in improving the human condition. Lifespans are ever expanding. Yet science often seems little interested in carefully measuring such gains against contemporary costs paid in human terms, such as those experienced by people like Henrietta Lacks or by those who are helplessly connected to technology near the end of their lives.

One of the greatest historical feats in this inward exploration into an unknown, yet personally owned, materiality, is the Human Genome Project (HGP). This scientific research and technological effort seeks to sequence and map all of the genes—together known as the genome—of members of our species, Homo sapiens. Completed in 2003, the HGP gives humanity the ability to read human matter (DNA) and glean from it nature's secret— the genetic blueprint for creating a human being.[55] By manipulating human genetic material, we not only exercise dominion over creation, but become creators ourselves. As with Dolly, the cloned sheep, we may soon know the name of a materially manufactured human being representing humanity's technological mastery of creation itself. With the scientific knowledge to unlock the secrets of DNA, not only will we understand that human beings are made in the image of God; we will make technological use of the material contained within us to make gods of us all.

Conclusion

Worship without Sacrifice

Americans from every conceivable walk of life find various ways to express and experience their ultimate concerns. These do not always include a church, temple, synagogue, or mosque. Many venerate the altars we describe in this book more frequently and arguably more fervently than their religious traditions. Scholars like H. Richard Niebuhr and Mircea Eliade analyzed lines of demarcation between popular culture (the secular) and religion (the sacred). Robert Bellah and others tried more simply to pinpoint religious expressions within broad swathes of American life in terms known as civil religion. Our task in this book has been different. We attempt to show how popular culture in our day has become a means through which Americans express their religiosity.

One might ask, what does this say about the current state of religious life in the United States? For many years, both scholars and pundits have declared that the United States is the great exception to the global patterns of secularization. There is no question that in Europe—as well as in other selected industrialized nations around the world—organized religion has suffered a considerable loss of cultural capital over the last century. The wealth of data concerning the observable secularization of these societies is virtually unassailable.[1] Whatever the metric—doctrinal beliefs, membership, church or synagogue or mosque or temple attendance, frequency of prayer, tithing practices, identification—the evidence shows a decline in traditional religiosity.[2]

Moreover, though the secularization debate is often posited strictly as a Western phenomenon, this trend of turning away from traditional religions has been just as dramatic in parts of the East. In 1970, there were 96,000 Buddhist temples throughout Japanese society; today that number is down to 75,000, a decline of 21,000 temples in roughly forty years. Of the remaining temples, approximately 20,000 are either understaffed or entirely unstaffed. The possession and use of Buddhist altars in Japanese households has declined dramatically; as few as 26 percent of city dwellers maintain altars in their homes.[3]

Some observers of religion claim that as beliefs decline, religious worldviews and modes of meaning making become less hegemonic, which in turn prompts routine participation in religious activities to drop. As a result, religion ends up playing a vastly diminished role in modern societies. A particularly compelling theory of secularization offered by Pippa Norris and Ronald Inglehart[4] asserts that a decline in religiosity at the national level may be inherently linked to a perceived sense of existential security. When most members of a given society experience a secure existence (food, water, shelter, jobs, education, access to medication, and so on), and life is relatively free, safe, and nonviolent, their commitment to religion weakens. In such locations, secularism gains strength. Despite what might be the wide and seemingly global applicability of the Norris and Inglehart thesis, secularization remains idiosyncratic; its forms are as unique as the societies within which it exists.

The United States offers no exception. We must remain tentative about broad attempts to explain secularization that ignore historical, national, and local differences. America, of course, possesses its own economic, political, geographic, ethnic, racial, sexual, religious, and artistic peculiarities. The United States is still the most religious of modern industrialized democracies. This designation does not mean much today, and, in fact, might be damning the United States with faint praise. Although religion still permeates public and cultural life in the United States, and although nonreligious Americans still constitute a clear minority, the numbers of the "nones" (those who identify themselves as religiously unaffiliated) are markedly rising in American life.[5] However, the "nones" are not necessarily irreligious. Around 55 percent of the "nones" describe themselves as either religious (18 percent) or spiritual (37 percent), and around 34 percent of "nones" continue to view religion as important in their lives.[6]

As religiously unaffiliated populations are growing, organized religions are declining. So-called secularization is also growing. These two declarative sentences are both true. As trends, they are undeniable in modern, industrialized societies. The first thing to note, however, is that religiously unaffiliated does *not* mean "not religious." The second thing to note is that the secularization of society does not sound the death knell of religion.[7] Religion in America continues to be public (and likely will remain so) in organized ways and connected to political parties and even government-funded, faith-based initiatives. We could also point to the 2014 Supreme Court decision declaring that Hobby Lobby as a privately held corporation possessed *religious* rights normally reserved for individuals.[8]

Nonetheless, statistics indicate that larger numbers of Americans are turning to private expressions of religion. Some in the country prefer a more inward and insular religion. This developing form of religious expression feeds an individualism that restricts meaningful public discourse and erodes public notions of the common good, *civitas*, or commonweal. Concern for the common good is replaced by devoting one's life to "what is good for me." Both these public and private expressions are religious quests, but they are quite different from one another.

Many Americans live in multiple religious worlds at once. They attend a traditional religious community once or twice a week—and then spend countless hours a week devoted to "what is good for me" through fervent attention to music or sports or big business. The "nones," having freed themselves from both the irrelevance of organized religion and the irreverence religious communities demonstrate toward their lifestyles, have taken control of their own lives and now meet their deepest needs through politics, economics, sports, or sex. It is not that they have no sacred regard, but rather that they experience it most dramatically in alternative ultimate concerns. For these "nones," organized religion sets humanity in opposition to itself, always making abstract demands that seem in direct opposition to their concrete realities.

Finding no salvation in religion, Americans have laid our fair share, if not our all, at the altars of body and sex, big business, entertainment, politics, sports, and science and technology. Organized religion has you shuffling between who you are and what you are expected to become, appearing to make religion an out-of-body experience more than an embodied one. For many Americans, religion attempts to make you "so heavenly minded that you are no earthly good." A good percentage of "nones," as well as a growing number of the American population, are looking for new places and spaces where they can find inspiration without being judged, where they can have both their humanity affirmed and their natural sensations nurtured. Americans are well able to invest time, energy, wealth, blood, sweat, and tears in a number of interests at once. To borrow a sentiment from the British novelist Graham Greene, "If you have abandoned one faith, do not abandon all faith. There is always an alternative to the faith we lose."[9]

Much of our work, implementing both thick description and analysis, has been inductive. We have trusted this process. Our collaboration began by looking at the relationship between religion and popular culture. The more we took seriously what we found, the better we were able to see what had initially seemed mostly theoretical. To be honest, and taking us a bit by surprise, the practices we discovered aligned rather dramatically with the theories of religion we knew. We found that popular culture had actually taken on the form of religion. Now, as we've come to the end of this project, in a work immersed in studying the practices and preferences of American people—be they religious in a typical sense or not—we believe an additional typology might be helpful in interpreting the implications associated with these altars.

Mohandas K. Gandhi, a man who struggled to reconcile his compassion for religious aspirations and his understanding of the crises many humans faced, sought to provide solace born in real-world experience. He lived and died to transform negative life circumstances into positive life chances. As a lawyer and Hindu, he pursued practical, palatable, and palpable solutions to real-world problems. As an exemplary advocate of religious pluralism and civil rights for all, Gandhi took the power of belief seriously. He knew one's beliefs affected both one's own quality of life and the lives of others. The natural laws and celebrated beliefs of our religions are indeed relevant to our sociopolitical conditions and realities. The former must never make a mockery out of the latter. So too, what we believe it means to be human must connect with how we live out our humanity. Human ideals and practices must be mutually affirming. Our practices cannot negate the meanings associated with our ideals.

Gandhi became one of the twentieth century's most influential religious figures engaged in sociopolitical activism. He identified seven social sins that potentially threatened the future of humanity, precisely because they represented human desires set in dire contrast with commonsense human ideals. These seven social sins he described as pleasure without conscience; commerce without morality; knowledge without character; politics without principle; wealth without work; science without humanity; and worship without sacrifice. He derived this list, first published in his weekly newspaper *Young India* on October 22, 1925, from his search for the roots of violence (which he called "passive violence"). Peter J. Gomes contends, "Years ago, I was much encouraged when I discovered that Gandhi had a list of seven social sins that, if not resisted, could destroy both persons and countries. . . . We live in a world in which these social sins flourish as much today as they did in Gandhi's time; surely the battle against them is still worth waging."[10]

While many contend today that organized religion has been tried and found wanting, the question now might be whether the emerging altars discussed in this book offer better alternatives. As we've contemplated that question, we wonder now whether Gandhi's axioms are as applicable as they are arresting. So we ask these questions. Is the American obsession with body and sex an example of seeking pleasure without conscience? Is the desire for profitability and prosperity that serves a shrinking elite of America's population, where 1 percent enjoys about 50 percent of all wealth, setting us on the road to a commerce utterly devoid of morality? In a context where comedy that parodies the news becomes more informative than the news itself, and the entertainment industry exemplifies and inculcates the directives and values that define our daily living, are we purveying knowledge without character? With America's deeply divided politics defined more by platitudes, platforms, and pejoratives than its care for the common good of its people, is there much doubt that contemporary politics are severely lacking in principle? While disciplined athletic efforts hone skills and develop talents, is the wealth associated with the few who play as profession in America comparable to the work product associated with them? Are the benefits of unfettered progress and the need for speed worth the costs as scientific advancements and technological innovations displace or destroy the humans they are supposed to serve?

We offer these questions as a new starting place for rigorous reflection concerning the "altar-ization" of these aspects of American culture. We cannot overstate the truth that religion is in crisis. The crisis is well noted and likely well deserved. Nonetheless, decreasing numbers at the altars of organized religions has not meant the cessation of worship. Worship continues at new altars. But, in Gandhi's words, is this "worship without sacrifice"? Drawing from the wisdom of John Milton, a classic figure in popular culture featured in *The Devil's Advocate*, "You sharpen the human appetite to the point where it can split atoms with its desire; you build egos the size of cathedrals; fiber-optically connect the world to every eager impulse; grease even the dullest dreams with these dollar-green, gold-plated fantasies, until every human becomes an aspiring emperor, becomes his own God . . . and where can you go from there?"[11]

A poet, T. S. Eliot, reframes Milton's final query with more urgency: "After such knowledge, what forgiveness?"[12]

Notes

Introduction

1. Martin Luther, as quoted in H. Richard Niebuhr, *Radical Monotheism and Western Culture* (New York: Harper & Row, 1960), 119.
2. Niebuhr, *Radical Monotheism*, 119.
3. "America's Changing Religious Landscape," Pew Research Center study, May 12, 2015, http://www.pewforum.org/2015/05/12/americas-changing-religious-landscape/.
4. http://www.gallup.com/poll/1690/religion.aspx.
5. See C. K. Hadaway, P. L. Marler, and Mark Chaves, "What the Polls Don't Show: A Closer Look at U.S. Church Attendance," *American Sociological Review* 58 (1993): 741–52.
6. http://www.gallup.com/poll/1690/religion.aspx.
7. http://www.pewforum.org/2015/05/12/americas-changing-religious-landscape /pr_15-05-12_rls-00/.
8. Pew study, http://www.pewforum.org/2012/0/09/nones-on-the-rise/.
9. Russell Chandler, *Racing toward 2001: The Forces Shaping America's Religious Future* (Grand Rapids: Zondervan; San Francisco: Harper, 1992), 191ff.
10. Wade Clark Roof, *A Generation of Seekers* (San Francisco: HarperSanFrancisco, 1993).
11. "Science in America: Religious Belief and Public Attitudes," Pew Research Center, December 18, 2007, http://pewforum.org/docs/?DocID=275.
12. Patti Davis, *The Way I See It: An Autobiography* (New York: Putnam, 1992).
13. Rice sociologist Michael Lindsay, in commenting on the 2008 Pew study, said, "Americans believe in everything. It's a spiritual salad bar." See Cathy Lynn Grossman, "Survey: More have dropped dogma for spirituality in U.S.," *USA Today*, July 2, 2008, http://www.usatoday.com/news/religion/2008-06-23 -pew-religions_N.htm.
14. Tom Beaudoin, *Virtual Faith: The Irreverent Spiritual Quest of Generation X* (New York: Jossey-Bass, 1998).
15. Ibid., 14.

16. David Chidester, *Authentic Fakes: Religion and the American Popular Culture* (Berkeley: University of California Press, 2005), 43.
17. See Ninian Smart, *The Religious Experience of Mankind*, 2nd ed. (New York: Scribner's, 1976).
18. Mircea Eliade, *The Sacred and the Profane* (New York: Harcourt, Brace, 1959), 25.
19. Smart, "Theravada Buddhism and the Definition of Religion," in Ugo Bianchi, ed., *The Notion of Religion in Comparative Research: Selected Proceedings of the XVIth Congress of the International Association for the History of Religions* (Rome: L'Erma di Bretschneider, 1994), 604.
20. Charles Long, *Significations: Signs, Symbols, and Images in the Interpretation of Religion* (Aurora, CO: Davies Publishers, 1986), 125–37.
21. Ibid., 161–68.
22. Ibid., 80–87.
23. Paul Tillich, *Dynamics of Faith* (New York: Harper & Row, 1957), 6.
24. Paul Tillich, *Theology of Culture* (New York: Oxford University Press, 1959), 42.

Chapter 1: Body and Sex

1. Lieve Spaas, ed., *Echoes of Narcissus* (New York: Berghahn Books, 2003).
2. Michel Foucault, *The History of Sexuality*, vol. 2: *The Use of Pleasure* (New York: Random House, 1989), 5.
3. Sigmund Freud, *Civilization and Its Discontents*, trans. and ed. James Strachey (New York: W. W. Norton & Co., 1961), 25–27.
4. bell hooks, *All about Love: New Visions* (New York: William Morrow Paperbacks, 2001), xxiii.
5. Michael Johns, *Moment of Grace: The American City in the 1950s* (Berkeley: University of California Press, 2003), 24.
6. See Susan Doll, "Marilyn Monroe's Later Career," www.entertainment.how stuffworks.com/marilyn-monroe-later-career.htm. See also Susan Doll, *Marilyn Monroe: Her Life and Legend* (London and Chester, NY: Omnibus Press, 1990).
7. *TV Guide* gave her this title in 2009; see https://learnodo-newtonic.com /marilyn-monroe-facts.
8. Elton John and Bernie Taupin, "Candle in the Wind," in the album *Goodbye Yellow Brick Road* (London: Trident Studios, 1973).
9. Edwin Mullins, *The Painted Witch: How Western Artists Have Viewed the Sexuality of Women* (New York: Carroll & Graf Publishers, 1985), 62–63.
10. Margaret Wolfe Hungerford, *Molly Bawn* ((Leipzig: Bernhard Tauchnitz, 1878).
11. http://www.psychologytoday.com/blog/it-s-man-s-and-woman-s-world/201403 /is-beauty-in-the-eye-the-beholder.
12. Audre Lorde, *Sister Outsider: Essays and Speeches* (Trumansberg, NY: Crossing Press, 1984), 55.
13. Carter Heyward, *Touching Our Strength: The Erotic as Power and the Love of God* (San Francisco: Harper & Row, 1989), 99.
14. Anthony Giddens, *The Transformation of Intimacy: Sexuality, Love, & Eroticism in Modern Societies* (Stanford, CA: Stanford University Press, 1992), 41.
15. Jill Gordon, *Plato's Erotic World: From Cosmic Origins to Human Death* (New York: Cambridge University Press, 2012), 225.

16. Ibid.
17. Sigmund Freud, *Civilization and Its Discontents*, trans. and ed. James Strachey (New York: W. W. Norton & Co., 1961), 25.
18. Ibid., 25–26.
19. Ibid., 26–27.
20. See Lisa Sowle Cahill, *Sex, Gender and Christian Ethics* (New York: Cambridge, 1996).
21. Klaus V. Meier examines the shift from Descartes to Merleau-Ponty in "Cartesian and Phenomenological Anthropology: The Radical Shift and Its Meaning for Sport," *Journal of the Philosophy of Sport* 2 (1975): 51–73.
22. Maurice Merleau-Ponty, *The Phenomenology of Perception*, 196–97, quoted in Meier, "Cartesian and Phenomenological Anthropology," 60.
23. Susan Parsons, *The Ethics of Gender* (London: Blackwell, 2002).
24. Linda Tschirhart Sanford and Mary Ellen Donovan, *Women and Self Esteem: Understanding and Improving the Way We Think and Feel about Ourselves* (New York: Viking Penguin, 1984), 375. See also *Men's Lives*, ed. Michael S. Kimel and Michael A. Messner, 4th ed. (Boston: Allyn & Bacon, 1998).
25. "How to Look Your Best All Your Life," *McCall's*, July 1979, 18, quoted in Sandra Lee Bartky, *Femininity and Domination: Studies in the Phenomenology of Oppression* (New York: Routledge, 1990), 33.
26. Susan Stanford Friedman, *A Woman's Guide to Therapy* (New York: Prentice-Hall, 1979), 369.
27. Sanford and Donovan, *Women and Self Esteem*, 371.
28. Judith Butler, *Gender Trouble* (London: Taylor & Francis, 1999).
29. Michel Foucault, *The History of Sexuality*, vol. 1: *An Introduction* (New York: Random House, 1978); *The History of Sexuality*, vol. 2: *The Use of Pleasure* (New York: Random House, 1989); Allan Rauch, *Useful Knowledge: The Victorians, Morality, and the March of Intellect* (Chapel Hill: Duke University Press, 2001); and Susan Medus and Jane Redall, eds., *Sexuality and Subordination* (New York: Routledge, 1989).
30. This poem, entitled "The New Colossus," is on the Statue of Liberty.
31. See Ronald Takaki, ed., *From Different Shores: Perspectives on Race and Ethnicity in America* (New York: Oxford University Press, 1994); Takaki, *A Different Mirror: A History of Multicultural America* (New York: Little, Brown & Co., 1993); and Nell Irvin Painter, *The History of White People* (New York: W. W. Norton and Co., 2010); and Jennifer Harvey, *Whiteness and Morality: Pursuing Racial Justice through Reparations and Sovereignty* (New York: Palgrave, 2007).
32. See Katie G. Cannon, *Black Womanist Ethics* (Atlanta: Scholars Press, 1988).
33. See Frances B. Cogan, *All-American Girl: The Ideal of Real Womanhood in Mid-Nineteenth-Century America* (Athens: University of Georgia Press, 1989).
34. Anthony B. Pinn, *Embodiment and the New Shape of Black Theological Thought* (New York: New York University Press, 2010); Meri Nana-Ama Danquah, *The Black Body* (New York: Seven Stories Press, 2009).
35. Joan Cocks, *The Oppositional Imagination: Feminism, Critique, and Political Theory* (New York: Routledge, 1989), 174–75.
36. Cornel West, *Prophesy Deliverance! An Afro-American Revolutionary Christianity* (Philadelphia: Westminster Press, 1982), 53–60; see also Hortense J. Spillers, *Black, White, and in Color: Essays on American Literature and Culture* (Chicago: University of Chicago Press, 2003), 205.
37. West, *Prophesy Deliverance*, 47.

38. Ibid., 54.

39. Susan M. Zimmermann, *Silicone Survivors: Women's Experiences with Breast Implants* (Philadelphia: Temple University Press, 1998), 56.

40. Kathy Davis, *Reshaping the Female Body: The Dilemma of Cosmetic* (New York: Routledge, 1994); and Sander L. Gilman, *Making the Body Beautiful: A Cultural History of Aesthetic Surgery* (Princeton, NJ: Princeton University Press, 1999).

41. Jacque Lacan, *Feminine Sexuality*, ed. Juliet Mitchell and Jacqueline Rose (New York: W. W. Norton & Co., 1982).

42. This is from a childhood "patty-cake" or "hand jive" song that thrived in black communities during Jim Crow; see the documentary *Black Is . . . Black Ain't*, produced and directed by Marlon Riggs, California Newsreel, 1995.

43. Nellie Wong, "When I Was Growing Up," used by permission of the poet.

44. W. E. B. DuBois, *Souls of Black Folk* (1903; New York: Vintage Books, 1990), 8–9.

45. Parsons, *The Ethics of Gender*, 62–63.

46. Sanford and Donovan, *Women and Self Esteem*, 378.

47. bell hooks, *Black Looks: Race and Representation* (Boston: South End Press, 1992), 21.

48. Sara I. McClelland, "What Do You Mean When You Say That You Are Sexually Satisfied?," *Feminism and Psychology* 24, no. 1 (2014): 74–96.

49. Julia Serano, *Whipping Girl: A Transsexual Woman on Sexism and the Scapegoating of Femininity* (Berkeley, CA: Seal Press, 2007), 117.

50. Anthony Giddens, *The Constitution of Society: Outline of the Theory of Structuration* (Cambridge: Polity Press, 1984), 24.

51. Pierre Bourdieu, *Language and Symbolic Power*, ed. John B. Thompson, trans. Gino Raymond (Cambridge, Harvard University Press, 1994), 119–21.

52. Joseph Carroll, Gallup Poll, "Americans: 2.5 Children Is 'Ideal' Family Size," June 26, 2007.

53. Betty Friedan, *The Feminine Mystique* (1963; New York: W. W. Norton & Co., 2001).

54. Stephanie Coontz as quoted in Kate Rice, "New 'Non-Traditional' American Families," January 19, 2004, http://abcnews.go.com/Health/story?id=118267.

55. George Ryley Scott, *The History of Prostitution* (London: Senate, 1996).

56. Steven D. Levitt and Stephen J. Dubner, *Super Freakonomics: Global Cooling, Patriotic Prostitutes, and Why Suicide Bombers Should Buy Life Insurance* (New York: William Morrow, 2009), 25.

57. See Leanne Italie, "50 Shades of Grey Marketing Phenom Goes Mainstream," Associated Press, August 15, 2012, http://bigstory.ap.org/article/50-shades-grey-marketing-phenom-goes-mainstream.

58. Jack Boulware, *Sex American Style: An Illustrated Romp through the Golden Age of Heterosexuality* (Venice, CA: Feral House, 1997).

59. See Philip Scranton, ed., *Beauty and Business: Commerce, Gender, and Culture in Modern America* (New York: Routledge, 2001).

60. Sandra Lee Bartky, *Femininity and Domination: Studies in the Phenomenology of Oppression* (New York: Routledge, 1990), 71.

61. Lynne Luciano, *Looking Good: Male Body Image in Modern America* (New York: Hill & Wang, 2001), 3.

62. Sanford and Donovan, *Women and Self Esteem*, 377.

63. Londa Schiebinger, *The Mind Has No Sex? Women in the Origins of Modern Science* (Cambridge, MA: Harvard, 1989), 203.

64. Mike Vacanti, "Why Gym Culture is Uniquely Enchanting" (a blog On the Regimen: Fitness, Psychology and Wellness and a Better Life), July 30, 2013, http://ontheregimen.com/2013/07/30/why-gym-culture-is-uniquely-enchanting/.
65. Mary F. Rogers, *Barbie Culture* (London: Sage Publications, 1999), 3.
66. http://www.wired.com/2016/01/like-real-people-barbie-now-comes-in-different-sizes/.
67. Rogers, *Barbie Culture*, 113.
68. Adapted from John 4:13.
69. Adapted from the 1905 hymn "Is Your All on the Altar," by Elisha A. Hoffman, in *The New National Baptist Hymnal: 21st Century Edition* (Nashville: R. H. Boyd Co., 2001), 220–21. Introducing Hoffman's words is a line from the hymn "Whosoever Will," written by P. P. Bliss in 1870; see http://hymnary.org/text/whosoever_heareth_shout_shout_the_sound.

Chapter 2: Big Business

1. David M. Kennedy, *Freedom from Fear: The American People in Depression and War, 1929–1945* (New York: Oxford University Press, 1999), 33.
2. Harvey Cox, "The Market as God: Living in the New Dispensation," *Atlantic Monthly* 283 (March 1999): 18–23.
3. Thomas Carlyle, quoted in Peter Groenewegen, "Thomas Carlyle, 'The Dismal Science,' and the Contemporary Political Economy of Slavery," *History of Economics Review* (June 2001): 74–94.
4. Harold C. Livesay, *Andrew Carnegie and the Rise of Big Business*, 2nd ed. (New York: Longman, 2000), 5.
5. Ibid., 15.
6. Ibid., 30.
7. David Nasaw, *Andrew Carnegie* (New York: Penguin Press, 2006), 229.
8. Andrew Carnegie, *The Gospel of Wealth and Other Timely Essays*. Selected and Introduced by David Nasaw (1901; repr., New York: Penguin, 2006).
9. Nasaw, *Andrew Carnegie*, 787.
10. Ibid.
11. Ibid.
12. Ibid.
13. Ibid., 350.
14. Ibid., 624–25.
15. Ibid., 49.
16. Ibid., 226–27.
17. Andrew Carnegie, *Autobiography of Andrew Carnegie* (1920; New York: Public Affairs, 2011), 339.
18. Nasaw, *Andrew Carnegie*, 625.
19. Ibid., 229.
20. Anyone interested in examining the life and times of Andrew Carnegie ought to begin with Andrew Carnegie, *Autobiography of Andrew Carnegie* (1920; New York: Public Affairs, 2011). See also Joseph Frazier Wall, *Andrew Carnegie* (New York: Oxford University Press, 1970); Burton J. Hendrick, *The Life of Andrew Carnegie* (New York: Doubleday, Doran and Co., 1932); Bernard Alderson, *Andrew Carnegie: From Telegraph Boy to Millionaire* (London: C. Arthur Pearson, Ltd., 1902); John K. Winkler, *Incredible Carnegie* (New York: The Vanguard Press, 1931); Louis Hacker, *The World of Andrew Carnegie* (Philadelphia, 1968); Alun Munslow, "Andrew Carnegie and the Discourse

of Cultural Hegemony," *Journal of American Studies* 22 (August 1988): 213–24; Harold C. Livesay, *Andrew Carnegie and the Rise of Big Business*, 2nd ed. (New York: Longman, 2000); and David Nasaw, *Andrew Carnegie* (New York: Penguin Press, 2006).

21. See http://en.wikipedia.org/wiki/Self-made_man.
22. Irvin G. Wyllie, *The Self-Made Man in America: The Myth of Rags to Riches* (New York: Free Press, 1954), 9–10; Robert V. Remini, *Henry Clay: Statesman for the Union* (New York: W. W. Norton & Co., 1991), 3; and Daniel Walker Howe, *Making the American Self: Jonathan Edwards to Abraham Lincoln* (Cambridge: Harvard University Press, 1997), 136–37.
23. Gary Scharnhorst, *Horatio Alger, Jr.* (Boston: Twayne, 1980); Gary Scharnhorst and Jack Bales. *The Lost Life of Horatio Alger, Jr.* (Bloomington: Indiana University Press, 1985).
24. http://www.aynrand.org/novels/the-objectivist.
25. Chris Matthew Sciabarra, *Ayn Rand: The Russian Radical* (University Park: Pennsylvania State University Press, 1995).
26. Amy Benfer, "And the Rand Played On: The Going Galt Movement Protests Obama With a Collective Shrug," *Mother Jones* on-line (July/August 2009), http://www.motherjones.com/media/2009/07/and-rand-played; Brian Doherty, "She's Back!" *Reason* 41, no. 7 (December 2009): 51–58.
27. Mimi Reisel Gladstein, *Ayn Rand* (New York: Continuum, 2009).
28. Benfer, "And the Rand Played On."
29. Corey Robin, "Garbage and Gravitas," *The Nation*, June 7, 2010.
30. Anne C. Heller, *Ayn Rand and the World She Made* (New York: Anchor Books, 2009), 139; Jennifer Burns, *Goddess of the Market: Ayn Rand and the American Right* (New York: Oxford University Press, 2009), 42–43.
31. Geoffrey James, "5 Reasons Ayn Rand Is Bad for Business," *Inc.*, August 16, 2012, www.inc.com/geoffrey-james/5-reasons-ayn-rand-is-bad-for-business .html.
32. Herbert Hoover, October 22, 1928, http://teachingamericanhistory.org /library/document/rugged-individualism/.
33. Scott A. Sandage, *Born Loser: A History of Failure in America* (Cambridge: Harvard University Press, 2005), 18.
34. Kennedy, *Freedom from Fear*, 45–47.
35. Kevin Phillips, *Bad Money: Reckless Finance, Failed Politics, and the Global Crisis of American Capitalism* (New York: Viking Press, 2008), 207.
36. See Huck Gutman, "Dishonesty, Greed and Hypocrisy in Corporate America," July 14, 2002, http://www.uvm.edu/~sgutman/Dishonesty,_Greed_and _Hypocrisy_in_Corporate_America.html.
37. Ibid.
38. Ibid.
39. Dick Cheney, quoted in ibid.
40. Liaquat Ahamed, "How Bernard Madoff Did It," *New York Times*, May 13, 2011, http://www.nytimes.com/2011/05/15/books/review/book-review-the -wizard-of-lies-bernie-madoff-and-the-death-of-trust-by-diana-b-henriques. html?pagewanted=all&_r=0. See also Diana B. Henriques, *The Wizard of Lies: Bernie Madoff and the Death of Trust* (New York: Times Books/Henry Holt, 2011).
41. See Diana B. Henriques, "Madoff Is Sentenced to 150 Years for Ponzi Scheme," *New York Times*, June 29, 2009, http://www.nytimes.com/2009/06/30/business /30madoff.html?pagewanted=all.

42. "Madoff Says from Prison that Banks 'Had to Know,'" *New York Times*, February 16, 2001, A-1.
43. Henriques, "Madoff Is Sentenced."
44. Thornstein Veblen, *The Theory of the Leisure Class* (1899; New York: Dover, 1994), 47.
45. Kerwin Kofi Charles, Erik Hurst, and Nikolai Roussanov, "Conspicuous Consumption and Race," *Quarterly Journal of Economics* 124, no. 2 (May 2009): 425-67.
46. Leigh Eric Schmidt, *Consumer Rites: The Buying & Selling of American Holidays* (Princeton, NJ: Princeton University Press, 1997).
47. See Taylor Clark, *Starbucked: A Double Tall Tale of Caffeine, Commerce, and Culture* (New York: Little, Brown, & Co., 2007); Noah Kerner and Gene Pressman, *Chasing Cool: Standing Out in Today's Cluttered Marketplace* (New York: Atria Books, 2007).
48. Veblen, *The Theory of the Leisure Class*, 43–62.
49. Karl Marx, "Human Requirements and Division of Labour under the Rule of Private Property," Economic and Philosophical Manuscripts of 1844, in Robert C. Tucker, ed., *The Marx–Engels Reader*, 2nd ed. (New York: Norton, 1978), 96.
50. Thomas Piketty, *Capital in the Twenty-First Century* (Cambridge: Belknap Press of the Harvard University Press, 2014), 105.
51. Adam Smith, *An Inquiry into the Nature and Causes of the Wealth of Nations*, ed. Edwin Cannan (1776; New York: Modern Library, 1994), book 1, chap. 5, 42.
52. See Mark Toulouse, *God in Public: Four Ways American Christianity and Public Life Relate* (Louisville, KY: Westminster John Knox Press, 2006).
53. Jason Goodwin, *Greenback: The Almighty Dollar and the Invention of America* (New York: Henry Holt, 2003), 7.
54. Ibid.
55. See Patricia Sullivan and Carlos Lozada, "Milton Friedman, 1912–2006, Economist Touted Laissez-Faire Policy," *Washington Post*, November 17, 2006, http://www.washingtonpost.com/wp-dyn/content/article/2006/11/16/AR2006111600592.html.
56. On Friedman, see Godfrey Hodgson, *The World Turned Right Side Up: A History of the Conservative Ascendancy in America* (Boston: Houghton Mifflin: 1996), 85, 197–203, 211–12; Kevin Phillips, *Wealth and Democracy: A Political History of the American Rich* (New York: Broady Books, 2002), 95, 334–35; "Milton Friedman: An Enduring Legacy," *The Economist*, November 17, 2006; Penn Bullock, "Bernanke's Philosopher," *Reason*, November 17, 2009; and Greg IP and Mark Whitehouse, "How Milton Friedman Changed Economics, Policy, and Markets," *Wall Street Journal*, November 17, 2006.
57. Cynthia J. Koepp and Steven Laurence Kaplan, "Introduction," in Kaplan and Koepp, eds., *Work in France: Representations, Meaning, Organization, and Practice* (Ithaca, NY: Cornell University Press, 1986), 17.
58. Adam Smith, *An Inquiry*, book 4, chap. 2, 484–85.
59. Anne Robert Jacques Turgot, "Observations sur un Mémoire de M. de Saint-Péravy." (1767) in *Œuvres de Turgot et Documents le Concernant, avec Biographie et Notes*, vol. 2, ed. Gustave Schelle (Paris: Librairie Féliz Alcan, 1914), 144.
60. John Maynard Keynes, *The General Theory of Employment, Interest, and Money* (1936; New York: Harcourt Brace, 1953); John Kenneth Galbraith, *Money: Whence It Came, Where It Went* (Boston: Houghton Mifflin, 1975), 268–82;

Alan Brinkley, *The End of Reform: New Deal Liberalism in Recession and War* (New York: Vintage, 1995), 265–71; and Kennedy, *Freedom from Fear*, 357–60.

61. John Kenneth Galbraith, *American Capitalism: The Concept of Countervailing Power* (1952; Boston: Houghton Mifflin, 1956), 80–82; and Daniel Yergin and Joseph Stanislaw, *The Commanding Heights: The Battle for the World Economy* (New York: Touchstone Books, 2002), 37–38.

62. Kenneth G. Crawford, "From Pump-Priming to Pumping," *Nation*, May 27, 1939, 606–7; Lauchlin Currie, "Comments on Pump Priming," *History of Political Economy* 10 (Winter 1978): 525–33.

63. John H. Williams, "Deficit Spending," *American Economic Review* 30 (February 1941): 52; E. Cary Brown, "Fiscal Policy in the Thirties: A Reappraisal," *American Economic Review* 46 (December 1956): 863–69; Udo Sautter, "Government and Unemployment: The Use of Public Works before the New Deal," *Journal of American History* 73 (1986): 59–86; Kenneth D. Roose, *Economics of Recession and Revival: An Interpretation of 1937–38* (New Haven, CT: Yale University Press, 1954), 79; John Kenneth Galbraith, *Economics and the Public Purpose* (Boston: Houghton Mifflin, 1973), 24–25; Alvin H. Hanson, *Full Recovery or Stagnation* (New York: W. W. Norton & Co., 1938), 269; Margaret Weir and Theda Skocpol, "State Structures and the Possibilities for Keynesian Responses to the Great Depression in Sweden, Britain, and the United States," in Peter B. Evans, Dietrich Rueschmeyer, and Theda Skocpol, eds., *Bringing the State Back In* (New York: Cambridge University Press, 1985), 107–10, 132–35.

64. Daniel Yergin and Joseph Stanislaw, *The Commanding Heights: The Battle for the World Economy* (New York: Touchstone Books, 2002), 21–24.

65. John Maynard Keynes, *Economic Possibilities for Our Grandchildren* (London: Macmillan, 1930); Oliver C. Cox, *Capitalism as a System* (New York: Monthly Review Press, 1964), 223–35.

66. For information on the impact of Keynesian economics since the Great Depression, see Alan Brinkley, *The End of Reform: New Deal Liberalism in Recession and War* (New York: Vintage, 1995).

67. Eric Hobsbaawm, *The Age of Extremes: A History of the World, 1914–1991* (New York: Vintage, 1994), 403–13; Eric Foner, *The Story of American Freedom* (New York: W. W. Norton & Co., 1998), 320–22; and Thomas Piketty, *Capital in the Twenty-First Century*, trans. Arthur Goldhammer (Cambridge, MA: Belknap Press of Harvard University Press, 2014), 98.

68. Ulrich Duchrow and Franz J. Hinkelammert, *Property for People, Not for Profit: Alternatives to the Global Tyranny of Capital* (London: Zed Books, 2004), 142; Naomi Klein, *The Shock Doctrine: The Rise of Disaster Capitalism* (New York: Metropolitan Books, 2007), 241–45; Kevin Phillips, *Bad Money: Reckless Finance, Failed Politics, and the Global Crisis of American Capitalism* (New York: Viking, 2008), 73–80; and Joerg Rieger, *No Rising Tide: Theology, Economics, and the Future* (Minneapolis: Fortress Press, 2009), 12–19.

69. Irvine H. Sprague, *Bailout: An Insider's Account of Bank Failures and Rescues* (New York: Basic Books, 1986).

70. Itzhak Swary, "Stock Market Reaction to Regulatory Action in the Continental Illinois Crisis," *Journal of Business* 59, no. 3 (1986): 451–73; Federal Open Market Committee meeting transcripts from May 21–22, 1984, http://www .federalreserve.gov/monetarypolicy/fomc_historical.htm; Federal Deposit Insurance Corporation, *History of the Eighties, Lessons for the Future*, vol. 1 (Washington, DC: FDIC, 1997); Frederick Furlong, "Market Responses

to Continental Illinois," *Federal Reserve Bank of San Francisco Weekly Letter* (August 31, 1984); Inquiry into Continental Illinois Corp. and Continental Illinois National Bank: Hearings before the Subcommittee on Financial Institutions Supervision, Regulation and Insurance, 98th Congress (1984); https://fraser.stlouisfed.org/title/?id=745.

71. For the definitive account of the 2008 crisis, see Andrew Ross Sorkin, *Too Big to Fail: The Inside Story of How Wall Street and Washington Fought to Save the Financial System—and Themselves* (New York: Viking, 2009).

72. "Bernanke—Causes of the Recent Financial and Economic Crisis," Federal reserve.gov. 2010-09-02, http://www.federalreserve.gov/newsevents/testimony /bernanke20100902a.htm.

73. Paul Wiseman and Gogoi Pallavi, "FDIC Chief: Small Banks Can't Compete with Bailed-Out Giants," *USA Today*, October 19, 2009.

74. Eric Dash, "If It's Too Big to Fail, Is It Too Big to Exist?," *New York Times*, June 21, 2009, http://www.nytimes.com/2009/06/21/weekinreview/21dash .html?_r=0.

75. Bernie Sanders, "Billions for Bailouts! Who Pays?," *Huffington Post*, http://www .huffingtonpost.com/rep-bernie-sanders/billions-for-bailouts-who_b_127882 .html.

76. Michael McKee and Scott Sanman, "Greenspan Says U.S. Should Consider Breaking Up Large Banks," *Bloomberg*, October 15, 2009, http://www.bloomberg .com/apps/news?pid=newsarchive&sid=aJ8HPmNUfchg.

77. Recent works that offer cogent critiques of the rampant risk and inequality inherent in the contemporary free-market economy brought forth by neo-liberal capitalism include Joerg Rieger, *No Rising Tide: Theology, Economics, and the Future* (Minneapolis: Fortress Press, 2009); Noam Chomsky, *Profit over People: Neoliberalism and Global Order* (New York: Seven Stories Press, 2011); and Tavis Smiley and Cornel West, *The Rich and the Rest of Us: A Poverty Manifesto* (New York: SmileyBooks, 2012).

78. For insight into development of this culture of greed, see Bethany McLean and Peter Elkind, *The Smartest Guys in the Room: The Amazing Rise and Scandalous Fall of Enron* (New York: Portfolio, 2003); Bethany McLean and Joseph Nocera, *All the Devils Are Here: The Hidden History of the Financial Crisis* (New York: Penguin, 2010); John Cassidy, *How Markets Fail: The Logic of Economic Calamities* (New York: Picador, 2010); Gillian Tett, *Fool's Gold: The Inside Story of J. P. Morgan and How Wall St. Greed Corrupted Its Bold Dream and Created a Financial Catastrophe* (New York: Free Press, 2010); David Wessel, *In FED We Trust: Ben Bernanke's War on the Great Panic* (New York: Three Rivers Press, 2009); Matt Taibbi, *Griftopia: A Story of Bankers, Politicians, and the Most Audacious Power Grab in American History* (New York: Spiegel & Grau, 2011); Michael Lewis, *The Big Short: Inside the Doomsday Machine* (New York: W. W. Norton & Co., 2011); Sebastian Mallaby, *More Money Than God: Hedge Funds and the Making of a New Elite* (New York: Penguin, 2011); and Scott Patterson, *Dark Pools: The Rise of the Machine Traders and the Rigging of the U.S. Stock Market* (New York: Crown, 2013).

79. Peter Laarman,"Gordon Gekko Gets God: The Heritage Foundation of Theology," Religion Dispatches, May 13, 2009, http://www.religion dispatches.org/books/1436/gordon_gekko_gets_god__the_heritage_foundation _of_theology.

80. Adam Smith, *An Inquiry*, book 1, chap. 1, 3.

81. Ibid., 13.

82. Adam Smith, *An Inquiry*, book 5, chap. 1, article 3, 637.

83. See Janet Byrne, ed., *The Occupy Handbook* (New York: Back Bay Books, 2012).

84. Tony Smith, "Hegel, Marx, and the Comprehension of Capital," in Fred Moseley and Tony Smith, ed., *Marx's Capital and Hegel's Logic: A Reexamination* (Chicago: Haymarket Books, 2014), 17–18.

85. Karl Marx, *A Contribution to the Critique of Hegel's Philosophy of Right* (1844), in Loyd D. Easton and Kurt H. Guddat, eds. and trans., *Writings of the Young Marx on Philosophy and Society* (Garden City, NY: Doubleday Anchor, 1967), 249–50.

86. Arthur F. McGovern, *Marxism: An American Christian Perspective* (Maryknoll, NY: Orbis, 1987); John Marsden, *Marxian and Christian Utopianism: Toward a Socialist Political Theology* (New York: Monthly Review Press, 1991); and Cornel West, *The Ethical Dimensions of Marxist Thought* (New York: Monthly Review Press, 1991).

Chapter 3: Entertainment

1. Steven Watts, *The Magic Kingdom: Walt Disney and the American Way of Life* (Boston: Houghton Mifflin, 1997), 145; see also Edward G. Smith, "St. Francis of the Silver Screen," *Progress Today* (January–March 1935): 44; Charles W. Brahares, "Walt Disney as Theologian," *Christian Century* (Aug. 10, 1938): 968–69; and Annalee R. Ward, *Mouse Morality: The Rhetoric of Disney Animated Film* (Austin: University of Texas Press, 2002).

2. Gary Laderman, "The Disney Way of Death," *Journal of the American Academy of Religion* 68, no. 1 (2000): 27–46.

3. Watts, *The Magic Kingdom*, 174.

4. Nicholas Sammond, *Babes in Tomorrowland: Walt Disney and the Making of the American Child, 1930–1960* (Durham, NC: Duke University Press, 2005), 26.

5. The idea of "treasure trove" came from Bob Iger, Disney's chief executive; see Lakshmi Antonios, "Disney Buys Marvel," http://www.ffxiah.com/forum /topic/4726/disney-buys-marvel/.

6. Christopher Finch, *The Art of Walt Disney from Mickey Mouse to the Magic Kingdoms* (New York: Harry N. Abrams, 1999); Marc Eliot, *Walt Disney: Hollywood's Dark Prince* (New York: Birch Lane Press, 1993); Steven Watts, *The Magic Kingdom: Walt Disney and the American Way* (Boston: Houghton Mifflin, 1997); Janet Wasko, *Understanding Disney: The Manufacture of Fantasy* (New York: Polity, 2001); Sammond, *Babes in Tomorrowland*; Neal Gabler, *Walt Disney: The Triumph of the American Imagination* (New York: Alfred P. Knopf, 2006); and Henry A. Giroux and Grace Pollock, *The Mouse That Roared: Disney and the End of Innocence* (Lanham, MD: Rowman & Littlefield, 2010).

7. Gabler, *Walt Disney*, xii.

8. Ibid., xv.

9. Watts, *The Magic Kingdom*, 453.

10. Gabler, *Walt Disney*, 632.

11. Thomas Doherty, *Pre-Code: Hollywood: Sex, Immorality, and Insurrection in America Cinema, 1930–1934* (New York: Columbia University Press, 1999), 5.

12. James Baldwin, *The Devil Finds Work: Essay* (New York: Random House, 1976), 35.

13. bell hooks, *Reel to Real: Race, Class, and Sex at the Movies* (New York: Routledge, 1996), 2.

14. Juan Floyd-Thomas, "Popular Religion and Popular Culture: Since the Mid-Twentieth Century," in Charles H. Lippy and Peter W. Williams, eds., *Encyclopedia of Religion in America* (Washington, D.C.: CQ Press, 2010), 1723–26.

15. Many works address the synergy between religion and film, including Margaret R. Miles, *Seeing and Believing: Religion and Values in the Movies* (Boston: Beacon, 1996); John C. Lyden, *Film as Religion: Myths, Morals, and Rituals* (New York: New York University Press, 2003); S. Brent Plate, *Representing Religion in World Cinema: Filmmaking, Mythmaking, Culture Making* (New York: Palgrave Macmillan, 2003); Judith Weisenfeld, *Hollywood Be Thy Name: African American Religion in American Film, 1929–1949* (Berkeley: University of California Press, 2007); Greg Garrett, *The Gospel according to Hollywood* (Louisville, KY: Westminster John Knox Press, 2007); and Adele Reinhartz, *Bible and Cinema: An Introduction* (London: Routledge, 2013).

16. Jeffrey L. Staley and Richard Walsh, *Jesus, the Gospels, and Cinematic Imagination* (Louisville, KY: Westminster John Knox Press, 2007).

17. Adele Reinhartz, *Jesus of Hollywood* (New York: Oxford University Press, 2009), 252.

18. Ibid., 10.

19. Laurence Maslon and Michael Kantor, *Superheroes: Capes, Cowls, and the Creation of Comic Book Culture* (New York: Crown, 2013).

20. For more detailed examination of superheroes, religion, and mythology, see Richard Reynolds, *Super Heroes: A Modern Mythology* (Jackson, MS: University Press of Mississippi, 1994); B. J. Oropeza, ed., *The Gospel Aaccording to Superheroes: Religion and Pop Culture* (New York: Peter Lang, 2005); Chris Knowles, *Our Gods Wear Spandex: The Secret History of Comic Books* (San Francisco: Weiser Books, 2007); Greg Garrett, *Holy Superheroes!: Exploring the Sacred in Comics, Graphic Novels, and Film*, rev. and exp. ed. (Louisville, KY: Westminster John Knox Press, 2008); Don Lo Cicero, *Superheroes and Gods: A Comparative Study from Babylonia to Batman* (Jefferson, NC: McFarland & Co., 2008); A. David Lewis and Christine Hoff Kraemer, eds., *Graven Images: Religion in Comic Boooks and Graphic Novels* (New York: Bloomsbury, 2010); Ben Saunders, *Do the Gods Wear Capes?: Spirituality, Fantasy, and Superheroes* (New York: Bloomsbury, 2011); Marco Arnaudo, *The Myth of the Superhero*, trans. by Jamie Richards (Baltimore, MD: Johns Hopkins University Press, 2013); and Wendy Haslem, Angela Ndalianis, and Chris Mackie, eds., *Super / Heroes from Hercules to Superman* (Washington, DC: New Academia Publishing, 2007).

21. See Russell Dalton, *Marvelous Myths: Marvel Superheroes and Everyday Faith* (St. Louis: Chalice Press, 2011).

22. Joseph Campbell, *The Hero with a Thousand Faces* (Novato, CA: New World Library, 2008), 23. See also Stephen Harper, "Supermyth!," in Glenn Yeffeth, *The Man from Krypton: A Closer Look at Superman* (Dallas, TX: Benbella Books, 2006), 93–100.

23. Marco Arnaudo, *The Myth of the Superhero*, trans. Jamie Richards (Baltimore: Johns Hopkins University Press, 2013), 12.

24. "Superman on Radio," The Superman Homepage. Accessed July 17, 2016. http://www.supermanhomepage.com/radio/radio.php?topic=r-radio.

25. See Dan Jurgens et al., *The Death of Superman* (New York: DC Comics, 1993); and Louise Simonson et al., *The Return of Superman* (New York: DC Comics, 1993).

26. See also Jill Lepore, *The Secret History of Wonder Woman* (New York: Knopf, 2014); Tim Hanley, *Wonder Woman Unbound: The Curious History of the World's Most Famous Heroine* (Chicago: Chicago Review Press, 2014); and Joseph J. Darowski, *The Ages of Wonder Woman: Essays on the Amazon Princess in Changing Times* (Jefferson, NC: McFarland, 2013).

27. See "How Superheroes Fade: Alan Moore's *Watchmen*," blog located at http:// jaiarjun.blogspot.com/2006/06/how-superheroes-fade-alan-moores.html.

28. For further consideration on ethics and morality in superhero comic books, see Mark D. White, ed., *Watchmen and Philosophy: A Rorschach Test* (Hoboken, NJ: Wiley, 2009); Mark D. White and Robert Arp, eds., *Batman and Philosophy: The Dark Knight of the Soul* (Hoboken, NJ: Wiley, 2008); Tom Morris and Chris Ryall, eds., *Superheroes and Philosophy: Truth, Justice, and the Socratic Way* (Peterborough, NH: Carus Publishing, 2008); Roz Kaveney, *Superheroes! Capes and Crusaders in Comics and Films* (New York: I. B. Tauris, 2008), 4–14; Danny Fingeroth, *Superman on the Couch: What Superheroes Really Tell Us about Ourselves and Our Society* (New York: Continuum, 2005), 155–68.

29. The showrunner is the person who has overall creative responsibility and management authority for a television series.

30. Brett Martin, *Difficult Men: Behind the Scenes of a Creative Revolution: From* The Sopranos *and* The Wire *to* Mad Men *and* Breaking Bad (New York: Penguin, 2013), 4–5.

31. Alan Sepinwall, *The Revolution Was Televised: The Cops, Crooks, Slingers, and Slayers Who Changed TV Drama Forever* (New York: Touchstone, 2013); Brett Martin, *Difficult Men*.

32. A. O. Scott, "Bad in the Bones: How Walter White Found His Inner Sociopath," *New York Times*, July 24, 2013, http://www.nytimes.com/2013/07/28 /arts/television/how-walter-white-found-his-inner-sociopath.html?pagewanted =all&_r=0.

33. David R. Koepsell and Robert Arp, eds., *Breaking Bad and Philosophy: Badder Living through Chemistry* (Chicago: Open Court Publishing, 2012).

34. Quotes in this paragraph come from Scott, "Bad in the Bones."

35. Friedrich Nietzsche, *Beyond Good and Evil*, trans. Helen Zimmern (1886; Buffalo, NY: Prometheus Books, 1989), 10.

36. This doctrine is not particularly applicable to the ethos of independent and "alternative" cinema that often surfaces in opposition to the dominant Hollywood system of the mid- to late-twentieth century; ironically, many of those filmmakers who once operated as mavericks outside the Hollywood film industry—Martin Scorsese, Robert Altman, Hal Ashby, and Francis Ford Coppola among others—have been co-opted by the industry they originally critiqued and railed against.

37. Cheryl Lu-Lien Tan, "Harry Is Still Meeting Sally, 12 Years Later," *Baltimore Sun*, February 11, 2001, http://articles.baltimoresun.com/2001-02-11 /entertainment/0102110320_1_harry-met-met-sally-romantic-comedy.

38. Ibid.

39. "Television and Children," in *Your Child: Development and Behavior Resources*, University of Michigan Health System, written and compiled by Kyla Boyce, R.N., and reviewed by Brad Bushman, PhD, August 2010, at www.med.umich .edu/yourchild/topics/tv.htm.

40. Ibid.

41. Sigmund Freud, *The Joke and Its Relation to the Unconscious* (1905; New York: Penguin, 2003); Joseph Boskin, *Rebellious Laughter: People's Humor in American*

Culture (Syracuse: Syracuse University Press, 1997); Nancy A. Walker, *What's So Funny?: Humor in American Culture* (Lanham, MD: Rowman & Littlefield, 1998); Simon Critchley, *On Humour* (London: Routledge, 2002); and John Limon, *Stand-Up Comedy in Theory, or Abjection in America* (Durham, NC: Duke University Press, 2010).

42. Dean Obeidallah, "Muslim comics have a special purpose this year, and Trump is their punch line," *Washington Post*, July 12, 2016 [https://www .washingtonpost.com/news/acts-of-faith/wp/2016/07/12/the-jokes-that-muslim -american-comics-hope-will-stop-president-trump/]

43. Victor Turner, "Frame Flow, and Reflection: Ritual and Dramas as Public Liminality," in Michael Benamou and Charles Caramello, eds., *Performance Postmodern Culture* (Madison: University of Wisconsin Press, 1977), 33.

44. Bruno Deschênes, "Toward an Anthropology of Music Listening" *International Review of the Aesthetics and Sociology of Music* 29, no. 2 (December 1998): 138–39.

45. Tricia Rose, *Black Noise: Rap Music and Black Culture in Contemporary America* (Middletown, CT: Wesleyan University Press, 1994).

46. Walter Freeman, "A Neurological Role of Music in Social Bonding," in Nils L. Wallin, Bjorn Merker, and Steven Brown, eds., *The Origins of Music* (Cambridge, MA: MIT Press, 2000), 420; see also Anthony Storr, *Music and the Mind* (London: Harper Collins, 1992); Robin Sylvan, *Traces of the Spirit: The Religious Dimension of Popular Music* (New York: New York University Press, 2002); Daniel J. Levitin, *The World in Six Songs: How the Musical Brain Created Human Nature* (New York: Dutton, 2008); and Gary Laderman, *Sacred Matters: Celebrity Worship, Sexual Ecstasies, the Living Dead, and Other Signs of Religious Life in the United States* (New York: The New Press, 2009), 24.

47. Anthony Storr, *Music and the Mind* (London: Harper Collins, 1992), 17.

48. "The Slaughter of the Spy-Journalist, the Jew Daniel Pearl," video released on February 21, 2002.

49. http://fullcomment.nationalpost.com/2012/06/13/luka-rocco-magnotta-video -teacher/.

50. http://www.torontosun.com/2012/06/09/was-luka-magnotta-born-evil.

51. Ty Burr, *Gods Like Us: On Movie Stardom and Modern Fame* (New York: Pantheon Books, 2012), xiii.

52. Daniel J. Boorstin, *The Image: A Guide to Pseudo-Events in America* (1962; New York: Vintage, 1992), 57–58.

53. Christopher Lasch, *The Culture of Narcissism: American Life in An Age of Diminishing Expectations* (New York: W. W. Norton & Co., 1979), 60.

54. http://www.forbes.com/sites/clareoconnor/2014/06/30/kim-kardashians-28 -million-year-how-she-made-more-than-ever-before/#404d6e773d70

55. Pamela Des Barres, *I'm with the Band* (Chicago: Chicago Review Press, 1987/2005), and *Take Another Little Piece of My Heart: A Groupie Grows Up* (Chicago: Chicago Review Press, 1993/2008), and *Let's Spend the Night Together: Backstage Secrets of Rock Muses and Supergroupies* (Chicago: Chicago Review Press, 2007).

56. John Hope Franklin, "Birth of a Nation—Propaganda as History" (1979), in Steven Mintz and Randy Roberts, eds., *Hollywood America: United States History through Its Films* (St. James, NY: Brandywine Press, 2001), 49.

57. Ellen C. Scott, *Cinema Civil Rights: Regulation, Repression, and Race in the Classical Hollywood Era* (New Brunswick, NJ: Rutgers University Press, 2015); Emi-

lie Raymond, *Stars for Freedom: Hollywood, Black Celebrities, and the Civil Rights Movement* (Seattle: University of Washington Press, 2015).

58. Steven W. Thrasher, "OscarsSoWhite: Chris Rock Exposed the Depths of the Industry's Race Problem," *The Guardian*, February 29, 2016, http://www.theguardian.com/film/filmblog/2016/feb/29/oscars-so-white-academy-awards-2016-chris-rock-diversity.

59. Grace Ji-Sun Kim, "Chris Rock Should Know that Racism Isn't Black and White," *Time Inc. Network*, February 29, 2016, http://time.com/4241460/chris-rock-racism/.

60. Karen Workman, "After Oscars, Hashtags Ask: Does One Minority Group Have to Fight for Another?" *New York Times*, March 2, 2016, http://mobile.nytimes.com/2016/03/03/arts/after-oscars-hashtags-ask-does-one-minority-group-have-to-fight-for-another.html?referer=&_r=0.

61. http://www.cardplayer.com/poker-news/20036-global-online-gambling-market-growing-at-11-percent-clip.

62. James Paul Gee, *What Video Games Have to Teach Us about Learning and Literacy* (New York: Palgrave Macmillan, 2003), 18.

63. See text of McGonigal's TED Talk: http://www.ted.com/conversations/44/we_spend_3_billion_hours_a_wee.html. See also Jane McGonigal, *Reality Is Broken: Why Games Make Us Better and How They Can Change the World* (New York: Penguin Books, 2011); http://www.barnesandnoble.com/w/reality-is-broken-jane-mcgonigal/1100817884?ean=9781101475492; Ian Bogost, *Persuasive Games: The Expressive Power of Videogames* (Cambridge MA: The MIT Press, 2010); Tom Bissell, *Extra Lives: Why Video Games Matter* (New York: Vintage, 2011).

64. This phrase is drawn from Penguin's promotional paragraph on Amazon for McGonigal, *Reality Is Broken*; see https://www.amazon.ca/Reality-Broken-Games-Better-Change/dp/0143120611.

65. McGonigal, *Reality Is Broken*, 4.

66. Steven Johnson, *Everything Bad Is Good for You: How Today's Popular Culture Is Actually Making Us Smarter* (New York: Riverhead Books, 2005), 42.

67. George Rawlinson, trans., with Henry Rawlinson and J. G. Wilkinson, *The History of Herodotus: A New English Version* (New York: D. Appleton, 1861), 182; http://archive.org/stream/historyofherodot03hero#page/n5/mode/2up.

68. Johnson, *Everything Bad*, 36.

69. "God game," Wikipedia, http://en.wikipedia.org/wiki/God_game.

Chapter 4: Politics

1. See *The Republic of Plato*, trans. with notes and an interpretive essay by Allan Bloom, 2nd ed. (New York: Basic Books, 1968).

2. On the role Plato's philosophy has had on the formation of Western civilization and government, see Stacey M. Floyd-Thomas and Miguel A. De La Torre, eds., *Beyond the Pale: Reading Ethics from the Margins* (Louisville, KY: Westminster John Knox Press, 2011), chap. 1.

3. Popper, Karl. *The Poverty of Historicism* (Abingdon, Oxon, UK: Routledge Classics, 2002).

4. Linnell E. Cady, *Religion, Theology, and American Public Life* (New York: SUNY Press, 1993), 10f. As examples of descriptions treating the "cultural crisis" America faces in these areas, Cady mentions the work of Daniel Bell and Christopher Lasch; see p. 17. Jeffrey Stout also points out that Luther's convictions about the nature of the secular order and the work of eighteenth-

century deists and nineteenth-century atheists all contributed to the secularization of public discourse. See Stout, *Ethics after Babel: The Languages of Morals and Their Discontents* (Boston: Beacon Press, 1988), 80.

5. Locke, *The Second Treatise of Civil Government*, edited with an introduction by J. W. Gough (Oxford : Basil Blackwell, 1946.), chap. 7, sec. 87–89.

6. http://avalon.law.yale.edu/19th_century/jefinau1.asp.

7. Charles Francis Adams, ed., *The Works of John Adams*, vol. 4 (Boston: Charles C. Little and James Brown, 1851), 375–76.

8. Jefferson's discussion of this topic can be found in Adrienne Koch and William Peden, eds., *The Life and Selected Writings of Thomas Jefferson* (New York: Modern Library, 1944), 261.

9. Quoted in ibid., 238.

10. Randy Boyagoda, *Richard John Neuhaus: A Life in the Public Square* (New York: Image Books, 2015). For an extensive discussion on the relationship of establishment to freedom of religion in the First Amendment, see Mark G. Toulouse, *God in Public: Four Ways American Christianity and American Public Life Relate* (Louisville, KY: Westminster John Knox Press, 2006), chaps. 1 and 2.

11. Toulouse, *God in Public*, 27.

12. James Madison, quoted in *God in Public*, 27.

13. Stephen E. Lucas, "Justifying America: The Declaration of Independence as a Rhetorical Document," in Thomas W. Benson, ed., *American Rhetoric: Context and Criticism* (Carbondale: Southern Illinois University Press, 1989), 67–130.

14. On the secular nature of the Constitution itself and the attempts of many groups to make it an explicitly religious document, see Toulouse, *God in Public*, 7–9.

15. See Jennifer Steinhauer, "Constitution Has Its Day (More or Less) in House," *New York Times*, January 6, 2011, http://www.nytimes.com/2011/01/07/us/politics/07constitution.html?_r=0. Robert Ratliff, our editor at Westminster John Knox suggested this parallel.

16. Freedland, "This Sacred Text Explains Why the US Can't Kick the Gun Habit," *The Guardian*, December 21, 2012, http://www.theguardian.com/commentisfree/2012/dec/21/sacred-text-us-gun-habit.

17. "A Modell of Christian Charity" (more commonly known as "City on a Hill"), delivered aboard the *Arabella* in 1630; see http://history.hanover.edu/texts/winthmod.html for a copy of the sermon.

18. For a discussion on manifest destiny and mission as forces in American political life, especially as they affect foreign policy, see Frederick Merk, *Manifest Destiny and Mission in American Life*, reprint ed. (Cambridge: Harvard University Press, 1996).

19. Sanford Levinson, *Constitutional Faith* (Princeton, NJ: Princeton University Press, 1988), 129–30, 133. Barbara Jordan's famous statement arose as she spoke to the nation from her position as a member of the committee considering the impeachment of Richard Nixon in 1974. Her statement, according to Levinson, inspired him to write *Constitutional Faith* in the first place.

20. Mark Hulliung, *The Social Contract in America: From the Revolution to the Present Age* (Lawrence: University Press of Kansas, 2007).

21. Garry Wills, *Lincoln at Gettysburg*, reissue ed. (New York: Simon & Schuster, 2006), 88.

22. Franklin Delano Roosevelt, first inaugural address, Saturday, March 4, 1933, http://www.bartleby.com/124/pres49.html.

23. John F. Kennedy, http://www.jfklibrary.org/Asset-Viewer/BqXIEM9F4024 ntFl7SVAjA.aspx.

24. Martin Luther King Jr., "I Have a Dream . . . ," https://www.archives.gov/press /exhibits/dream-speech.pdf, 1–2.

25. Lyndon B. Johnson, http://www.lbjlib.utexas.edu/johnson/archives.hom /speeches.hom/640522.asp.

26. King, "The Causalities of the War in Vietnam," February 25, 1967, The Nation Institute, Los Angeles 1967, http://www.aavw.org/special_features /speeches_speech_king02.html.

27. http://www.whitehouse.gov/the-press-office/2013/01/21/inaugural-address -president-barack-obama.

28. Will Herberg, *Protestant, Catholic, Jew: An Essay in American Religious Sociology* (Chicago: University of Chicago Press, 1955), 79.

29. "The National Archives and Records Administration Annual Report 1999," U.S. National Archives and Records Administration.

30. See Toulouse's analysis of President George W. Bush's rhetoric in *God in Public*, 54–56.

31. Steven Waldman, "Palin and Religion: What's Scary, What's Not?" Huffington Post, May 25, 2011, http://www.huffingtonpost.com/steven-waldman /palin-religion-whats-scar_b_125305.html.

32. Steve Schmidt, "Palin Believed Candidacy 'God's Plan,'" Huffington Post, March 18, 2010, http://www.huffingtonpost.com/2010/01/10/steve-schmidt -palin-belie_n_417977.html.

33. Shadee Ashtari, "GOP Lawmaker Sends Every Member of Congress a Bible for 'Decision Making' Instruction," Huffington Post, August 7, 2014, http://www .huffingtonpost.com/2014/08/06/steven-palazzo-congress-bible_n_5656160 .html?utm_hp_ref=religion-and-politics.

34. Shadee Ashtari, "Michele Bachmann: Gays Pushing Laws Allowing Adults 'To Freely Prey On Little Children Sexually,'" Huffington Post, July 25, 2014, http://www.huffingtonpost.com/2014/07/25/michele-bachmann-gay -marriage_n_5621344.html?utm_hp_ref=religion-and-politics.

35. Sidney E. Mead, *The Lively Experiment: The Shaping of Christianity in America* (New York: Harper & Row, 1976), 152.

36. Abraham Lincoln, "Second Inaugural Address (March 4, 1865)," in Conrad Cherry, ed., *God's New Israel: Religious Interpretations of American Destiny*, rev. and updated ed. (Chapel Hill: University of North Carolina Press, 1998), 202.

37. Evelyn Nieves, "Judges Ban Pledge of Allegiance from Schools, Citing 'Under God,'" *New York Times*, June 27, 2002. See Toulouse, *God in Public*, 71.

38. "Fast Chat: Out From Under God," *Newsweek*, August 18, 2002, http://www .newsweek.com/fast-chat-out-under-god-144201.

39. http://www.prnewswire.com/news-releases/newsweek-cover-under-god-under -fire-78004762.html.

40. *Newdow v. United States of America*, United States Court of Appeals for the Ninth Circuit, 2002, http://www.constitution.org/usfc/9/newdow_v_us.htm.

41. Newdow; Pat Doe; Jane Doe; DoeChild; Jan Poe; PoeChild; RoeChild-1 v. Rio Linda Union School District and the United States of America, http:// cdn.ca9.uscourts.gov/datastore/opinions/2010/03/11/05-17257.pdf.

42. Ibid.

43. http://www2.kenyon.edu/Depts/Religion/Fac/Adler/Politics/newdow.irons.pdf.

44. Quoted in Karen M. Seeley, *Therapy after Terror: 9/11, Psychotherapists, and Mental Health* (Cambridge: Cambridge University Press, 2008), 151–52.
45. David L. Atheide, *Terror Post 9/11 and the Media* (New York: Peter Lang, 2009), 28.
46. http://www.metrolyrics.com/god-bless-the-usa-lyrics-lee-greenwood.html.
47. http://www.defense.gov/News/NewsArticle.aspx?ID=65272.
48. Simon Hall, *American Patriotism, American Protest: Social Movements since the Sixties* (Philadelphia: University of Pennsylvania Press, 2011), 7.
49. Toulouse, *God in Public*, 59.
50. Mead, *The Lively Experiment*, 66–68.
51. James Madison to Henry Lee, June 25, 1824, http://founders.archives.gov /documents/Madison/99-02-02-0247.
52. Richard Hofstadter, *Anti-Intellectualism in American Life* (New York: Vintage, 1962), 154.
53. Kaplan, "Reaganism, Capitalism, and Sheilaism," Huffington Post, posted August 5, 2013, http://www.huffingtonpost.com/marty-kaplan/reaganism -capitalism-and-_b_3704958.html.
54. U.S. Department of Defense News Briefing of Secretary of Defense Donald H. Rumsfeld and General Richard Myers, February 12, 2002; the question was, "He asked you if you knew of evidence that Iraq was supplying—or willing to supply weapons of mass destruction to terrorists." This was Rumsfeld's reply. www.defense.gov/transcripts/transcript.aspx?transcriptid=2636.
55. Sabine Lang, *NGOs, Civil Society, and the Public Sphere* (Cambridge: Cambridge University Press, 2012).
56. Toulouse, *God in Public*, 58.
57. Ibid., 62.

Chapter 5: Sports

1. Will Blythe, *To Hate Like This Is to Be Happy Forever: A Thoroughly Obsessive, Intermittently Uplifting, and Occasionally Unbiased Account of the Duke-North Carolina Basketball Rivalry* (New York: HarperCollins, 2006), 89.
2. Tom Krattenmaker, ed., *Onward Christian Athletes: Turning Ballparks into Pulpits and Players into Preachers* (Lanham, MD: Rowman & Littlefield, 2010), 167–88; see chap. 9, "A Match Made in Heaven—Or Hell: The Dissonance between the Values of Jesus and the Values of Big-Time Sports."
3. Tony Ladd and James Mathisen note the anniversary of the Cornell/ Dartmouth game in their book *Muscular Christianity: Evangelical Protestants and the Development of American Sport* (Ada, MI: Baker Books, 1999).
4. Krattenmaker, *Onward Christian Athletes*, 169–70.
5. Richard Lischer, "Legends of the Game," *Christian Century*, July 24, 2013, 32.
6. Ibid., 33.
7. For example, for religion scholars, see Robert J. Higgs, *God in the Stadium: Sports and Religion in America* (Lexington: University Press of Kentucky, 1995); Robert J. Higgs and Michael C. Braswell, *An Unholy Alliance: The Sacred and Modern Sports* (Macon, GA: Mercer University Press, 2004); Krattenmaker, *Onward Christian Athletes*; Joseph Price, ed., *From Season to Season: Sports as American Religion* (Macon, GA: Mercer University Press, 2001); Jeffrey Scholes and Raphael Sassower, *Religion and Sports in American Culture* (New York: Routledge, 2014). For scholars of sport, see Adam Brown, ed., *Fanatics! Power, Identity, and Fandom in Football* (London: Routledge, 1998); Norbert Elias and

Eric Dunning, *Quest for Excitement: Sport and Leisure in the Civilizing Process* (Oxford: Blackwell, 1986); Garry Robson, '*No One Likes Us, We Don't Care': The Myth and Reality of Millwall Fandom* (Oxford: Berg, 2000). For sociological analysis, see Daniel Burdsey, *British Asians and Football: Culture, Identity, Exclusion* (London, Routledge, 2007); Johan Huizinga, *Homo Ludens: A Study of the Play Element in Culture* (Boston: Beacon Press, 1950); Kristin Walseth and Kari Fasting, "Islam's View on Physical Activity and Sport: Egyptian Women Interpreting Islam," *International Review for the Sociology of Sport* 38, no. 1: 45–60. For anthropological analysis, see Thomas F. Carter, *In Foreign Fields: The Politics and Experiences of Transnational Sport Migration* (London: Pluto Press, 2011); Susan Brownell, *Beijing's Games: What the Olympics Mean to China* (Lanham, MD: Rowman & Littlefield), 2008. For an excellent overview of these different approaches to religion and sport, see anthropologist Thomas F. Carter's essay, "God Does Not Play Dice with the Universe, or Does He?: Anthropological Interlocations of Sport and Religion," *Religion and Society: Advances in Research* 3 (2012): 142–62.

8. This biography over the next few pages is dependent on Arnold Rampersad, *Jackie Robinson: A Biography* (New York: Ballantine Books, Random House, 1997), 12.

9. Ibid., 12–17.

10. Ibid., 23.

11. Ibid., 27.

12. Ibid., 31f.

13. Ibid., 53–57

14. Ibid., 75.

15. In 1946, the fall before Robinson integrated baseball, Washington and Strode became the first two black football players to integrate the modern National Football League. When the Cleveland Rams moved to Los Angeles, the commissioners of the Los Angeles Coliseum mandated that the team had to be integrated in order to use the stadium; the Rams picked up both Washington and Strode. Washington played for three years, and Strode for one.

16. Rampersad, *Jackie Robinson*, 70–73.

17. Ibid., 91.

18. David Chidester, "The Church of Baseball, the Fetish of Coca-Cola, and the Potlatch of Rock 'N' Roll," in B. Forbes and J. Mahan, eds., *Religion and Popular Culture in America* (Berkeley: University of California Press, 2005), 215.

19. For the previous paragraph's discussion and this quote, see Chidester, 216–18.

20. William J. Baker, *Playing with God: Religion and Modern Sport* (Cambridge: Harvard, 2007), 172.

21. Joseph Dorinson and Joram Warmund, eds., *Jackie Robinson: Race, Sports, and the American Dream* (Armonk, NY: M. E. Sharpe, 1998), 107.

22. Martin Luther King, quoted in Joseph Dorinson, "Hank Greenberg, Joe DiMaggio, and Jackie Robinson: Race, Identity, and Ethnic Power," in Dorinson and Warmund, *Jackie Robinson: Race, Sports, and the American Dream*, 112.

23. Patrick Henry, "Kareem's Omission? Jackie Robinson, Black Profile in Courage," in Dorinson and Warmund, *Jackie Robinson: Race, Sports, and the American Dream*, 209.

24. Samuel O. Regalado, "Jackie Robinson and the Emancipation of Latin American Baseball Players," in Dorinson and Warmund, *Jackie Robinson: Race, Sports, and the American Dream*, 157–64.

25. Dorinson and Warmund, *Jackie Robinson: Race, Sports, and the American Dream*, 148.

26. Christopher H. Evans, "Baseball as Civil Religion: The Genesis of an American Creation Story," in Christopher H. Evans and William R. Herzog II, eds., *The Faith of 50 Million: Baseball, Religion, and American Culture* (Louisville, KY: Westminster John Knox Press, 2002), 13–33.

27. See section on Babe Dedrikson in Allen Barra, "Hit or Myth,"*Village Voice* (December 28, 1999), http://www.villagevoice.com/news/hit-or-myth-6420179.

28. John R. Tunis, "The Great Sports Myth," *Harper's Monthly Magazine*, March 1, 1928, 422-31.

29. A. Bartlett Giamatti, *Take Time for Paradise: Americans and Their Games* (Bloomsbury: New York, 1989), 73, quoted in Joseph Price, *From Season to Season*, 126.

30. Allen Barra, *Mickey and Willie, The Parallel Lives of Baseball's Golden Age* (New York: Random House, 2013). See also the review by Bill Savage, found in the *Chicago Tribune*, http://articles.chicagotribune.com/2013-05-17/features/ct -prj-0519-mickey-mantle-willie-mays-allen-barra-20130517_1_mickey-and -willie-mantle-mays.

31. http://latino.foxnews.com/latino/sports/2013/04/03/over-28-percent-players -were-foreign-born-in-mlb-opening-day/.

32. Jimmie Lee Solomon, "Percentage of Major League African-American Players Has Fallen Drastically," in Huffington Post online, http://www .huffingtonpost.com/jimmie-lee-solomon/african-american-baseball-players _b_4923689.html.

33. Richard Lapchick, "2013 Racial and Gender Report Card: National Football League," published October 22, 2013, by The Institute for Diversity and Ethics in Sport, http://www.tidesport.org/RGRC/2013/2013_NFL_RGRC.pdf.

34. For this comment, see Bob Oates, "A Sports Myth for Black Youth," *The Wilson Quarterly* (Autumn 1979): 187.

35. Joshua Kjerulf Dubrow and Jimi Adams, "Hoop Inequalities: Race, Class, and Family Structure Background and the Odds of Playing in the National Basketball Association," *International Review for the Sociology of Sport* 47, no. 1: 43–59.

36. Peter Keating, "Next Level," *ESPN The Magazine*, http://espn.go.com/espn /story/_/id/6777581/importance-athlete-background-making-nba.

37. David Leonhardt and Ford Fessenden, "Black Coaches in NBA Have Shorter Tenures," in *New York Times*, http://www.nytimes.com/2005/03/22/sports /basketball/22coaches.html?_r=2&pagewanted=print&position=&.

38. Tom Ziller, "The NBA's Race Problem for Coaches Is Staring Us in the Face," SB Nation, http://www.sbnation.com/nba/2014/5/16/5723170/nba-race-problem -coaches-gms-owners.

39. Lapchick, "2013 Racial and Gender Report Card," http://www.tidesport.org /RGRC/2013/2013_MLS_RGRC.pdf.

40. Farrell Evans, "Too Few Good Men: Minorities Struggle to Find Jobs as PGA Pros," *Sports Illustrated*, February 8, 2011, http://www.golf.com/tour -and-news/too-few-good-men-minorities-struggle-find-jobs-pga-pros.

41. During the summer of 2016, fans seem especially hopeful.

42. See chapter 4 of Joseph L. Price, *Rounding the Bases: Baseball and Religion in America* (Macon, GA: Mercer University Press, 2006), as he discusses "Conjuring Curses and Supplicating Spirits," 93–110.

43. http://espn.go.com/new-york/mlb/story/_/id/7612606/new-york-yankees-derek -jeter-lot-muhammad-ali.

44. For a variety of Lombardi quotes on this topic, see http://www.vincelombardi
.com/quotes.html.

45. Anson Dorrance gave this note to Mia Hamm in 1992 when he witnessed her training on her own. She used it in her own book, *Go for the Goal* (New York: HarperCollins, 1999). Later, it inspired the title of Dorrance's book, *The Vision of a Champion* (Chelsea, MI: Sleeping Bear Press, 2002).

46. http://www.allblacks.com/Teams/Haka.

47. Carl Diem, quoted in Alois Koch, SJ, "Sport—A Secular Religion," http://www.con-spiration.de/koch/english/religion-e.html#-22.

48. Johan Huizinga, *Homo Ludens: A Study of the Play-Element in Culture* (London: Routledge & Kegan Paul, 1949), 18; see also Carter, "God Doesn't Play Dice," 144.

49. Carter, "God Doesn't Play Dice," 150, who discussed and quoted Vincent Turner concerning this point.

50. Luke Cyphers, "The Song Remains the Same," ESPN Magazine, http://espn.go.com/espn/story/_/id/6957582/the-history-national-anthem-sports-espn-magazine.

51. See Joseph Price's excellent section on ethics in baseball in his book *Rounding the Bases*, 157.

52. Ken Belson, "NFL Domestic Violence Policy Toughened in Wake of Ray Rice Case," *New York Times*, August 28, 2014, http://www.nytimes.com/2014/08/29/sports/football/roger-goodell-admits-he-was-wrong-and-alters-nfl-policy-on-domestic-violence.html?_r=2.

53. Price, *Rounding the Bases*, 160.

54. Marney made this statement in the hearing of Mark Toulouse, when he was a seminary student in 1975.

55. Robert J. Higgs, *God in the Stadium: Sport and Religion in America* (Lexington: University Press of Kentucky, 1995), 194.

56. Price, *Rounding the Bases*, 120.

57. Wallace, http://www.nytimes.com/2006/08/20/sports/playmagazine/20federer.html?pagewanted=all&_r=0.

58. "Is Sports a Religion?" Nigel Barber's blog, "The Human Beast," in *Psychology Today*, http://www.psychologytoday.com/blog/the-human-beast/200911/is-sport-religion.

59. Christopher Carter's blog, "Religion and More," where he refers to this quote, http://religionandmore.wordpress.com/2010/09/30/just-how-religious-is-sport/.

60. Ana Gamboa, http://www.philly.com/philly/sports/soccer/worldcup/20140612_For_Latinos__soccer_virtually_a_religious_experience.html.

61. See a discussion of these kinds of sport experiences in Shirl Hoffman, *Sport and Religion* (Champagne, IL: Human Kinetics, 1992), 67.

62. See, for example, Tracy J. Trothen, "Hockey: A Divine Sport?—Canada's National Sport in Relation to Embodiment, Community, and Hope," *Studies in Religion* 35, no. 2 (2006): 291–305.

63. Klaus V. Meier examines the shift from Descartes to Merleau-Ponty in Meier, "Cartesian and Phenomenological Anthropology: The Radical Shift and Its Meaning for Sport," *Journal of the Philosophy of Sport* 2 (1975): 62–63.

64. Ibid., 69.

65. Ibid., 69–71.

66. Clifford Putney, *Muscular Christianity: Manhood and Sports in Protestant America, 1880–1920* (Cambridge: Harvard University Press, 2001); Betty DeBerg, *Ungodly Women: Gender and the First Wave of American Fundamentalism* (Macon, GA: Mercer University Press, 2000).
67. DeFord, "Religion and Sport," *Sports Illustrated*, April 19, 1976, 88–102.
68. Eleanor J. Stebner and Tracy J. Trothen, "A Diamond Is Forever? Women, Baseball, and a Pitch for a Radically Inclusive Community," in *The Faith of Fifty Million: Baseball, Religion, and American Culture*, ed. Christopher H. Evans and William R. Herzog II (Louisville, KY: Westminster John Knox Press, 2002), 167–84.
69. http://en.wikipedia.org/wiki/Legends_Football_League.
70. http://bleacherreport.com/articles/1326619-100-hottest-athletes-of-all-time is an example.
71. Helen Jefferson Lenskyj, "Reflections on Communication and Sport: On Heteronormativity and Gender Identities," *Communication and Sport*, vol.1, June 2013, 145.
72. Helen Jefferson Lenskyj, *Out on the Field: Gender, Sport and Sexualities* (Toronto: Women's Press, 2003).
73. Lenskyj, "Reflections on Communication and Sport," 143.

Chapter 6: Science and Technology

1. David C. Lindberg, *The Beginnings of Western Science: The European Scientific Tradition in Philosophical, Religious, and Institutional Context, Prehistory to A.D. 1450*, 2nd ed. (Chicago: University of Chicago Press, 2008).
2. http://www.heritage.org/initiatives/first-principles/primary-sources/woodrow-wilson-asks-what-is-progress"What Is Progress?"
3. https://er.jsc.nasa.gov/seh/ricetalk.htm.
4. See Richard Conniff, "What the Luddites Really Fought Against," *Smithsonian Magazine*, March 2011, http://www.smithsonianmag.com/history-archaeology/What-the-Luddites-Really-Fought-Against.html.
5. Donald Kraybill, quoted in Jeff Brady, "Amish Community Not Anti-Technology, Just More Thoughtful," September 2, 2013, http://www.npr.org/blogs/alltechconsidered/2013/09/02/217287028/amish-community-not-anti-technology-just-more-thoughful.
6. http://www.thespoof.com/news/science-technology/83952/luddite-invents-machine-to-destroy-technology-quicker.
7. David F. Noble, *The Religion of Technology: The Divinity of Man and the Spirit of Invention* (New York: Alfred A. Knopf, 1997), 17.
8. Ibid., 140.
9. Ibid., 162.
10. Ibid., 191.
11. Jeff Goodell, "The Steve Jobs That Nobody Knew," *Rolling Stone*, October 27, 2011, 38.
12. The following paragraphs are drawn from a few sources: Goodell, "The Steve Jobs That Nobody Knew," 36–45; and Walter Isaacson, *Steve Jobs* (New York: Simon & Schuster, 2011).
13. Goodell, "The Steve Jobs That Nobody Knew," 38.
14. Steve Jobs, quoted in ibid., 40.
15. Ibid., 41.

16. Isaacson, *Steve Jobs*, 110.

17. Ibid., 118.

18. Ibid., 122.

19. Ibid.

20. Ibid., 252.

21. Goodell, "The Steve Jobs That Nobody Knew," 44.

22. Ibid., 45.

23. Isaacson, *Steve Jobs*, 565.

24. Russell W. Belk and Gülnur Tumbat "The Cult of Macintosh," *Consumption Markets & Culture* 8, no. 3, September 2005, 207–8.

25. See Belk and Tumbat, "The Cult of Macintosh," 205–17; Alan Deutschman, *The Second Coming of Steve Jobs*, 1st ed. (New York: Broadway Books, 2000); Leander Kahney, "Worshipping at the Altar of Mac," *Wired*, December 5, 2002, http://www.wired.com/gadgets/mac/commentary/cultofmac/2002/12/56674?currentPage=all; Isaacson, *Steve Jobs*; and Brett T. Robinson, *Appletopia: Media Technology and the Religious Imagination of Steve Jobs* (Waco, TX: Baylor University Press, 2013); and Craig Detweiler, *iGods: How Technology Shapes Our Spiritual and Social Lives* (Grand Rapids: Brazos Press, 2013).

26. Isaacson, *Steve Jobs*, 143.

27. Ibid., 166.

28. Ibid., 138.

29. Ibid., 115.

30. Samsung lost an important patent battle with Apple in 2012 and, as of November 21, 2013, a jury concluded that Samsung must pay Apple $290,456,793 in damages. In a second trial concerning violation of patents, Samsung ended up paying Apple an additional $119.6 million.

31. http://www.theguardian.com/technology/2013/nov/17/apple-mavericks-upgrade-naughton.

32. For a full discussion of Buber's "I-Thou" philosophy, see Martin Buber, *I and Thou* (New York: Scribner, 1958).

33. http://www.foxnews.com/science/2013/05/17/why-still-love-star-trek/.

34. See Lawrence M. Krauss, *The Physics of Star Trek*, rev. ed. (New York: Basic Books, 2007), xi.

35. Margaret Atwood, "The Road to Ustopia," *The Guardian*, October 14, 2011, http://www.guardian.co.uk/books/2011/oct/14/margaret-atwood-road-to-ustopia.

36. See blog, "Eye of Horus (Subliminals)," http://hollywoodsubliminals.wordpress.com/franchise/the-matrix/the-matrix/eye-of-horus/.

37. Quoted in John Dear, *Put Down Your Sword: Answering the Gospel Call to Creative Nonviolence* (Grand Rapids, MI: Eerdmans, 2008), 114.

38. Craig Georgianna, Tom Underhill, and Chad Kelland, *Hyperstimulation: Teens, Porn, and Online Addictions* (Brea, CA: The Center for Psychotherapy, 2010).

39. http://library.timelesstruths.org/music/Is_Your_All_on_the_Altar/.

40. http://www.theatlantic.com/magazine/archive/2013/04/the-touch-screen-generation/309250/.

41. techland.time.com/2013/05/19/what-is-tumblr/.

42. http://clinicalexcellence.blogs.hopkinsmedicine.org/2011/03/01/rituals-in-medicine/.

43. Matthew Herper, "The Medical Power of Ritual," *Forbes*, December 23, 2010, http://www.forbes.com/sites/matthewherper/2010/12/23/the-medical -power-of-ritual/.

44. Sanjay Gupta, *Monday Mornings: A Novel*, reprint ed. (New York: Grand Central Publishing, 2013).

45. Ginny Jaques, "Are Electronic Devices Appendages to Your Body?," www .bloggingbistro.com/are-electronic-devices-appendages-to-your-body/.

46. Brian Fung, "Inside Former NSA Chief Michael Hayden's 'Interview' with an Amtrak Live-Tweeter," *Washington Post*, http://www.washingtonpost.com /blogs/the-switch/wp/2013/10/24/inside-former-nsa-chief-michael-haydens- interview-with-an-amtrak-live-tweeter/.

47. Observation Baltimore, "Handheld Devices: Addiction or Obsession?" Observationbaltimorecom/blog/2011/11/handheld-devices-addiction-or -obsession/.

48. http://www.itu.int/en/ITU-D/Statistics/Pages/stat/default.aspx#.

49. http://www.statista.com/statistics/216573/worldwide-market-share-of-search -engines/.

50. Pamela Jones Harbour, "The Emperor of All Identities," *New York Times*, Op-Ed, December 18, 2012, http://www.nytimes.com/2012/12/19/opinion /why-google-has-too-much-power-over-your-private-life.html?_r=0.

51. See the online PBS special, "College Inc.," on this phenomenon, http://www .pbs.org/wgbh/pages/frontline/collegeinc/. Accreditation connected to these schools asks questions about whether or not appropriate autonomy from the parent corporation exists. A number of more traditional schools and universities have developed "massive open online courses (MOOC)." While these courses extend publicity and notoriety for professors and universities, most are trying to understand where the revenue stream can be attached to the MOOC phenomenon.

52. http://observationbaltimore.com/blog/tag/which-technology-devices-are-most -associated-with-addiction-to-the-internet/.

53. http://www.eecg.toronto.edu/~mann/.

54. See http://www.technologyreview.com/news/416104/implantable-silicon-silk -electronics/page/1/ a http://www.forevergeek.com/2011/07/qr-code-tattoo/.

55. http://www.genome.gov.

Conclusion: Worship without Sacrifice

1. Steve Bruce, *Secularization* (New York: Oxford University Press, 2011); Steve Bruce, *God is Dead: Secularization in the West* (Malden, MA: Blackwell, 2002); Ian Reader, "Secularization, RIP? Nonsense! The 'Rush Hour Away from the Gods' and the Decline of Religion," *Journal of Religion in Japan* 1 (2012): 7–36; David Voas and Siobhan McAndrew, "Three Puzzles of Non-religion in Britain," *Journal of Contemporary Religion* 27, no. 1 (2012): 29–48; Phil Zuckerman, "Atheism: Contemporary Numbers and Patterns," in *The Cambridge Companion to Atheism*, ed. Michael Martin (New York: Cambridge University Press, 2007); Jack Shand, "The Decline of Traditional Christian Beliefs in Germany," *Sociology of Religion* 59 (1998): 179–84; and Anthony B. Pinn, ed., *Theism and Public Policy: Humanist Perspectives and Responses* (New York: Palgrave Macmillan, 2014), 1–11, 37–52.

2. For example, in Canada a hundred years ago, only 2 percent of the population claimed to have no religion. Today, nearly 30 percent of Canadians openly

claim such a designation, and one in five Canadians profess not to believe in God. A century ago in Australia, less than 1 percent of the population claimed no religious identity, but, by comparison, approximately 20 percent of Australians claim as much today, including the current Prime Minister of Australia, Julia Gillard, who is an open atheist. In Holland, in the early twentieth century, around 10 percent of the population claimed to be religiously unaffiliated; today, it is over 40 percent. In contemporary Great Britain and Sweden, nearly half of the people now claim no religious identity at all. Percentages for the following countries are similar and growing: the former Czech Republic (61 percent), Estonia (49 percent), Slovenia (45 percent), Bulgaria (34 percent), and Norway (31 percent). Significant percentages of the populations in France (33 percent), Belgium (27 percent), and Germany (25 percent) do not believe in God or any sort of universal spiritual life force—and these are all the highest rates of nonbelief ever recorded for these nations. See Bruce, *Secularization*; and Bob Altemeyer, "Non-Belief and Secularity in North America," in *Atheism and Secularity*, ed. Phil Zuckerman (Santa Barbara, CA: Praeger, 2009); Reginald Bibby, *Restless Gods* (Toronto: Stoddart, 2002). On Holland, see also Loek Halman, "Atheism and Secularity in the Netherlands," in *Atheism and Secularity*, vol. 2, ed. Phil Zuckerman (Santa Barbara, CA: Praeger, 2010); for Britain, see Samuel Bagg and David Voas, "The Triumph of Indifference: Irreligion in British Society," in *Atheism and Secularity*, vol. 2; Alasdair Crockett and David Voas, "Generations of Decline: Religious Change in 20th Century Britain," *Journal for the Scientific Study of Religion* 45, no. 4 (2006): 567–84; R. Gil, C. K. Hadaway, and P. L. Marler, "Is Religious Belief Declining in Britain?" *Journal for the Scientific Study of Religion* 37 (1998): 507–16; and for Sweden, Lars Ahlin, *Pilgrim, Turist Eller Flykting? En Studie av Individuell Religiös Rörlighet i Senmonderniteten* (Stockholm: Brutus Östlings Bokförlag Symposium, 2005); for Europe, see Inglehart et al., *Human Beliefs and Values: A Cross-Cultural Sourcebook Based on the 1999–2002 Value Surveys* (Buenos Aires: Siglo Veintiuno Editores, 2004); For no belief in either God or any spiritual source, see Eurobarometer Report, "Social Values, Science, and Technology," European Commission, 2005, accessed July 24, 2014, http://ec.europa.eu/public_opinion /archives/ebs/ebs_225_report_en.pdf; Jack Shand, "The Decline of Traditional Christian Beliefs in Germany," *Sociology of Religion* 59 (1998): 179–84.

3. For example, consider the situation in postwar Japan: in the 1940s, about 60 percent of Japanese said they had religious beliefs, in the 1970s, religious belief had fallen to 33 percent, and today it is around 20 percent. Faith in the existence of spiritual beings (such as Shinto gods) has also declined dramatically in Japan—down to 13 percent today. See Reader, "Secularization, RIP? Nonsense!"

4. Pippa Norris and Ronald Inglehart, *Sacred and Secular: Religion and Politics Worldwide* (New York: Cambridge University Press, 2004).

5. "Rapid Growth of Unaffiliated," http://www.pewforum.org/2015/05/12 /americas-changing-religious-landscape/pf_15-05-05_rls2_unaffiliated200px-2/.

6. See " 'Nones' on the Rise," Pew Forum Report, http://www.pewforum.org /Unaffiliated/nones-on-the-rise.aspx.

7. See Jose Casenova, *Public Religions in the Modern World* (Chicago: University of Chicago Press, 1994). Casanova argues that secularization is a complex phenomenon. As a thesis, it is most convincing when considered as the emancipation of political, legal, cultural, and economic spheres of society from the

influence of religion. However, if one means by secularization the decline of religious belief and practice, only western Europe really fits. Finally, Casanova attempts to prove that secularization does not necessarily equate with the privatization of religion. Religion actively engages with politics, society, and even economics. Extensive scholarly debate and discussion surrounds the very meanings and definitions of secularization. See William Swatos and Daniel Olson, *The Secularization Debate* (Lanham, MD: Rowman & Littlefield, 2000).

8. *Burwell v. Hobby Lobby*, decided June 30, 2014, Supreme Court of the United States.

9. Graham Greene, *The Comedians* (London: The Bodley Head, 1966), 286.

10. Peter J. Gomes, *The Scandalous Gospel of Jesus: What's So Good about the Good News?* (New York: HarperCollins, 2007) 170–71.

11. *The Devil's Advocate*, Warner Brothers, 1997.

12. T. S. Eliot, "Gerontion," in *The Wasteland and Other Poems* (Toronto: Broadview Press, 2011), 41.

Index

CPSIA information can be obtained
at www.ICGtesting.com
Printed in the USA
LVHW021624191121
703844LV00016B/1300

9 780664 235154